W9-ACN-489

Revolution by Judiciary

Revolution by Judiciary

The Structure of American Constitutional Law

Jed Rubenfeld

Harvard University Press

Cambridge, Massachusetts, and London, England | 2005

Library of Congress Cataloging-in-Publication Data

Rubenfeld, Jed, 1959–

    Revolution by judiciary : the structure of American constitutional law / Jed Rubenfeld.

      p. cm.

    Includes bibliographical references and index.

    ISBN 0–674–01715–3 (alk. paper)

    1. Constitutional law—United States. 2. Law—United States—Interpretation and construction. 3. Judicial process–United States. I. Title.

KF4550.R83 2005

342.73—dc22   2005040211

To Amy,
without whom nothing

Contents

Acknowledgments

Unfortunately I did not have an opportunity to acknowledge those who helped me with my previous book, *Freedom and Time*. Therefore to the many debts I incurred in writing the present book, I must add the compounded debts I owe in connection with the earlier one. Intellectually my greatest thanks and obligations are due to Bruce Ackerman, a man I only wish I could emulate, personally as well as professionally. Michael Sandel guided and encouraged me in more ways than he knows. Other friends and colleagues who provided invaluable help, comments, and criticism include Akhil Amar, Ian Ayres, Jack Balkin, Kate Bartlett, Yochai Benkler, Michael Bratman, Amy Chua, Jules Coleman, Anne Dailey, Chris Eisgruber, Stanley Fish, Owen Fiss, Jim Fleming, Bob Gordon, Don Horowitz, Paul Kahn, Harold Koh, Andy Koppelman, Tony Kronman, Daniel Markovits, Frank Michelman, Philip Pettit, Jeff Powell, Larry Sager, Chris Schroeder, Scott Shapiro, Reva Siegel, Nomi Stolzenburg, Jim Whitman, and Bill van Alstyne. I profited enormously from conversations all around the country at workshops whose organizers and participants are far too many to name. For brilliant, painstaking research and editorial assistance, I cannot thank Barbara Merz enough.

I

The Structure of Constitutional Law

1

Introduction: Radical Reinterpretation

It was a great century for constitutional law—wasn't it?—the third consecutive century of constitutional revolution in America.

As of 1900, the Supreme Court had not struck down a single statute under the First Amendment; today, that amendment is an inexhaustible font of case law. In 1900, states could keep blacks out of white train cars and women out of the legal profession; today, the Fourteenth Amendment renders such exclusions unthinkable. In 1900, Congress's commerce power reached buying and selling across state lines; a century later, the commerce power extended to virtually everything we do in our working lives and much of what we do in our own homes. At the same time, new fundamental rights continually emerged on the scene: the liberty of contract, the right of privacy, the freedom of expressive association.

The most extraordinary feature of these twentieth-century constitutional revolutions was this: they were accomplished without amendment. Each and every one came about through radical judicial reinterpretation.

There was just one problem: constitutional law has no account of radical reinterpretation. What, if anything, makes it legitimate for judges to re-read the Constitution radically, breaking profoundly from both past and present understandings? What, if anything, guides or structures this power? What, if anything, limits it? American constitutional law not only has no answers to these questions; it does not even ask them.

There was little need to do so prior to the twentieth century. After 1803, when *Marbury v. Madison* affirmed the power of judicial review, that power lay largely dormant for half a century. The Court did not invalidate another federal law until *Dred Scott v. Sandford,* decided in 1857—a decision that claimed to be based almost entirely on original intentions. After the Civil War, the justices were too busy cutting back on the rights and powers created by the Fourteenth Amendment—that is, too busy vindicating *old* constitutional understandings—to impose on the nation radically new ones.

Hence when, in the twentieth century, the justices began in earnest to engage in radical reinterpretation, they had little preexisting practice, and no account of this practice, to call on. This lacuna was never filled. By 2000, constitutional law had developed to a point where it could no longer explain itself. It could not justify its most important cases as an interpretive matter. This was so both of the Court's unenumerated-rights decisions, such as *Roe v. Wade,* and of its purportedly enumerated-rights decisions, such as *Brown v. Board of Education, Miranda v. Arizona, Boy Scouts v. Dale* or *Bush v. Gore.*

Which is why, as the twentieth century passed into the twenty-first, it had become hard to believe in constitutional law. Hard to take it seriously— as law. We knew too much. We knew that the politics of our justices were inseparable from their decisions. We knew they could make it up as they went along. We knew they did. We had seen the rationalization, the greedy result-seeking barely disguised under a patina of pitiful legal reasoning—and not in trivial cases, but in cases of the greatest pitch and moment. To be sure, you and I might name different decisions from different decades as exemplars, but we can all name names.

Is it fair, however, to judge constitutional law by cases like *Roe v. Wade* or *Bush v. Gore?* Surely we will have a distorted view of constitutional law (it might be said) if we take stock of it by singling out its most controversial cases. Shouldn't we ask instead how constitutional law handles more standard or more conventional cases?

Here we come to the heart of the matter. American constitutional law lacks an accepted account not only of radical reinterpretation, but also "standard" interpretation. Incredibly, American constitutional case law has almost nothing to say about what judges are supposed to be doing when they go about the business of interpreting the Constitution.

A Subject on Which Constitutional Law Is Silent

When judges are called on to interpret *statutes,* well-known precepts apply. These precepts are not informal; they are not unspoken. They are matters of law, in the sense that they are expressly laid out in hundreds of cases, and lower court judges can be reversed for failing to follow them.

These interpretive precepts leave considerable room for maneuver, to be sure, but they do set out the basic shape and structure of statutory interpretation. The most important of them is this: when interpreting statutes, courts are supposed to ascertain and effectuate legislative intent. This rule, contestable though it often is, furnishes judges with a basic grasp of what it means to interpret a statute rightly.

In administrative law too, when the meaning of legal texts is challenged before a judge, well-known interpretive protocols are established. The general rule is that courts must defer to an agency's construction of the statutes and regulations it administers unless the agency's construction contradicts the plain meaning of the text. Again this rule supplies a tolerably clear picture of the business of interpretation.

In constitutional law, however, there are no such overarching interpretive precepts or protocols. There are no official interpretive rules at all. In any given case raising an undecided constitutional question, nothing in current constitutional law stops a judge from relying on original intent, if the judge wishes. But nothing stops a judge from ignoring original intent. Or suppose a plaintiff comes to court asserting an unwritten constitutional right. Under current case law, judges are fully authorized to dismiss the right because the Constitution says nothing about it. Another admissible option, however, is to uphold the right on nontextual grounds. Evolving American values? Judges can consult them or have nothing to do with them.

Practitioners know they can argue from text, precedent, original meaning, morality, tradition, structure, and so on. But there is no knowing why or whether or when or in what priority these "modalities" of argument will be considered in any given case.[1] There is no law of constitutional interpretation.

Thus is constitutional law, which speaks to so many issues today, silent on one subject: itself. It has nearly nothing to say about the connection between the Constitution and the enormous web of doctrine spun judicially around that document. It tells judges virtually nothing about what they are supposed to be doing when they go about the business of reading and applying the Constitution. Lacking an account of interpretation, constitutional law produces but cannot explain its acts of radical reinterpretation. It cannot explain when such revisions are justified, what they mean, or what is going on when they occur.

In 2000, five justices of the Supreme Court—the same five who have decided so many of the Court's groundbreaking cases since 1995—held that the Boy Scouts had a constitutional right to expel a homosexual scoutmaster.[2] According to the Court, New Jersey's law prohibiting discrimination on the basis of sexual orientation violated the Boy Scouts' "First Amendment freedom of association." Within a few months, citing *Boy Scouts,* lower courts would be dutifully testing anti-discrimination laws under the "Freedom of Association Clause of the First Amendment."[3]

The only difficulty: there is no "Freedom of Association Clause" in the First Amendment (or anywhere else in the Constitution). The point is not that *Boy Scouts* was wrong because the word "association" does not appear in the Constitution. The point is not even that the Constitution has become so ill-read in standard American legal practice that no one apparently notices when courts refer to a clause that does not exist. The point is simply that this mistake makes no difference. Constitutional law today does not tell a judge to do anything differently depending on whether the actual text of the Constitution does or does not guarantee the right that the judge is supposed to be applying.

I am not condemning unenumerated rights. (Incidentally, the *Boy Scouts* justices were not the inventors of this one; the "First Amendment freedom of association" was a creation of the Warren Court.) But a court that enforces some unenumerated rights has a question to answer. Why did the justices in *Boy Scouts* recognize this particular unwritten right when they would not and do not recognize many others? There has to be some account of how this particular unwritten right gets read into the First Amendment, when the same judges reject most other unwritten rights in most other constitutional contexts. On this little question, constitutional law has nothing to say.

But *Boy Scouts,* it might again be objected, is one of those utterly controversial decisions like *Roe v. Wade* or *Bush v. Gore.* There is something misguided in asking for methodological or interpretive explanations when it comes to such cases, which in a sense stand at the edges or outer reaches of constitutional law. One should not generalize, someone might say, from such cases.

Cases like *Boy Scouts* or *Roe* or *Bush v. Gore* are not the problem; or, rather, they are not the only problem. Constitutional law's inability to account for itself is not limited only to "nonstandard" or "noncentral" decisions, or to holdings about which millions disagree. On the contrary, constitutional law cannot even say why its most widely accepted cases are rightly decided. Just consider *Brown v. Board of Education.*

The Strange Obscurity of *Brown*

No decision of the last century was more radical than *Brown;* none is more respected today. None is more central to the entire corpus of contemporary constitutional law. After fifty years, you might think there would be some well-reasoned or at least well-accepted account of why this explosive yet exemplary case was rightly decided. But there isn't.

Academics, of course, have numerous explanations of why the case was rightly decided as an interpretive matter, but their efforts to justify *Brown* are astonishingly obtuse and unsatisfactory. Originalists, for example, say that *Brown* "can be rested" on "the original understanding,"[4] which seems a bit of a stretcher, since *Brown* contradicted the original understanding.[5] Others claim the emergence in the 1950s of a majority consensus against segregation,[6] which may at least be factually correct, but which, if it is supposed to explain *Brown*'s rightness, makes majority will the predicate for minority rights—not a very appealing result, from a constitutional point of view. "Moral readers" of the Constitution condemn segregation on moral grounds,[7] which is easy to do, but this does not help much unless you think the equal protection clause licenses five justices to strike down virtually every law they deem immoral.

How unsettled is *Brown*'s interpretive pedigree? So unsettled that one eminent constitutional theorist says the case can be explained solely by the operation of unwritten constitutional amendments, which were apparently "enacted" around 1940, only to be discovered—by this same theorist—some fifty years later.[8]

Lawyers and judges, by contrast, are unpuzzled. For them, *Brown* is a given. It is a fixed juridical star, a holding to which all laws are answerable. But this givenness does not explain why *Brown* was right. Rather, it makes the absence of an explanation more glaring. Cutting anchor from original intent, but refusing to set sail into pure moralizing, twentieth-century constitutional law remained baffled by its most celebrated decision.

The really remarkable thing is that *Brown* was and is an easy case. Easy not only as a matter of justice, but as a matter of interpretation. No torturing of method is necessary to understand *Brown,* no unwritten amendments, no surrender to the idea that the Constitution must follow current majority will. There is a simple, enduring interpretive structure to American constitutional law, and *Brown* exemplifies it. In a moment, I will explain. First, I want to say a few words about how judges and scholars have tried to deal with the problem of radical reinterpretation—often by denying that it exists.

Denying or Domesticating Radical Reinterpretation

Here is what I have said so far: constitutional law presents us with a body of decisions unable to account for its own existence. In this unaccounted-for interpretive system, our justices periodically effect revolutionary doctrinal transformations. Five justices may be doing so again today. But we have no criteria by which—no framework within which—to evaluate these episodes of radical reinterpretation.

It should be no surprise, therefore, that the charge of judicial activism is cried anew in every generation. All that changes is the identity of the criers. We are so inured by now to such accusations that they hardly register, but the charge of activism will always have sting as long as constitutional law purports to be law. As a result, judicial revolutions, like political revolutions, are often clothed in a rhetoric of restoration.

The rhetoric of restoration explains radical changes in constitutional law by claiming that these changes merely restore the Constitution to its true, original meaning. The Constitution was lost, but now it's found. Because judges are merely rediscovering or enforcing original meanings, radical interpretive innovation is not in play.

But it is a nice trick to make this rhetoric stick when the Court restores the Constitution to a past it never had. There was no constitutional liberty of contract that the *Lochner* era Court could "recover." There was no pre-twentieth-century tradition of free speech law that modern First Amendment jurisprudence could "restore." *Brown v. Board* can be described as having found the lost meaning of the equal protection clause, but the fact is that segregated public schools had existed from the day of enactment of the Fourteenth Amendment. None of these doctrinal revolutions can be plausibly understood through a rhetoric of restoration.

Today's Court faces the same problem. Today's justices have held, for example, that all governmental measures employing explicit racial classifications, including measures designed to benefit racial minorities ("affirmative action"), must satisfy the usually fatal "strict scrutiny" standard of review. But Congress in the 1860s repeatedly made use of racial classifications, both to segregate blacks and in several instances to assist blacks in the allocation of benefits.[9] If, therefore, today's law is to be called a recovery of lost meaning, then we are dealing with a sense of "lost" that was lost on the framers themselves.

The point of the rhetoric of restoration is to deny that judges are engaged in radical reinterpretation, where this term implies the creation of genuinely innovative constitutional law—decisions that break profoundly from both past understandings and present doctrines. The charge of activism is not the only reason why some judges and scholars have trouble embracing radical reinterpretation. Another is that in most standard accounts of legal interpretation, radical reinterpretation should never take place. If judges had read the Constitution rightly the first time around, on this view, there could be no occasion to re-read it. The rhetoric of restoration accepts this claim; it maintains, therefore, that earlier judges failed to read the Constitution correctly.

By contrast, at least three important tropes or ideas can be found in the American constitutional literature that do recognize the propriety of doctrinal change even when the Constitution may have been interpreted correctly the first time around.[10] None of them, however, gets quite to the heart of the matter. Instead, each finds a new way to tame or deny the phenomenon of radical reinterpretation.

The first, simplest thought is that changed circumstances sometimes require new doctrine in order to keep the law faithful to the Constitution's purposes. The federal commerce power provides an obvious example. Congress was always intended (it could be said) to have control over "truly national" commerce or "nationwide commercial problems." The sphere of "truly national" commerce may have been small in 1789, but it has expanded spectacularly in the last two centuries. Congress's commerce power must therefore expand with it.

The changed-circumstances idea is essentially originalist. It assumes that the judicial job is to effectuate original purposes; doctrinal change is permitted because these purposes sometimes require new outcomes in a changing world.[11] This may well be an improvement over more rigid forms of originalism, but it does not grasp the nettle of radical reinterpretation.

Radical reinterpretation is, precisely, a new interpretation of the basic principles or purposes behind a constitutional provision. Through this act of reinterpretation, new constitutional purposes or principles replace the original ones. The changed-circumstances idea provides no handle on, no conceptual space for, the introduction of radically new constitutional meaning.

A second idea, equally familiar in American constitutional jurisprudence, comes closer. It is the idea of "the living Constitution," which builds on the changed-circumstances idea but breaks away from its originalist moorings. A living Constitution (it is said) must evolve and adapt to contemporary needs and values. It must grow with the society that surrounds it, even if in the process it outgrows the original purposes.[12]

The metaphor of the living Constitution, limp though it has now become, had a real virtue. It captured, better than do the dominant academic schools of interpretation (originalism, textualism, proceduralism, and so on), the reality that constitutional law undergoes significant interpretive shifts over time, as a result of which new meanings come into play. Unfortunately, talk of a living Constitution is not much help in thinking through these shifts.

If the Constitution is alive, and our criteria for evaluating doctrinal innovations are those of evolution or organic growth, then there is little room for a distinctively *interpretive* account of radical change in constitutional law. The changed-circumstances thought is at least an interpretive thought; it demands doctrinal change in the name of fidelity to intended meaning. Demanding fidelity to intended meaning is one obvious way of demanding that a text be interpreted properly. But the natural measure for evaluating a living Constitution is naturalistic; it is pragmatic, not interpretive. If we believed in the living Constitution, we would ask whether our courts had generated doctrine well adapted to the country's needs.

Pragmatism is in vogue in many legal quarters today, but the turn to pragmatism is a turn away from the entire discipline of interpretation. As the chief contemporary proponent of legal pragmatism candidly acknowledges, a truly pragmatic judge denies that he has a "moral or even political duty to abide by constitutional or statutory text."[13] By contrast, a judge who considers himself engaged in reinterpretation understands that his first duty is, precisely, to abide by the Constitution: to deliver a just reading of that document according to interpretive criteria. Reinterpretation may be innovative—it may break profoundly from past and present understandings—but it remains an instance of interpretation; hence it must answer to the discipline, the norms, and the practices of constitutional interpretation. The metaphor of a living Constitution is not inconsistent with this aspiration, but offers little help in achieving it.

Finally, there is the idea, pioneered by Bruce Ackerman, of "constitutional moments," at which the law undergoes a "regime change," following periods of extraordinary political mobilization and decisive national electoral outcomes.[14] Ackerman may have been the first to try to systematize the reality and the legitimacy of periodic, radical doctrinal shifts in constitutional law. But his story is a story of amendment; it offers no account of radical reinterpretation in the absence of amendment.

At successful "constitutional moments," says Ackerman, the Constitution is amended, even if the formal requirements of Article V have not been satisfied, and only by recognizing such amendments can we explain and justify the path-breaking judicial decisions that follow. For example, the Court's eventual acceptance of the New Deal is explained on the ground that the Constitution was actually amended some time around 1940 to expand federal regulatory powers. This way of putting things forces Ackerman to embrace a picture of constitutional interpretation in the absence of amendment that is surprisingly conservative—indeed almost originalist. His argument, in strongest form, is that if the 1940s Court had only the unamended commerce clause before it, proper interpretation would have required the Court to continue striking down New Deal legislation, because that legislation plainly transgressed original intentions. That is why, the argument goes, a "New Deal amendment" is necessary to explain and legitimize the post-1940s case law.

The same reasoning pushes Ackerman toward the view that *Plessy v. Ferguson* was correctly decided. Ackerman wants to explain *Brown* by reference to the same New Deal amendment that authorized an activist state. As a result, he cannot admit that *Plessy* was wrong in its own time and place. For if it was, then *Brown* would be easy to explain without reference to any unwritten amendments. But this commits Ackerman, once again, to an originalist picture of interpretation (in the absence of amendment). In effect, his argument runs as follows: since *Plessy* conformed with original intentions, while *Brown* did not, we can explain and legitimize the shift from *Plessy* to *Brown* only when we see that, appearances to the contrary, the Constitution was amended some time between those two cases.

To be sure, once the Constitution is amended, Ackerman's judges can and must become quite creative interpreters, because they are then called on to "synthesize" the nation's various "constitutional moments." But absent amendment, radical nonoriginalist interpretation is impermissible; it cannot be part of the story, because it undermines the case for uncodified amendments. Because Ackerman wants to tell a story of constitutional amendment outside the Article V process, his story of constitutional change, bold as it is in so many ways, adheres to a highly conservative picture of constitutional interpretation, offering no account of interpretive innovation absent amendment.

Each of these three ideas—changed circumstances, the living Constitution, and constitutional moments—responds, in one form or another, to the reality of doctrinal change over time. Each rejects the notion that if interpretation is done rightly the first time around, doctrinal change should never take place. But none of these tropes ultimately gives us a handle on the problem that most needs to be confronted: the problem of radical reinterpretation in the absence of amendment.

Giving Up on Interpretation

Once this problem is recognized, what then? What is left to say about constitutional interpretation, if, without change in the constitutional text, judges are free radically to alter the Constitution's meaning, breaking profoundly from all past and contemporary understandings? In what sense are judges who engage in this kind of constitutional revolution interpreting the Constitution at all?

One natural and tempting response is to give up the whole idea of constitutional interpretation as a bad job. This response comes in a number of styles. There is, for example, the realist-cynical style ("it's all politics"), the vulgar-deconstructive style ("there is no such thing as a 'right' or 'wrong' interpretation of any text"), and the consequentialist-pragmatic style ("never mind 'interpreting' the Constitution; the only important thing is to get the most socially useful results"). Today, this attitude is so common it is no longer subversive. It is the complaisant attitude of aging poststructuralist professors and Seventh Circuit judges alike. It is also the path of least resistance. It requires the least energy, demands the least acumen, and, because it claims to turn its back on the ideal of constitutional interpretation, has the least effect on anything, leaving the law and those who play the game exactly as they were.

The other path is of course to set one's shoulders yet again to the law's ancient labor of interpretive reconstruction. This was Alexander Bickel's effort, and John Hart Ely's too. They claimed, in the midst of all the constitutional cacophony, hypocrisy, and rationalization, to have discovered the hidden keys and stops of constitutional interpretation, the internal precepts that not only explained much of what the Supreme Court had done but also justified American-style judicial review against the charge of activism—justified it in the broadest sense, under the principles of self-government itself—and at the same time yielded criteria by which to say where the Court had gone off the rails.

This book makes another argument of this form. Despite everything, and even through periods of revolutionary change, American constitutional law has in fact conformed to a determinate interpretive structure. This interpretive structure, although largely or even completely unrecognized, explains a good deal about American constitutional law; it emerges from the deepest democratic commitments of constitutional law, and it provides the framework within which to evaluate episodes of radical reinterpretation. Such, at least, is the three-part thesis of this book.

This enduring interpretive structure is not at all complex. It is easy to describe and to discern, as soon as one or two new concepts have been introduced. But it does not fit into any of the boxes described by the major schools of contemporary constitutional thought. It is historicist without being originalist. It is substantive (as opposed to proceduralist) without implying a judicial power to read into the Constitution whatever fundamental values the justices prefer. It recognizes that judges must ultimately do justice when they interpret, but it is much more historically oriented than a "moral reading" of the Constitution would be. And it derives ultimately from the imperative of self-government, but not in the way that this imperative has usually been understood—as, for example, by Bickel and Ely.

Here is the interpretive structure to which I refer.

The Structure of American Constitutional Law

Constitutional law has in fact been dominated by historical meanings—but only by *some* historical meanings. One particular subset of historical meaning has maintained a powerful, almost inviolable, doctrine-shaping status. Outside this subset, history routinely ends up in the constitutional dustbin. This asymmetry is inadmissible according to almost all contemporary constitutional thinking. Whether friendly or hostile to historical understandings, nearly everyone agrees that judges cannot pick and choose among them.[15] That would be cheating. It would license "roaming through history looking for one's friends."[16]

But consider the following, impossibly simple distinction. Specific understandings about a constitutional right can take two different forms: there can be specific laws or practices that the right is understood to *prohibit*; and there can be specific laws or practices that the right is understood *not* to prohibit. Virtually all the important historical understandings of the former kind—specific understandings of what a right prohibited—are alive and well throughout constitutional law, playing a foundational role in the doctrine. By contrast, where constitutional doctrine has departed from important historical understandings, it has virtually always departed from understandings of the latter kind—concerning what a right did not prohibit.

The freedom of speech was understood originally to prohibit prior restraints. It is still so understood today. On the other hand, the freedom of speech was originally understood not to prohibit laws banning blasphemy, pornography, or the use of indecent words in public. Today these historical understandings are—history.

How to label this distinction? Constitutional rights are prohibitory (meaning that their function is to prohibit at least some acts by some actors). Let us say, as a shorthand, that a prohibitory law *applies* to those actions it prohibits, and that it does *not apply* to those actions it does not prohibit. So I will call specific understandings of what a constitutional right prohibits *Application Understandings,* and of what it does not prohibit, *No-Application Understandings.* Moreover, for reasons I will clarify later, I will call the original Application Understandings of a constitutional right its *foundational* or *core* applications.

Similarly, with respect to constitutional power-granting provisions (such as the commerce clause), which authorize certain actors to take certain actions, I will call Application Understandings any specific understandings of what such a provision authorizes, while the No-Application Understandings are specific understandings of what such a provision does not authorize. Here, too, we will see that the foundational or core applications remain very much alive in contemporary constitutional doctrine, while important No-Application Understandings have been discarded.

For any given constitutional right, it is possible to identify innumerable No-Application Understandings, which cover the entire universe of laws and practices not prohibited. The First Amendment was originally understood not to prohibit the U.S. Navy or the sale of flour in ten-pound bags. By contrast, there will typically have been only a few definitive, original core applications. Then as now, "deep divisions" surrounded "the meaning and the application of the Constitution," even "among those who . . . supported its adoption."[17] But for every right, there were nearly always a few, core Application Understandings: understandings, shared overwhelmingly by supporters and opponents alike, that the right would unquestionably abolish this or that particular practice once and for all. Almost invariably, these core Application Understandings remain in force today.

The freedom of speech still prohibits, as I have said, prior restraints. The establishment clause still prohibits a national church and compulsory support for a designated faith. The Fourth Amendment still prohibits "general warrants." The takings clause still prohibits uncompensated exercises of eminent domain; the self-incrimination clause, the "cruel trilemma"; the equal protection clause, "black codes."[18]

By contrast, consider the original understanding that *Brown* overturned: the understanding that segregated public schools were constitutional. This was a No-Application Understanding. It was an understanding of something the Fourteenth Amendment did *not* forbid. So was the understanding that the equal protection clause did *not* prohibit state actors from denying women a seat on juries or other important rights and privileges.

What possible reason is there for differentiating in constitutional interpretation between Application and No-Application Understandings? Answering this question will occupy a hundred pages of this book, but I will summarize the basic thought in one sentence here. No-Application Understandings are not commitments.

Commitments are not the same as intentions, and No-Application Understandings are, at most, intentions. Originalism holds that all original intentions are equally binding; that is its flaw. Constitutional interpretation is not and should not be intentionalist in this sense. The point of constitutional law is to hold the nation to its self-given, fundamental commitments over time, and discharging this task requires courts to distinguish, as they have, between commitments and mere intentions. The foundational applications of a right or power are definitive of the Constitution's commitments, while No-Application Understandings, even if held by every framer and ratifier, are not commitments at all. As a result, constitutional interpretation is bound by the former, but not by the latter.

These are unfamiliar ideas. They require explaining. To my knowledge, no constitutional scholar has observed the enormous doctrinal role played by the distinction between Application and No-Application Understandings. Nor has anyone tried to distinguish between those historical understandings that count as commitments and those that are, at most, mere intentions. Nor has anyone argued that constitutional law is properly concerned with commitments, as opposed to mere intentions, and is therefore bound to adhere to historical Application Understandings, while free to disregard historical No-Application Understandings.

Paradigm Cases, Paradigm Shifts

Out of this simple distinction between Application and No-Application Understandings a determinate structure of constitutional interpretation emerges. The Constitution's core applications serve as *paradigm cases*.

They provide the reference points for the construction of doctrinal frameworks.

Judges build interpretive frameworks or paradigms around the Constitution's paradigmatic Application Understandings. In this process they regard themselves as free to break from No-Application Understandings. But more than one interpretive paradigm can always be fashioned around a given set of paradigm cases. As a result, constitutional law is always open to—and has periodically undergone—paradigm shifts, even while it remains organized around the foundational paradigm cases.

For example, although modern equal protection jurisprudence is profoundly nonoriginalist, the Fourteenth Amendment's core applications continue to anchor and organize the doctrine. The foundational application of the equal protection clause—its abolition of the black codes— plays a special, structuring doctrinal role, serving as a paradigm case and anchoring everything the Court has ever said about "suspect classes," the organizing concept for all modern constitutional antidiscrimination doctrine.[19] In working out the meaning and implications of suspect classes, the Court has bulldozed over once well-established, highly important No-Application Understandings (concerning racial segregation, for instance, and sex discrimination). In doing so, the Court brought about a fundamental paradigm shift in equal protection law, radically altering our understanding of the Fourteenth Amendment's basic purposes and principles. Today another paradigm shift might be taking place, as the Court shifts the locus of the doctrine from the concept of suspect classes to that of suspect classifications (moving the doctrine closer to strict color-blindness).

Reasoning from paradigm cases is a variegated business—incorporating considerations of text, policy, and justice; requiring ineluctably normative, even ideological judgment—but it is the primary business of constitutional interpretation. Judges interpret constitutional texts in light of their paradigm cases; in so doing, they build up the interpretive paradigms through which the texts are applied. At the same time, they lay down new paradigm cases, which, like *Brown*, can come to be regarded as landmark precedents. Every time the Supreme Court holds that a constitutional right prohibits a particular law or practice, it creates a new paradigm case—although these precedent-based Application Understandings rarely have the same inviolable status as the foundational Application Understandings. Extrajudicial historys can also create new paradigm cases; the Sedition Act of 1798 became a paradigmatic example of a First Amendment violation, even if the First Amendment's original understanding would not have viewed it as such.

In the course of paradigm case reasoning, judges periodically tear down the interpretive paradigms they have constructed, replacing them with new ones. This occurs for a wide variety of reasons, principally having to do with the appointment of justices whose constitutional instincts differ from those who preceded them. When such paradigm shifts take place, constitutional law retains its fundamental structure: it remains organized around historical Application Understandings, while No-Application Understandings are left behind.

This simple structure explains why originalism—maintaining that *all* original understandings must be adhered to—can never capture the real shape of American constitutional law, or, for that matter, the true role of original understanding within it. At the same time, the relatively ahistorical views of constitutional law (whether of the cynical variety, according to which judges basically decide any way they like, or of the more high-minded variety, according to which judges basically decide as moral philosophy instructs) equally fail to capture the structure of constitutional law. They fail to see that constitutional provisions have core, historical meanings, impervious or almost impervious to judicial rewriting, given by the concrete political battles fought and won, sometimes at great price, in the nation's revolutionary past.

Paradigm cases do not dictate unique answers to most constitutional questions. Different judges will see the paradigm cases differently; it will almost always be possible to capture the paradigmatic applications of a particular constitutional right or power within more than one interpretive paradigm. This means that five justices of the Supreme Court can, at any given moment, redetermine the basic meaning of the paradigm cases. There is nothing inherently wrong with such transformative reinterpretations. *Brown v. Board of Education* marked such a reinterpretation of the Fourteenth Amendment's paradigm cases.

But if what I have said so far is correct, then there are interpretive criteria for evaluating constitutional paradigm shifts. Judges who engage in radical reinterpretation of the Constitution must still answer to the Constitution's foundational paradigm cases. The new doctrine labors under the continuing obligation to do justice to the paradigm cases—or, more precisely, to do justice to the text in light of its paradigm cases.

Frank Michelman and Laurence Tribe were among the first to use the Kuhnian terms *paradigm* and *paradigm shift* in connection with constitutional law.[20] Both suggested a critical attitude toward these terms. Michelman observed, correctly in my opinion, that the idea of paradigm shifts can mislead if taken to imply that the shifts occur all at once, in great epistemological (or constitutional) moments, implying that dominant modes of understanding are not constantly contested and subject to revision even in "ordinary" cases. I am not, however, using these terms in the same way that Thomas Kuhn did in his *Structure of Scientific Revolutions*.

The concept I take to be primary is that of the paradigm case. Interpretive paradigms and paradigm shifts are built around these paradigm cases. This idea of how interpretation works long predates Kuhn and is consistent with a number of other interpretive theories. In legal circles, paradigm-case reasoning can be found in centuries-old common law decisions and is strongly associated with H. L. A. Hart's jurisprudence.[21] In philosophical circles, there have been suggestions that paradigm cases and paradigm-case reasoning provide the basic building blocks through which we create and comprehend many of our concepts.

Summary

This book describes a new way of looking at constitutional law. This new perspective has three dimensions: descriptive, theoretical, and evaluative. The book's three parts correspond to these three dimensions.

Part I is descriptive. Its point is to demonstrate the remarkable ubiquity, throughout constitutional law, of a basic interpretive structure—the doctrinal structure described earlier, with its asymmetric relation to historical understandings. In field after field, constitutional law reveals a paradigmatic fidelity to history's Application Understandings, combined with a reckless infidelity to No-Application Understandings. Although Part I is descriptive, it has normative implications (because the actual practice of legal interpretation helps generate its norms). Once we see the fundamental structure of constitutional interpretation, the revolutionary holding in a case like *Brown* will no longer seem difficult to justify as a matter of interpretation. On the contrary, treating the abolition of black codes as paradigmatic, while regarding the original No-Application Understandings as nonbinding, will permit *Brown* to be seen for what it is: an easy case, not only as a matter of justice but as a matter of interpretation, requiring no exegetical gyrations and no hidden constitutional amendments to legitimize it.

Part II is theoretical. It asks what reasons there might be for constitutional law's asymmetrical treatment of Application and No-Application Understandings. It finds these reasons in a theory of constitutional self-government that rests on a distinction between commitments and intentions. If, as I will argue, the judiciary's essential task in constitutional cases is to hold the nation to its constitutional commitments, both originalism and the ahistorical schools of interpretation are necessarily flawed. Originalism wants judges to adhere to all original intentions, failing to see that some of these intentions—the No-Application Understandings—are not commitments and therefore command no special interpretive deference. By contrast, the ahistorical approaches (such as moralism and process-based interpretation) do not acknowledge the binding force of specific, substantive commitments laid down in the past, and therefore fail to see that some of the original understandings—the Application Understandings—remain inviolable. Part II is an exercise in constitutional theory; those who have no taste for such things are forewarned.

Part III is evaluative. It takes the conclusions arrived at in Parts I and II and applies them to some of the Court's most important recent constitutional decisions. It asks whether a new paradigm shift is occurring today in constitutional law and whether the Court's transformative decisions are consistent or inconsistent with the Constitution's foundational paradigm cases.

2

Rights

American constitutional law in the twentieth century was dominated by a series of radical judicial reinterpretations. Throughout these transformations, however, the law conformed to a determinate interpretive structure. In virtually every field, No-Application Understandings were the understandings that fell away, while core Application Understandings remained not only intact but central to the doctrinal frameworks that emerged.

The only way to make this showing is by going through a significant number of doctrines and decisions. The rights most changed by, and most important in, contemporary constitutional law are probably the freedom of speech; the freedoms of religion; the protection against unreasonable searches and seizures; the self-incrimination privilege; the takings clause; and the equal protection guarantee. I will consider each of these rights in turn in this chapter. The next chapter will look at the congressional powers most changed by, and most important in, contemporary constitutional law: the spending power and the commerce power. It will also discuss the separation of powers.

Most of what I will say in this chapter is familiar. The paradigmatic applications of most constitutional rights or powers—and the continuing pertinence of those paradigmatic applications today—are known to every student of constitutional law. But the familiarity of the discussion cannot be avoided; the point is to show the structure of what constitutional law takes for granted.

I want to emphasize one point at the outset. I am not saying that paradigm-case reasoning *caused* the case law to develop as it did. I am not saying that the judges who decided the cases to be discussed were aware of the distinction between Application and No-Application Understandings. They may have reached their decisions through any number of approaches, out of any number of motivations, with any number of biases. The extraordinary fact is that all these approaches, motives, and biases have played themselves out within a determinate interpretive structure.

On the other hand, in many cases, judges have in fact explicitly invoked core historical Application Understandings as authority for their decisions and have consciously built on those understandings in elaborating doctrine. In these cases, judges have expressly engaged in paradigm-case reasoning. But I am not claiming that this was so in all or even most of the case law to be discussed. The claim is solely that American constitutional law has in fact systematically adhered to and expanded from core historical Application Understandings even while discarding important historical No-Application Understandings.

Freedom of Speech

Before the twentieth century, there was virtually no Supreme Court free-speech case law at all.[1] Today the freedom of speech protects, to name just a few things, profanity, pornography, blasphemy, nude dancing, paintings of the Virgin adorned with dung, advertising, campaign financing, insults, falsehoods concerning public figures, and the advocacy of unlawful conduct short of imminent incitement.

It is as certain as history can be that the freedom of speech was originally understood not to apply to at least some of the types of expression just listed.[2] It is possible that the First Amendment was not intended to stop Congress from prohibiting *any* of them.[3] In other words, contemporary free-speech law spurns a vast range of original No-Application Understandings.

Originalists will shake their head at this fact, complaining that constitutional law today is heedless of historical meaning. But it isn't so. First Amendment law remains very much attached to certain powerful, historical understandings—Application Understandings.

There are two core historical applications of the freedom of speech. The first is called *prior restraint*. Whatever else it might mean, the freedom of speech in the United States has always been understood first and foremost as a prohibition against "previous restraints" on publication.[4] The paradigmatic prior restraint was the requirement (existing in England until the end of the seventeenth century and in the colonies until the early eighteenth) that every work to be published on a printing press had to be submitted to crown officials, who were empowered to strike out offending passages and from whom a license had to be obtained before the work could be legally published. Violations of the licensing system were punishable as crimes.

Despite the manifest ahistoricity of much of modern free-speech doctrine, the original understanding that the First Amendment applied to such prior restraints has never been shaken.[5] The bar against prior restraints was invoked in one of the most important First Amendment cases of the Vietnam War period, in which the Supreme Court reversed a lower court's order enjoining publication of the "Pentagon Papers."[6] Modern judges still refer to prior restraints as "the most serious and least tolerable infringement on First Amendment rights."[7] Moreover, when doing so, judges unabashedly cite historical meaning: "Prior restraint upon speech suppresses the precise freedom which the First Amendment sought to protect against abridgment"; the "elimination of prior restraints was a 'leading purpose' in the adoption of the First Amendment."[8]

All this is well known, but it ought to strike contemporary readers as puzzling. After all, there is a case to be made that First Amendment law should be considerably more tolerant of prior restraints. Consider speech of uncertain constitutional protection—for example, a story so explicit in its depictions of sex that it might cross the line into (unprotected) "obscenity." Why exactly is a system of prior restraints for such speech so much less tolerable than a law punishing obscenity after publication? At least in a prior-restraint system, writers or publishers could find out beforehand what they may and may not legally publish, while an after-the-fact criminal law subjects them to such potentially high costs (perhaps even imprisonment) if they guess wrong that they may be excessively cautious and produce less protected speech overall.

Now consider clearly unprotected speech, such as deliberate misrepresentations falsely describing some private person's secret sex life. Under a system of post-utterance penalties, a publisher of such speech may be punished only after the fact, when irreparable damage may already have been done. Why should First Amendment law ban a system of prior restraints that would prevent publication of this sort of speech? There are possible responses to these questions, of course, but many think that these responses are not satisfactory.[9]

I am not saying prior restraints ought to be upheld. The point is that in a free speech jurisprudence as untroubled about original understandings as ours, there is something puzzling about the fact that judges should continue to call prior restraints "the most serious and least tolerable infringement on First Amendment rights," and that judges should cite the original understanding as if it were almost conclusive authority for this proposition, seemingly unaware that in countless other respects contemporary law ignores original understandings.

The explanation is simple: we deal here with a foundational Application Understanding. Modern judges feel free to depart from No-Application Understandings, but Application Understandings are treated differently. That is why, despite the manifest non-originalism of today's free speech law, a modern court will say, without apparent embarrassment, "Prior restraint upon speech suppresses the precise freedom which the First Amendment sought to protect against abridgment."[10] This formulation refers to a historical Application Understanding, giving this bit of historical meaning a priority and an authority lacking in history's No-Application Understandings—which the same court would have no difficulty rejecting.[11]

Turn now to the second historically paradigmatic violation of free speech—seditious libel laws. The English common law crime of seditious libel covered "any written censure upon any public man whatever for any conduct whatever, or upon any law or institution whatever."[12] There is some doubt about whether the First Amendment was originally understood to prohibit seditious libel laws. But one eighteenth-century seditious libel prosecution was so notorious in the American colonies that it may well have served as a foundational paradigm case for the First Amendment.

In 1735, New York printer John Peter Zenger was tried for criticizing the colonial governor. His acquittal—apparently by a nullifying jury—was celebrated throughout the colonies as a victory for the freedom of speech. According to most accounts, it served as a benchmark in the founding American understanding of the First Amendment.[13] Nevertheless, despite the fame of the Zenger trial, some have claimed that the freedoms of speech and press originally extended only to a freedom from prior restraints.[14] This may have been the view of President John Adams and his fellow Federalists, who passed the federal Sedition Act of 1798, which essentially made it a crime to criticize Adams or his fellow Federalists.[15] The Supreme Court never ruled on the constitutionality of the Sedition Act of 1798, but the law was enforced by a number of (Federalist) judges, and several prominent critics of the Adams administration were imprisoned or fined for violating it.

If the understanding that the First Amendment prohibited seditious libel laws was not at first universal, it was very considerably strengthened after the election contest of 1800. The Sedition Act became a central issue in Thomas Jefferson's presidential campaign. He and his Republican supporters repeatedly attacked the Sedition Act as a blatant violation of the First Amendment. The Kentucky and Virginia Resolutions made the same point in inflammatory language. After election, Jefferson pardoned individuals who had been convicted under the act, and Congress rescinded their fines. Jefferson's victory is widely regarded by contemporary historians as a decisive condemnation of the Sedition Act and the prosecutions thereunder.[16]

Today the unconstitutionality of "seditious libel" laws is a piece of First Amendment bedrock,[17] and courts will explicitly say, when they declare such laws unconstitutional, that they are honoring the First Amendment's historical meaning. "It goes without saying," our otherwise deeply un-originalist twenty-first-century judges will happily say, "that such stigmatization of speech critical of public officials was among the chief evils that the First Amendment sought to combat."[18] Which is to say: even while the First Amendment's historical No-Applications Understandings are routinely flouted, its two core historical Application Understandings remain authoritative.

More than this, these two core applications were central to the revolutionary expansion in free-speech law that occurred over the course of the twentieth century. In Holmes's great *Abrams* dissent, to which a good deal of modern free-speech law can be traced, he expressly relied on the nation's repudiation of the Sedition Act of 1798.[19] A half century later, in *New York Times Co. v. Sullivan*,[20] the full Court held that "the central meaning of the First Amendment" could be discerned in that episode.

New York Times is the case in which the Court held that the First Amendment represented a "profound national commitment to the principle that debate on public issues should be uninhibited, robust, and wide-open, and that it may well include vehement, caustic, and sometimes unpleasantly sharp attacks on government and public officials." The facts, briefly, were these: a local police commissioner sued the *Times* after the newspaper ran a fund-raising advertisement, signed by the "Committee to Defend Martin Luther King," recounting reports of police abuses and assaults on King in Montgomery, Alabama. Finding that some of the statements in the advertisement were false, an Alabama jury awarded plaintiff $500,000 in damages. The Supreme Court reversed:

[N]either factual error nor defamatory content suffices to remove the constitutional shield from criticism of official conduct. . . . This is the lesson to be drawn from the great controversy over the Sedition Act of 1798, 1 Stat. 596, which first crystallized a national awareness of the central meaning of the First Amendment. . . . Although the Sedition Act was never tested in this Court, the attack upon its validity has carried the day in the court of history. Fines levied in its prosecution were repaid by Act of Congress on the ground that it was unconstitutional. Jefferson, as President, pardoned those who had been convicted . . . and remitted their fines. Its invalidity has been assumed by Justices of this Court. These views reflect a broad consensus that the Act, because of the restraint it imposed upon criticism of government and public officials, was inconsistent with the First Amendment.[21]

With *New York Times,* modern free speech law had expressly placed seditious libel at the "center" of the First Amendment, treating the Sedition Act of 1798 as a paradigmatic First Amendment violation.[22] Indeed, *New York Times* is a classic instance of paradigm-case reasoning, expanding on the core case to find that ordinary civil libel laws could also, in certain circumstances, violate the First Amendment. The Court recognized the paradigm case and built on it, interpreting and elaborating that case in formulating new doctrine.

But *New York Times* (like *Abrams*) involved criticism of public authorities, so that, by itself, it did not call for the First Amendment to protect all the forms of once-punishable expression that constitutional law protects today. Instead, it was by combining the First Amendment's two historical paradigm cases—sedition laws and prior restraints—that the Court produced the radically new interpretive paradigm that would have this result.

Today the First Amendment could be described in terms of an antiorthodoxy or anticensorship paradigm, in which, on virtually all matters of opinion, ideas, or taste, state actors are not permitted to penalize people for expressing any particular view or to force them to express a government-sanctioned view. And it was in prior-restraint doctrine that the Court first interpreted the freedom of speech as standing against "censorship."

A court reasoning from paradigm cases has to offer an account of why the paradigm cases *are* paradigm cases: what was it about the English licensing systems that made them core violations of the freedom of speech? Say that statute A has been struck down as a prior restraint; now some plaintiff brings suit against statute B, which differs (slightly or considerably) from A, but which, says the plaintiff, is still a prior restraint. To resolve the case, the court is obliged to identify definitive features of prior restraints, and in doing so, the court will, if it does its job tolerably well, tie these features into some account of what it is about prior restraints that makes them a violation of the First Amendment. A court will do this in the ordinary course of articulating and applying the operative law, so that people know what to look for in order to recognize prior restraints in future.

But in the course of this entirely standard practice of legal reasoning, the court may introduce defining terms or principles capable of radically altering the doctrinal framework it is elaborating. With respect to free speech law, a critical decision of this kind was handed down in 1938.[23] The case concerned a municipal ordinance prohibiting the distribution "within city limits" of "literature of any kind" without permission from the "City Manager." The ordinance was not directed at publishers of newspapers or books (as paradigmatic prior restraints were); nor was there any procedure set up through which the City Manager could strike out offending portions of the material. Rather, the ordinance was applied to stop a Jehovah's Witness from distributing materials in the street or house-to-house. Was this the kind of prior restraint that the First Amendment prohibited?

In holding that it was, the Court explained that this ordinance would permit state actors to perpetrate the very evil that the bar against prior restraints served to combat. What was that evil? The Court's answer was "censorship":

> We think that the ordinance is invalid on its face. Whatever the motive which induced its adoption, its character is such that it strikes at the very foundation of the freedom of the press by subjecting it to license and censorship. . . . Legislation of the type of the ordinance in question would restore the system of license and censorship in its baldest form.[24]

The Court here suggested an explanation of why prior restraints were categorically unconstitutional: because they so clearly instantiated governmental censorship—"censorship in its baldest form." At first blush, this way of explaining the unconstitutionality of prior restraints seems natural and unremarkable. What is a prior restraint if not an act of censorship?

But to conceptualize prior restraints as "censorship in its baldest form" is to point the way toward a radical reinterpretation of the basic principles behind the First Amendment. For after all, laws that punish speech *after* the fact can also be said to censor. After-utterance punishment will stop many people from speaking the forbidden speech in the first place. So long as the law tells people what they legally can and cannot say, the state can easily be said to be censoring speech—regardless of whether the coercive power of the state comes in before or after utterance. The idea of censorship is not easy to cabin within the confines of prior-restraint doctrine. Once the evil of prior restraints is conceptualized in terms of censorship, the question becomes whether the condemnation of censorship should be limited, for some reason, *only* to prior restraints.

And in answering that question, the paradigmatic unconstitutionality of sedition laws was critical. The case of seditious libel laws showed that the freedom of speech was not limited to prior restraints. Taken together, the two paradigm cases generated a radically expansive freedom of speech. Each gave to free-speech law a critical element the other did not.

The concept of prior restraint was limited to laws that restrain speech before utterance, but it had no inherent subject-matter limitation (it was not limited, for example, to political speech). The prohibition of sedition laws stretched beyond prior restraint, but it was limited by subject matter (applying only to speech criticizing government officials or policy). When, however, these two paradigm cases are put together, the First Amendment can become a bulwark against *all* state efforts to impose orthodoxies on individuals' opinions, regardless of subject matter and regardless of whether the restrictions apply before or after the speech has been uttered. If prior-restraint doctrine shows that government cannot censor speech, and if sedition doctrine shows that such unconstitutional censorship can occur through after-the-fact punishment, the path is cleared for a revolutionary expansion of free-speech jurisprudence.

That is the position the Court mapped out in 1943, when it struck down a law requiring children to salute and pledge allegiance to the U.S. flag. A passage from this case is famous. It begins as follows:

It is now a commonplace that censorship or suppression of expression of opinion is tolerated by our Constitution only when the expression presents a clear and present danger of action of a kind the State is empowered to prevent and punish.[25]

Note how Justice Jackson, in his opinion for the Court, runs together the ideas of "censorship" and "suppression of expression," so that the concept of censorship, first articulated in the prior-restraint cases, becomes applicable outside the domain of prior restraints. Note as well that the Court here implicitly refers to its earlier sedition cases (in which Justice Holmes had first formulated the "clear and present danger" test). But Jackson's famous passage extends far beyond seditious speech, condemning state-imposed orthodoxies of *any* kind:

> [I]f there is any fixed star in our constitutional constellation, it is that no official, high or petty, can prescribe what shall be orthodox in politics, nationalism, religion, or other matters of opinion or force citizens to confess by word or act their faith therein. If there are any circumstances which permit an exception, they do not now occur to us.[26]

This passage expresses the basic paradigm through which the First Amendment is understood today, suggesting an almost absolute protection of speech on all "matters of opinion." It represented a revolutionary shift in free-speech law, for it opened the way to the protection of all the forms of expression listed at the beginning of this section. Once it was established that state actors may not "prescribe what shall be orthodox" in any matter of opinion, it could not be long before the freedom of speech would protect blasphemy, pornography, the words "Fuck the draft" on the back of a jacket, a painting of the Virgin adorned with excrement, and so on.

Is this radically expanded free speech paradigm consistent with the original understanding? The only possible answer is—yes and no.

On the one hand, modern doctrine has plainly rejected some of the most important historical No-Application Understandings. On the other, modern doctrine has retained and built on the First Amendment's historical Application Understandings. Blasphemy laws offer a particularly clear example.

Blasphemy convictions were repeatedly upheld in the nineteenth century.[27] They were viewed as especially unproblematic when the defendant had dared to impugn Christ, as opposed to "impostors" such as "Mahomet" or the "grand Lama."[28] Abusive language was not necessary; mere declarations of disbelief in Christ were sufficient.[29] Today, of course, a law forbidding blasphemy or atheistic speech, and especially a law singling out blasphemy against Christian doctrine, would be struck down without hesitation,[30] not only as a violation of the religion clauses but as a clear violation of the freedom of speech.[31] Why?

The result is in a sense overdetermined; it derives from many causes. But as a matter of constitutional doctrine, the explanation is that the anti-orthodoxy or anticensorship vision of free speech, first articulated by the Court in the 1930s and 1940s, with roots in both sedition and prior-restraint cases, is now the law of the land. If "no official, high or petty, can prescribe what shall be orthodox" in "matters of opinion," the unconstitutionality of blasphemy laws requires very little further discussion.

Is this rejection of blasphemy laws, despite its contradiction of the original understanding, still consistent with the overarching original purposes behind the First Amendment? Can it be "translated" into the language of the framer's original intentions, particularly if we consider the "changed circumstances" of modern America?

These are the wrong questions. Constitutional law does not answer to original purposes or intentions as such. It does not bear the same relationship to *all* historical intentions. Some intentions retain a specially privileged position; others are of no consequence at all. The modern freedom of speech cannot be reconciled with the original No-Application Understandings. But it adheres to and builds on the historical Application Understandings. Such is the characteristic structure of American constitutional law, to which free-speech law conformed even as it underwent revolutionary expansion in the twentieth century.

Religious Freedom

Of the large purposes or principles that originally lay behind the Constitution's religion clauses, widely disparate things have been said. On one view, the First Amendment was enacted to create a "wall of separation" between church and state. On another view, the framers believed that there was nothing wrong with state laws supporting religion as a whole, or Christianity more particularly, or even Protestantism, so long as those laws neither penalized nor preferred any particular denomination.[32]

The truth is that fundamental disagreements existed then, just as they do now, about the proper relation between church and state. In a few states—notably Virginia—the commingling of church and state had been categorically condemned by leading Revolutionary figures, such as Jefferson and Madison, and by legislation. Separationists complained that the original text of the Constitution (that is, the Constitution as it existed before the Bill of Rights) did not expressly prevent Congress from establishing a national church or from violating rights of conscience.[33] But many others had the opposite complaint. The problem with the original Constitution, they said, was that it failed to acknowledge God, to endorse Christianity, or to prevent Congress from trying to impose church-state separationism on states that didn't want it. Outside Virginia, most of the new American states had ecclesiastical laws that would strike us today as plainly establishing religion. Most of the states imposed religious tests for office, sometimes compelling religious worship and often guaranteeing civil and political rights only to Christians or Protestants.[34] Throughout New England, towns were empowered to tax their residents for "the support and maintenance" of "Protestant" ministries.[35]

The First Amendment was enacted against this contradictory background, and it shows. The establishment clause, as originally understood, was apparently a "two-edged" sword, prohibiting Congress from either establishing or disestablishing religion, from passing "any law *disfavoring* as well as any law *favoring* an establishment of religion."[36] Given the conflicting views then prevailing in the United States, it seems likely that there was no shared original understanding about the proper overarching shape of church-state relations.

But what can be identified with much greater clarity is a set of specific, original, core Application Understandings. The religion clauses prohibited Congress from creating a national church, like the Church of England.[37] It prohibited Congress from prosecuting or penalizing Baptists, Jews, or others who worshiped at the "wrong" church.[38] It prohibited Congress from levying taxes to support a particular faith. These core applications—of the establishment clause and of the free-exercise clause—still go without saying today, and they are obviously central to modern American conceptions of the separation between church and state. As the Court said in the landmark *Everson* case, the establishment clause

> means at least this: Neither a state nor the Federal Government can set up a church. Neither can pass laws which aid one religion, aid all religions, or prefer one religion over another. . . . Neither can force nor influence a person to go to or to remain away from church against his will or force him to profess a belief or disbelief in any religion. No person can be punished for entertaining or professing religious beliefs or disbeliefs, for church attendance or non-attendance. No tax in any amount, large or small, can be levied to support any religious activities or institutions.[39]

But as to the No-Application Understandings, modern doctrine as expressed in *Everson* and its progeny is heedless of them. For example, in 1789 it is very unlikely that the religion clauses were understood to prohibit prayer in public schools. Indeed, the most important original No-Application Understanding of the establishment clause was that it would *not* prohibit *states* from establishing a religion or preferring Christianity through taxes or other legal measures,[40] and this No-Application Understanding has been categorically rejected. As *Everson* holds, the establishment clause now applies, through the Fourteenth Amendment, with equal force against the states and the federal government. To cite just one example, the clear original understanding of the religion clauses was that they did not prohibit religious tests for *state* office, but today courts hold that the establishment clause does prohibit such tests.[41]

This particular expansion of the establishment clause—its application against the states—has been the subject of heated debate.[42] The originalists' objection has been that incorporation of the establishment clause (through the Fourteenth Amendment) against the states makes no historical sense. The originalists say, quite rightly, that the establishment clause was a federalism clause, protecting state sovereignty over religious matters. Therefore (the argument goes) it makes no logical sense to hold that the Fourteenth Amendment "incorporates" the establishment clause against the states, just as it would make no sense to hold that the Fourteenth Amendment incorporates the Tenth Amendment, which says that the powers not conferred upon the federal government remain with the states.[43] "While many specific Bill of Rights incorporations have been criticized, none are so thoroughly contradicted by the historically discernible intentions of our forefathers than that of the establishment clause."[44]

The originalists have a point, but their point does not prove what they suppose. It is true that in incorporating the establishment clause, the Court displayed a remarkably limited or distorted sense of the pertinent history. The Court wrote *Everson* as if all the framers of the First Amendment had embraced a broad principle demanding separation of church and government. The Court thus vindicated one-half of the original meaning of that clause (the half that prohibited national establishment of religion) while suppressing or ignoring the other half (the half that deliberately left states free to establish a religion if they chose).

What the originalists fail to see is that this selective treatment of historical meaning is neither arbitrary nor unusual. It is part of the basic structure of American constitutional law. The understanding that the establishment clause left states free to pass whatever ecclesiastical laws they liked was a No-Application Understanding. In *Everson,* and in all the cases that followed, the Court privileged and built upon the core Application Understandings, at the expense of original No-Application Understandings.

Searches and Seizures

Today's constitutional law of criminal procedure is notoriously unteth-ered to original understandings or practices.[45] In particular, the Supreme Court has dramatically expanded the Constitution's guaran-tees governing police conduct, such as searches, arrests, and question-ing. The original understanding of the Bill of Rights did not prohibit the introduction of evidence "tainted" by an unreasonable search, nor did it prohibit the introduction of statements made by people who were arrested but not read their "*Miranda* rights." Yet in the midst of all this un-originalist law, the Constitution's foundational applications not only have remained intact but have played a central role in the development of doctrine.

If the Fourth Amendment was intended to prohibit anything, it was intended to prohibit indiscriminate "general warrant" searches of the kind famously condemned by Lord Camden in a case widely celebrated in revolutionary America.[46] On the basis of this original understanding, courts today will unhesitatingly invalidate an insufficiently particularized search warrant, explaining that "[i]t is familiar history that . . . 'general warrants' were the immediate evils that motivated the framing and adop-tion of the Fourth Amendment."[47] In one such case, the Supreme Court held, "we think it is clear that this warrant was of a kind which it was the purpose of the Fourth Amendment to forbid—a general warrant" and "[t]herefore . . . must . . . be set aside."[48] Why do such seemingly origi-nalist formulations raise no eyebrows in our quite non-originalist Fourth Amendment law? Because they concern foundational Application Under-standings.

By contrast, the Fourth Amendment's No-Application Understandings have been systematically forgotten. For example, as Akhil Amar has empha-sized, one of the most important original understandings of the Fourth Amendment was that it did not generally prohibit warrantless searches or seizures. The Amendment was intended to limit the issuance of warrants, which were viewed with suspicion because they immunized searches and seizures from subsequent attack in court. Another original No-Application

Understanding was that the Fourth Amendment did not generally prohibit searches or seizures on less than probable cause. A warrant could be issued "only upon probable cause," but this clause (written to make it harder for officers to obtain warrants) did not imply a general rule that searches or seizures could not occur without a warrant or on less than probable cause.[49]

Today, these No-Application Understandings have been jettisoned. Modern Fourth Amendment doctrine holds that "warrantless searches are presumptively unconstitutional,"[50] as are searches on less than probable cause.[51] These broad rules are responsible for a good deal of the tremendous expansion in Fourth Amendment doctrine over the last several decades.

The selective forgetting of history implicit in modern Fourth Amendment doctrine is once again grist for the originalist mill.[52] But it could not conform better to the pattern I have been observing. The Court has reasoned from the paradigmatic unconstitutionality of general warrants to the principle that the Fourth Amendment stands against unconstrained police discretion and unjustified intrusions into personal privacy. On the basis of this principle, rooted in history (that is, rooted in the historical, paradigmatic Application Understanding), modern Fourth Amendment doctrine has left historical No-Applications Understandings behind, prohibiting a great deal of police conduct to which the Fourth Amendment would originally not have applied.

Self-Incrimination

A defendant's right not to be "compelled in a criminal case to be a witness against himself" provides one of the clearest examples in constitutional law of the force of a historical paradigm case.

The original understanding of the self-incrimination clause is in many respects unknown. There are virtually no discussions of the clause in the debates over the Constitution.[53] The rationale behind it is obscure.[54] In a sense, *all* we know with certainty about the historical meaning of the privilege is its foundational paradigm case: the practice of interrogating an accused under oath while threatening harsh sanctions against him for refusal to answer.

This was the device employed four centuries ago against dissenters, including the Puritans, in certain English courts such as the Star Chamber, the abolition of which in the seventeenth century "remain[s] among the most celebrated landmarks of English political and legal history."[55] A guilty defendant in the Star Chamber faced three highly unattractive options. If he answered truthfully, he would condemn himself. If he stood silent, he would be imprisoned for refusing to answer. But if he denied the charges, he would perjure himself—which was not only a crime in itself but a mortal sin, given that the accused had sworn an oath before God.[56]

Why exactly was it considered intolerable to put a guilty person in this position? There is no settled answer to this question. What is settled, however, is that prohibiting this "cruel trilemma" represents the core application, the one fixed star, in American self-incrimination doctrine. "At its core, the privilege reflects our fierce 'unwillingness to subject those suspected of crime to the cruel trilemma of self-accusation, perjury or contempt' that defined the operation of the Star Chamber."[57]

Invoking and building on this foundational application, the Supreme Court explicitly engaged in paradigm-case reasoning when, in the 1960s, it began radically to expand self-incrimination doctrine.[58] In the process, following the usual pattern, important original No-Application Understandings passed away. Modern scholarship has persuasively shown that the privilege as applied today prohibits trial practices considered routine throughout the eighteenth and early nineteenth centuries.[59]

An especially significant example involves the famous *Miranda* warnings. According to the best historical evidence, the privilege against self-incrimination was originally understood *not* to prohibit compulsory unsworn testimony.[60] But today, as the *Miranda* warnings illustrate, the privilege protects an accused even when he is not under oath. *Miranda* thus contradicts the original understanding, not only because it applies to police questioning (rather than in-court questioning), but also because it involves questioning an individual without putting him under oath. Nevertheless, *Miranda* rests on paradigm-case reasoning. A "cruel trilemma," the Court held in *Miranda* and subsequent cases, of the very same kind that the privilege was enacted to prohibit, can exist even when an individual is questioned outside the sworn-testimony context.[61] According to the Court, a guilty individual interrogated in police custody, unwarned of his right to remain silent, may well feel forced to choose among the same three unattractive options: a self-incriminating truth, a self-exonerating lie, or punishment if he refuses to answer.

Modern self-incrimination doctrine is untroubled that this choice, as it is presented to a suspect arrested and questioned by the police, would not originally have been viewed as remotely comparable to the Star Chamber scenario. The oath was crucial to the predicament of the accused before the Star Chamber, because the oath supposedly caused the accused to believe that he faced eternal damnation if he perjured himself. Thus in the original understanding, the privilege would have had No Application to unsworn police questioning. In other words, the Court has expanded on the core application while running roughshod over central historical No-Application Understandings.

Takings

Modern takings doctrine is often said to be so confused that is almost unintelligible. In fact, however, it conforms to the same basic structure we have been observing, and its intelligibility improves considerably when this structure is laid bare. Takings law offers another strong illustration of both the vitality of paradigm cases in constitutional law and the power of paradigm-case reasoning to illuminate present doctrine.

Today's takings law is far removed from anything resembling the original understanding. (I'll say more about this in a moment.) That is not, however, why so many find it so confused. Most commentators try to make sense of takings law not through original understandings, but through one of two quite different lenses: fairness or economics. In other words, they want to know how the Court's takings cases can be said to make sense either in terms of economic efficiency or in terms of a fairness principle such as the notion that individuals should not be made to shoulder an undue share of the cost of public benefits or burdens. If these are the terms in which takings law must make sense, takings law is indeed difficult to understand.

The problems are often traced to the landmark 1922 Supreme Court case of *Pennsylvania Coal v. Mahon*,[62] which struck down, as an uncompensated taking, a state statute prohibiting coal companies from mining in such a way as to cause subsidence damage to houses, streets, or other structures overhead. Justice Holmes, writing for the Court, famously held that this law went "too far." *Pennsylvania Coal* was one of the first Supreme Court cases to find a "regulatory taking"—to find, in other words, that a mere regulation of property amounted to a taking. The difficulty ever since has been to say what it means for a regulation of property to go "too far."

Holmes's delphic phrase has usually been construed to refer primarily to the law's economic impact on the subject property, implying that if a law causes too great a diminution in the value of someone's property, there is a taking. Intuitively, this focus on economic loss seems to many exactly right: if a regulation reduces A's property's value to zero, A's loss is no different from what it would have been if the state had simply seized his property. If A is to be compensated when his property is taken away from him, then why shouldn't he also be compensated if a regulation deprives his property of all value?

Unfortunately—and here is where the claims of unintelligibility begin—takings law routinely allows government to destroy the economic value of people's property without compensating them. For example, well over a century ago, some states began enacting liquor prohibition laws. Manufacturers of spirits, unsurprisingly, brought suit. These laws, the manufacturers pointed out, rendered their inventories, not to mention their breweries and distilleries, valueless. In some cases, breweries were actually seized or shut down. But the Supreme Court upheld such laws,[63] and to this day, the case law expressly permits government to pass new contraband laws—laws declaring that some previously legal commodity can no longer be bought or sold—thus allowing the law totally to destroy the (legal) worth of some previously valuable and lawful property holdings.[64]

Similarly, the Court has expressly allowed state actors to destroy one person's property in order to save someone else's from damage. In an early case, state actors felled one man's cedar trees because a pest that resided in those trees threatened damage to a nearby apple orchard. The cedar owner's property was destroyed, but no taking was found.[65]

Sometimes it is said that all these cases can be explained by the fact that the state was acting to prevent harmful activity. This harm idea seems to many people a neat and proper solution to the difficulty: government *can* render property economically valueless when the government does so to prevent harm. The harm principle, it is said, covers not only the cedar tree case but also cases involving prohibition of liquor or other contraband articles. When a state legislature has deemed a substance harmful, the law can constitutionally ban traffic in the substance even if in doing so it totally deprives some property of all value.

The problem, however, is that many cases where courts have found a taking are also cases in which the government was acting to prevent harm. *Pennsylvania Coal* itself was an example; the law in that case clearly protected persons and buildings overhead from the harm of subsidence damage.[66] Indeed, Justice Brandeis pointed out in dissent in *Pennsylvania Coal* that the case fit squarely into the line of precedent allowing states to regulate property to prevent harm. Hence the clear meaning of *Pennsylvania Coal*—if anything can be said to be clear about that case—is that some land-use regulations can "go too far" even if they are harm-preventing.

Today's regulatory-takings cases adhere to this view. For example, in an important case called *Lucas,* a state law prevented virtually all development of an individual's beachfront property. The Supreme Court reversed a finding that this law had effected no taking, even though the Court explicitly accepted the state's claim that the development ban would prevent harms to the environment, diminution of other owners' property values, and potential storm damage to inland property.[67]

So modern takings law sometimes allows the government to destroy most or all of the economic value of certain property, but sometimes does not. Another line of taking cases that seems confusing to many holds that compensation is categorically required whenever the state authorizes a permanent or indefinite physical "occupation" or "invasion" of someone's property, no matter how small. Thus a law requiring installation of a small cable television box on the roof of an apartment building (so that the residents could have access to cable television) was found to be a taking.[68] So was a law requiring the owners of a private lake to allow their waters to be used by the public for recreational purposes (the lake provided good access to the ocean).[69] On the other hand, in the absence of a physical invasion, the case law permits governmental regulations of property that cause much greater decreases in property value.

These cases infuriate both law-and-economists and fairness-minded explicators of takings law. If a state puts a cable-box on your building, inflicting $10 of damages in the process, you are entitled to compensation, but if the state declares your New York City building a landmark, reducing its market value by 75% and costing you millions of dollars in damages, you get nothing.[70] If a city runs a road through your property, you will be compensated, even though your property value went down by, say, only 15%, but if the city passes a zoning ordinance, reducing your property value by 75% or perhaps even more, you will get nothing.[71] If the government takes over your mine for a few years, you will be compensated, but if the government shuts down your mine for the same number of years, you will get nothing.[72] These disparate results can seem baffling as a matter of economics or fairness, and have led scholars into a competition to find the most cutting epithets to describe the supposed incoherence of modern takings law.

Consider, however, how the paradigm-case method can clear up a great deal of this confusion. The foundational paradigm case for the takings clause is well known. It was the exercise of the so-called "eminent domain" power: the government's prerogative to seize land or other private property, dispossess its owner, and devote the property to uses such as laying a road, constructing a mill, or feeding soldiers. Occasionally, colonial American governments ruled that property owners did not necessarily have to be compensated when their property was seized in eminent domain. But Americans in the Revolutionary period did not take this view. The takings clause established the "sacred principle" that individuals whose property was taken for public use had to be justly compensated.[73] From the beginning and still today, the one clear, unquestioned application of the takings clause is that it requires compensation when the government exercises its eminent domain power.[74]

According to the original understanding, the takings clause seems to have applied *only* to eminent domain takings. Thus the takings clause had No Application to land-use regulations or other governmental actions that did not involve "the actual physical appropriation of property or a divesting of title."[75] Modern regulatory takings law rejects this original No-Application Understanding. In every case in which a regulatory taking is found, from *Pennsylvania Coal* on, the Court requires compensation for an owner whose property is neither physically nor legally taken out of his hands. Hence, as one commentator puts it, "[t]o the extent that the Court is willing to apply the original meaning of the Takings Clause to its interpretation, the Court should abandon the regulatory takings doctrine altogether."[76] On this view, Justice Holmes's famous opinion in *Pennsylvania Coal* is simply irreconcilable with "original meaning."[77]

But modern regulatory takings law, and *Pennsylvania Coal* in particular, are irreconcilable with "original meaning" only in one sense. They transgress important original No-Application Understandings. But they are eminently reconcilable with the original paradigm cases.

The paradigm-case method sets one task for constitutional interpretation: doing justice to the text in light of its paradigm cases. As noted, this means that judges are called on to explain what it is about the paradigm cases (here, classic exercises of eminent domain) that make them a paradigmatic violation of the constitutional clause at issue. In the case of the compensation clause, one strong, clear answer to this question would run as follows: in eminent domain cases, private property is not merely taken, but rather, just as the compensation clause specifies, it is "taken *for public use.*"

The crucial feature of a "using" is what distinguishes eminent domain from other ways in which governments deprive individuals of their property. In traditional cases of eminent domain, there is always both a taking and a using. The government takes over someone's land or chattel and impresses it into specific, state-directed use. The element of a using was well understood by nineteenth-century treatise writers, who relied on the fact that "eminent domain exacts specific property for specific uses" to distinguish takings from taxes and ordinary regulations, both of which also deprived owners of property and decreased property values.[78]

But as property regulations became more complex and pervasive, it became possible for government to accomplish an eminent domain result—the impressment of a person's things into state-dictated use—under the rubric of mere regulation. With this simple insight, twentieth-century takings law suddenly becomes much more intelligible.

Consider *Pennsylvania Coal.* As noted above, Holmes's opinion in that case is typically read to stand for the proposition that compensation must be made when a law takes away too much of the value of the subject property.[79] But the law at issue in *Pennsylvania Coal* did not merely diminish value. On the contrary, there was, in *Pennsylvania Coal,* both a taking and a using. A law that requires owners of underground real estate to leave pillars of land intact, in order to support buildings, streets, or other structures overhead, literally and physically takes private property for public use; it takes over and impresses this private property into state-directed service. While Pennsylvania's statute was, formally speaking, a mere land-use regulation, it was not like most other land-use regulations. Most land-use regulations merely forbid certain activities; they do not have the aim or effect of affirmatively directing that any particular property be put to any particular use. The statute in *Pennsylvania Coal* was an instance of the rare land-use regulation that actually conscripts private property into public use.

When a law merely deprives people of property or property value, but does not impress property into a specific use—as when government bans the sale of liquor, shuts down a mine, prohibits certain land uses, or orders the destruction of one man's cedar trees in order to save another's apple orchard—courts almost never find a taking.[80] By contrast, almost every case in which the Supreme Court has ordered compensation involved both a taking and a using. Most of those cases naturally involved usings, because they were traditional eminent domain cases, but a using was also present in almost every non-eminent-domain case in which the Court has found a taking.[81]

Commentators may have been largely oblivious to this pattern in takings law, but courts have not. On many occasions, judges have explicitly referred to the presence or absence of a using in deciding whether a compensable taking has occurred.[82] In one particularly clear case, the Supreme Court denied compensation to an owner of property destroyed by retreating U.S. soldiers during World War II in order to keep the property from falling into enemy hands. The Court recognized the longstanding rule that owners must be compensated when their property is conscripted by the army into wartime use. But, said the Court, the rule is different when the property is merely destroyed, not impressed into use. The earlier cases, held the Court, "involved equipment which had been impressed by the Army for subsequent use by the Army." By contrast, plaintiff's property here "was destroyed, not appropriated for subsequent use."[83]

This distinction—between merely destroying someone's property and taking it over for a specific state-dictated use—will seem unintelligible to those trying to understand the takings clause in terms of property owners' economic losses or even in terms of the maxim that property owners are to be compensated when unfair burdens are imposed on them. But the distinction is perfectly intelligible from the point of view of the paradigm-case method. The Court has identified a distinguishing feature of the takings clause's foundational applications—the element of a using, definitive of the eminent domain power—and built modern doctrine around it.

When seen in the light of paradigm-case reasoning, the modern case law on regulatory takings and physical-invasion takings shows a surprising overall coherence.[84] For example, the permissibility of contraband laws follows easily once a using is seen as a decisive element of a compensable taking. A newly enacted contraband law might seem grossly unfair to those whose property it suddenly renders worthless and illegal, but it does not require compensation, because it does not put their property to any state-dictated use. As a matter of fact, the cases in which the Court has denied compensation to owners whose property suffered a total or near-total loss of value all involved no using, while the cases in which the

Court has ordered compensation have almost always involved a using. The permanent physical occupation line of cases also becomes much easier to understand, because in most situations in which the government orders a permanent physical occupation of someone's property, it puts that property to a specific, state-dictated use. In other words, while modern takings law has jettisoned historically well-established No-Application Understandings, it has consistently built on the foundational applications.

Equal Protection

Equal protection law is another field that displays this same doctrinal structure. Let's begin with *Brown,* which has proven so difficult for constitutional theory to explain. The paradigm-case method makes *Brown* what it should be—an easy case.

As noted earlier, even originalists have conceded that "those who ratified the amendment did not think it outlawed segregated education or segregation in any aspect of life."[85] In other words, *Brown* rejected an original No-Application Understanding. But how does *Brown* stand in relation to the Fourteenth Amendment's original Application Understandings?

In 1865, the Southern states began promulgating laws singling out blacks for unequal treatment in matters of labor, land ownership, criminal penalties, and so on.[86] The motives behind this movement were obvious. Those who had been slaves were now officially free. This was a very unappealing development for the white South, especially in states where blacks outnumbered whites. The Southern answer to this state of affairs was to pass "black laws," or "black codes," designed to replicate the conditions of black servitude as nearly as possible, given that actually owning blacks was no longer possible.

The struggle to abolish these black codes was famously central to, and definitive of, the act of constitution-writing that became the Fourteenth Amendment.[87] The Fourteenth Amendment was enacted, in the most concrete, historically determinate sense, to abolish the black codes. Even in the earliest cases to reach the Supreme Court, when the Justices seemed determined to interpret the Fourteenth Amendment almost into oblivion, there was never doubt about its core applications.

Thus in 1873, in the famous *Slaughter-House Cases,*[88] in which the Supreme Court all but eradicated the Fourteenth Amendment's privileges and immunities guarantee,[89] the Court still could not bring itself to transgress against the foundational paradigm case: the abolition of the black codes. The *Slaughter-House* Court saw in the Amendment "one pervading purpose": "the protection of the newly-made freeman and citizen from the oppressions of those who had formerly exercised unlimited dominion over them." The Court offered a partial catalogue of those "oppressions":

> [Blacks] were [forbidden] to appear in the towns in any other character than menial servants. They were required to reside on and cultivate the soil without the right to purchase or own it. They were excluded from many occupations of gain, and were not permitted to give testimony in the courts in any case where a white man was a party.[90]

The Fourteenth Amendment, the Court correctly stated, had been enacted to abolish these "oppressions."

A few years later, the Court returned to the black codes and engaged in clear paradigm-case reasoning when it confronted a state law excluding blacks from jury service. Presumably because such statutes were common in the North as well as the South, and presumably because jury eligibility was denied to many other groups as well (women, persons without freeholds, and so on), this bit of racial discrimination was thought by some to have remained constitutional despite the Fourteenth Amendment. But in *Strauder v. West Virginia*,[91] the Court struck it down.

Both the majority and dissent in *Strauder* show the powerful attraction of paradigm-case reasoning in constitutional law. The dissent acknowledged the abolition of the Southern black codes as central to the Fourteenth Amendment's meaning, and even granted that this implied the unconstitutionality of "hostile and discriminating legislation" directed against blacks, but reasoned that the black codes, and hence the Fourteenth Amendment, involved only "civil rights," not "political rights."[92] Because jury service was a "political right," the Fourteenth Amendment did not apply to it.

The *Strauder* majority also started with the significance of the black codes, but the majority likened those codes to the exclusion of blacks from jury service in the following terms: "The very fact that colored people are singled out . . . is practically a brand upon them, affixed by the law, an assertion of their inferiority."[93] The Fourteenth Amendment, held the Court, stood against such laws. It conferred an "immunity" on blacks "from legal discriminations" "implying inferiority in civil society."[94]

Strauder was in some respects a very modest example of paradigm-case reasoning. The anti-inferiorization principle articulated by the *Strauder* Court was not understood, by the Justices at any rate, to apply to groups other than racial minorities. For example, the Court took pains to assert in dictum that states would still be free to exclude women from juries.[95] But *Strauder* is unquestionably an example of paradigm-case reasoning. Through an interpretation of the black codes, the Court derived a principle according to which "legal discriminations" against blacks "assert[ing] their inferiority" or "implying their inferiority in civil society" were unconstitutional. The Court then applied this principle to the jury-exclusion statute and, accordingly, struck it down.

Such reasoning, once begun, exerts a kind of hydraulic normative force. It pushes outward, in the familiar common-law style, available for the next set of plaintiffs as a basis for argument. Paradigm-case reasoning is common-law reasoning; it is the font of constitutional law's common-law-ishness.

If *Strauder*'s paradigm-case reasoning was modest in one way, it was profound in another. For there is no difficulty in seeing *Brown* as an elaboration on—indeed an application of—*Strauder*'s anti-inferiorization principle. "To separate [black children] from others of similar age and qualifications solely because of their race," wrote the Court in *Brown*, "generates a feeling of inferiority as to their status in the community that may affect their hearts and minds in a way unlikely ever to be undone."[96] This "inferiority as to their status in the community" is a formulation very close to *Strauder*'s "inferiority in civil society."

To be sure, *Strauder* does not logically compel the revolutionary result in *Brown*. A discriminating lawyer in 1954 could certainly have argued that "separate-but-equal" was not a form of "discrimination" against blacks "implying inferiority in civil society." A solid originalist argument could have backed up this claim. The original understanding of the Fourteenth Amendment was probably better reflected in the *Strauder* dissent. The thought was that there were two or three separate spheres of equality—"civil and political," or "civil, political and social"—and that the Fourteenth Amendment guaranteed only "civil" equality. This thinking is one of the main reasons why the framers of the Fourteenth Amendment, despite its guarantees of equal protection and of the privileges and immunities of citizenship, could believe that it did not prohibit states from denying blacks the suffrage. Voting was a political right. Similarly, segregation in schools and elsewhere also involved only political or social equality and hence was not forbidden by the equal protection clause.

One reply often made by those who valiantly try to make *Brown* safe for originalism is that *Brown* can be reconciled with the framers' original conception of equality. Public education, they say, had so increased in importance by 1954 that it had by then become a "civil right" or a fundamental part of "civil equality," regardless of whether this was so in 1867.[97] But this claim, if it does some good for *Brown*, undermines the numerous decisions, following close on the heels of *Brown*, in which the Court tore down America's racial separation regime in all its governmental forms, from segregated golf courses to public beaches.[98] It does not seem appealing to say that golfing had so increased in importance by the 1950s that it too was a civil right.

The truth is that *Brown* and its progeny broke not only from original No-Application Understandings but also from the entire interpretive framework through which the framers of the Fourteenth Amendment understood it—the framework in which states had to guarantee civil equality to blacks, but remained free to discriminate against them in matters of social or political equality. *Brown* ran a bulldozer over this original, tripartite conception of equality. It is not possible to imagine, after *Brown*, that the equal protection clause allows states to deny blacks the vote (even without considering the Fifteenth Amendment), the right to be elected to political office, the right to be named a judge, or any other political right. Does this make *Brown* difficult to accept as a matter of constitutional interpretation? Does it mean that *Brown* can be embraced only by accepting an essentially ahistorical, "moral reading" of the Constitution?

Not at all. From the point of view of paradigm-case interpretation, *Brown* requires only the following, simple logic. Begin with the black codes. Even the *Slaughter-House* Court got this far. What is it about the black codes that makes them clearly unconstitutional under the Fourteenth Amendment? This question can be answered in a number of ways.

One answer is to derive from the abolition of the black codes an anti-inferiorization principle along precisely the lines laid out in *Strauder* or, in a slight variation, an anticaste principle along the lines laid out by Justice Harlan in his famous dissenting opinion in *Plessy v. Ferguson:* "[I]n view of the constitution, in the eye of the law, there is in this country no superior, dominant, ruling class of citizens. There is no caste here."[99] Justice Harlan's anticaste formulation may be viewed as a restatement of *Strauder*'s anti-inferiorization principle or as a modification of it. For present purposes, it doesn't matter. Either formulation states a wholly plausible and justifiable reading of the Fourteenth Amendment in light of its foundational paradigm cases.

Finally, apply this principle to separate-but-equal. Did separate-but-equal discriminate against blacks in a manner that implied inferiority or subject them to a lower caste status, as the black codes had?

The question answers itself. America's racial separation laws were untouchability laws. To quote Justice Harlan again, they "proceed[ed] on the ground that colored citizens are so inferior and degraded that they cannot be allowed to sit in public coaches occupied by white citizens,"[100] or to drink from the same water fountains as whites, or otherwise to have intercourse with them. Untouchability is a universal marker of inferiority and caste. Separate-but-equal was a regime designed to keep blacks in their place, just as the black codes were. That is all that needs to be said to explain *Brown,* notwithstanding the various contortions that today's schools of interpretation deploy to reach the same result.[101]

The black codes do not, however, have to be read as instances of inferiorization or of lower-caste treatment. They could be read, for example, as departures from color-blindness (although this hardly captures their specific gravity), another principle that would vindicate *Brown.* I am not saying that *Brown* is logically compelled by every possible reading of the abolition of the black codes. Paradigm cases are never self-interpreting, and it would be possible to deliver an account of the unconstitutionality of the black codes under which racial segregation remained perfectly constitutional. In fact, the *Plessy* majority offered an interpretation of the black codes that attempted to justify exactly this result.

The *Plessy* Court essentially recapitulated the *Strauder* dissent, emphasizing the civil-political equality distinction already noted, but another ingredient in the Court's reasoning is also worth mentioning. Acknowledging the critical interpretive significance of the black codes, the *Plessy* majority redescribed those codes in an interesting way. The Fourteenth Amendment, the *Plessy* majority stated, was written to protect members of "the colored race from certain laws . . . curtailing their rights in the pursuit of life, liberty, and property to such an extent that their freedom *was of little value.*"[102] Not all "distinctions based upon color" were thereby ruled out, for not all such distinctions were so "onerous." Not all of them so "curtailed [blacks'] rights" "that their freedom was of little value." As long as states provided blacks with equal accommodations, the equal protection clause was satisfied.[103]

Plessy too, therefore, was an example of paradigm-case reasoning. It just happens to have been a very bad example.

The *Plessy* interpretation fails strikingly to capture the black codes themselves. Consider a statute excluding blacks from, say, professional occupations, such as law or medicine. This kind of exclusion presumably does not render black freedom "of little value." Yet this exclusion was precisely the kind of "black law" that the Fourteenth Amendment was centrally enacted to prohibit. The evil of such an exclusion is of course the invidious inequality to which it subjects blacks, regardless of whether it makes their liberty "of little value." Or again, consider the common black-code provision imposing on blacks greater criminal penalties than those imposed on whites who had committed the same offenses. In what way does this discrimination render blacks' freedom "of little value"?

The *Plessy* Court offered an interpretation of the black codes in terms of a liberty principle, instead of an equality principle. This effort not only failed to capture the black codes in themselves, but also failed to capture them as instances of the textual guarantee in question—as instances of a violation of the equal protection guarantee.

Paradigm-case interpretation is emphatically textualist. Judges engaging in paradigm-case reasoning are not grappling with the paradigm cases as free-floating entities detached from the Constitution. They are trying to do justice to a text in light of its paradigm cases. The *Plessy* Court claimed to be interpreting the equal protection clause, but instead of doing justice to this clause in light of its paradigm cases, the Court delivered a wholly unsuccessful account of the black codes in terms of a liberty principle.

On the other hand, the *Plessy* Court could have written an opinion solely based on the distinction between social and civil equality, holding that segregated train cars do not entrench on civil equality. Such an opinion would have had the virtue of conforming with the Fourteenth Amendment's original No-Application Understandings. All that I have said here, and all that it is necessary to say in order to explain *Brown*, is that judges are not bound by this original No-Application Understanding, and that there is a direct, compelling path to *Brown* from the Fourteenth Amendment's foundational applications, a path marked out by the Supreme Court itself as long ago as the 1870s, when it decided *Strauder.*

If this understanding of *Brown*'s radical holding seems almost too easy, it should. The paradigm-case method captures *Brown* the way it ought to be captured: as an easy case, not only morally but as a matter of interpretation. *Brown* was rightly decided because ending segregation was a matter of living up, finally, to the nation's constitutional commitment to end the legalized degradation of blacks.

Brown is not by any means the only example of a modern equal protection case defying original understandings. Contemporary equal protection doctrine is massively anti-originalist, systematically violating deeply held original understandings, such as the understanding that the Fourteenth Amendment would not bar sex discrimination. It just so happens that every one of these now-obsolete original understandings was a No-Application Understanding.

At the same time, contemporary equal protection law remains wholly structured by its foundational applications. The entire doctrinal framework of equal protection jurisprudence—imposing heightened means-ends review on state action burdening "suspect classes"—rests on and takes its intelligibility from the fact that invidious discrimination against blacks is paradigmatically prohibited. The fact that this framework, rooted in the Fourteenth Amendment's paradigm cases, generates results at odds with original No-Application Understandings is not a cause for consternation. It is, rather, the characteristic mark of American constitutional interpretation.

3

Powers

I have so far been discussing constitutional rights. I turn now to constitutional powers. To show how the distinction between Application and No-Application Understandings works in the case of powers, I am going to engage in some pretty fine, unpleasantly technical distinctions. For this, I beg the reader's pardon. I can only plead necessity.

The general difference between rights and powers is that the former are prohibitions, while the latter are authorizations. Constitutional rights prohibit certain actors (usually governmental actors) from taking certain actions. Constitutional powers authorize certain actors (usually governmental actors) to take certain actions.

There is, however, a complication. Sometimes a constitutional power is not merely authorizing, but also prohibitory. This is so when a constitutional power is *exclusive,* prohibiting anyone other than the designated actor(s) from exercising the power in question. The declaration-of-war clause *exclusively* authorizes Congress to declare war (or so it is generally understood). As a result, it prohibits the President or other actors from doing so.

But even when constitutional powers are exclusive, there is another sense in which they are still not prohibitory. They are not prohibitory with respect to the agents to whom they grant power. The declaration-of-war clause is not prohibitory with respect to Congress. It authorizes Congress to do something (declare war), but it imposes no prohibitions on Congress. The declaration-of-war clause cannot be thought to prohibit Congress from doing that which it does not authorize Congress to do, for then it would prohibit Congress from, say, regulating interstate commerce.

The powers originally granted to Congress were, taken together, intended to be *exhaustive,* as the Tenth Amendment confirms. This means

48

that Congress can do nothing that does not fall within one of its enumerated powers. The point, however, is that none of Congress's particular powers, taken by itself, can be read as imposing any prohibition on Congress. If Congress's commerce power does not apply to marriage laws, for example, it is not accurate to say that the commerce clause *prohibits* Congress from enacting marriage laws. The commerce clause merely does not permit it; another one of Congress's powers might.

Only with these distinctions in mind can we distinguish between Application and No-Application Understandings of Congress's powers. Each particular Article I power authorizes Congress to do something, while prohibiting nothing (to Congress). As a result, it follows that original understandings of what a particular Article I power did *not* authorize Congress to do are No-Application Understandings of that power. What does the declaration-of-war clause have to say about a congressional statute regulating the interstate sale of insurance contracts? Nothing. It neither authorizes nor prohibits such a law. It simply has No Application thereto.

Hence, just as the No-Application Understandings of a *prohibitory* text are specific understandings of what the text does *not prohibit*, the No-Application Understandings of an *authorizing* text (with respect to the actors to whom it grants power) are specific understandings of what the text does *not authorize*. And just as the core applications of a constitutional right consist of laws or actions that the right was centrally enacted to forbid, the core applications of a constitutional power (with respect to the actors to whom it grants power) consist of laws or actions that the power was centrally enacted to authorize.

On the other hand, when we deal with *exclusive* grants of power, a power can also have *prohibitory* Application Understandings. Because it was exclusive, the declaration-of-war clause was almost certainly originally intended to prohibit the President from unilaterally declaring war. This is an Application Understanding. If the President sought to take unauthorized unilateral military action deemed to be a declaration of war, we could say that the declaration-of-war clause applies to and prohibits what he is trying to do.

With these basic terms in mind, this chapter addresses three of the most important contemporary disputes concerning the Constitution's power-granting provisions: the reach of Congress's "spending power," the reach of the commerce clause, and the basic structure of the Constitution's separation-of-powers principles.

The Spending Power

The first power granted to Congress by the Constitution is the power to "lay and collect Taxes . . . to pay the Debts and provide for the common Defence and Welfare of the United States."[1] The meaning of this "spending clause"—the name by which our courts today refer to it, even though the word "spend" does not appear—was fundamentally contested from the beginning. Could Congress spend money on public education across the nation? Could the federal government fund roads or build a canal? Today, such spending is the basic stuff of Washington politics, and its permissibility would have been supported in the early period by such eminent figures as Hamilton and Story.[2] But many others, including Madison and Jefferson, took a far narrower view.

According to the narrow view, Congress's "spending power" was confined to "carrying out those enumerated and limited powers vested in Congress—and no others."[3] Thus as president, Jefferson maintained that a constitutional amendment would be necessary in order for Congress to fund "public education, roads, rivers, canals, and . . . other objects of public improvement,"[4] because none of those matters was placed within Congress's authority by any of the powers granted to Congress in Article I or any other article of the Constitution. Madison too, as president, vetoed an internal improvements bill on the ground that it exceeded Congress's powers.[5]

How did Madison, Jefferson, and other proponents of the narrow view deal with the fact that the "spending power" seems to be plenary on its face, authorizing Congress to "provide for the common Defence and Welfare"—an extremely capacious phrase?

Those who took the narrow view had a good textualist answer to this question. After "the spending clause," Article I goes on to grant Congress many other specific powers. These specific powers, proponents of the narrow view argued, would have been entirely otiose if the "spending clause" implied a general power to spend federal revenues for the common defense and welfare. Consider, for example, Congress's expressly granted power to "provide and maintain a Navy." Why would this specific power be granted—why would it have been necessary—if Congress already had, under the spending power, independent authority "to provide for the common Defence" however Congress saw fit? On the expansive reading of the spending power, the naval power would have been absurdly superfluous.

Or again, Congress is explicitly given a limited power to purchase land from states and to erect there "Forts, Magazines, Arsenals, dock-Yards, and other needful Buildings."[6] Didn't this provision imply that Congress did not, simply by virtue of the taxing power, have a general authority to use federal funds for the "general welfare" or "common defense"? As then-Congressman Madison said, "It would be absurd to say, first, that Congress may do what they please, and then that they may do this or that particular thing."[7]

Some claim that Jefferson's election in 1800 was a cementing victory for the narrow view of the spending clause, which had been an issue in his campaign. Andrew Jackson famously rejected the broad view during his presidency. Indeed, from 1800 through the latter part of the nineteenth century, U.S. presidents, with the exception of John Quincy Adams, consistently vetoed public works appropriations on the ground that Congress lacked any general constitutional authority to engage in public works or internal improvement spending. Although it has been said that no court ever endorsed the Madisonian (narrow) interpretation of the spending power, at least indirect support for it can be found in the famous case of *McCollough v. Maryland*—precisely because Marshall invokes nearly every congressional power *but* the "spending power" to justify a federal bank.[8]

In other words, while the historical record leaves room for debate, there was clearly a much-supported, long-held, early understanding, perhaps solidified by Jefferson's and Jackson's presidencies, that insisted on a narrow construction of the spending power. The narrow view reflected both Application and No-Application Understandings. The unquestioned, core Application Understanding, common to both the Hamiltonian (capacious) and Madisonian (narrow) views, was that the spending clause enabled Congress to raise and spend revenue to carry out its various *enumerated* powers, such as establishing post offices, maintaining a navy, or coining money. This core Application Understanding remains unquestioned today.

By contrast, the key elements of the Madisonian view—the elements by which it narrowed the reach of the clause—were No-Application Understandings: that the clause did not apply to internal improvements appropriations, and more generally, that it did not authorize Congress to spend money outside the sphere of carrying out of its enumerated powers. Thus even if this understanding was shared by most framers or ratifiers of the Constitution, and even if it was reinforced by Jefferson's or Jackson's presidency, it established no paradigm case. All that was established, at most, was a No-Application Understanding, and in modern spending power doctrine, as in so many other fields of constitutional law, this historical No-Application Understanding is history.

Under present doctrine, a federally funded dam or highway project is utterly unproblematic. As the Court put it in 1950, "the power of Congress to promote the general welfare through large-scale projects for reclamation, irrigation, or other internal improvement, is now . . . clear and ample."[9] Congress need only determine that such a project serves "the general welfare"—a requirement so lenient that it may not even raise a justiciable question.[10] The spending power has broken entirely free from the No-Application requirement that money be spent only in effectuating other powers granted by Article I. Thus has the federal fisc become the universal trough that we take for granted today.

At the same time, the core Application Understanding continues to play an important role in shaping the doctrine's expansion. One of the most debated questions today in spending power doctrine involves *conditional* federal funding, in which federal grants of money to states (or other parties) are conditioned on compliance with specified requirements.[11] Case law has suggested that conditional funding might be unconstitutional when inducement passes into "coercion."[12] In attempting to apply this difficult concept, at least one appellate court has distinguished between exercises of the spending power that fall within the paradigm case—spending to carry out goals within Congress's enumerated powers—and those that fall outside this core.

In a case involving the federal Highway Act, which denied 95% of federal highway funds to states that refused to adopt a 55-mile-per-hour speed limit, the Ninth Circuit reasoned as follows:

> We first explain why the provisions relating to the national speed limit must be upheld if Congress could impose those limits under an enumerated power, other than the Spending Power. . . . The central debate of the Spending Power cases has always been whether Congress may exercise authority beyond the strict limitations imposed by the other enumerated powers specified in the Constitution. . . . No one has yet questioned the right of the federal government to act, under the Spending Power, within the ambit of those other enumerated powers.

Nevada, however, argues that the federal government cannot engage in coercive conduct in the exercise of its Spending Power, even when the particular exercise is within the limitations of the Commerce Clause. We . . . reject[ ] appellant's theory. . . .[13]

Finding that the Highway Act was an exercise of the spending power to carry out a commerce clause objective, the Ninth Circuit concluded that "the coercion test is simply inapplicable, whether or not that test applies in Spending Power cases not involving actions within the scope of the other enumerated powers."[14]

This passage illustrates how core Application Understandings retain unquestioned status in modern constitutional law, even while courts are happy to reconsider and reject historical No-Application Understandings. At the same time, the Ninth Circuit's decision also shows how courts recur to these paradigmatic applications to answer difficult interpretive questions even as the doctrine expands beyond its historical limits. The Ninth Circuit here uses the unquestioned status of the Application Understanding to try to reason its way through the difficult "coercion" issue.

The Commerce Clause

The revolution in commerce clause doctrine that occurred after 1940 is well known. This revolution consisted entirely of demolishing earlier No-Application Understandings. Indeed, until recently, the locomotive of post-1940 commerce clause doctrine flattened virtually every No-Application Understanding in its path.

As originally understood, according to most commentators, the commerce clause did not empower Congress to regulate most manufacturing, agriculture, or labor relations within the several states.[15] These results followed from basic, widely shared No-Application Understandings: the commerce clause did not apply to the *production* of goods—only to commerce in goods—and it did not apply to wholly in-state activity. Today, however, the commerce power gives Congress nearly plenary authority to regulate manufacturing, agriculture, and labor relations, provided only that the activity regulated—for example, the growing of wheat—has in the aggregate a substantial effect on some aspect of interstate commerce, which nearly all activity does.[16]

What about the original Application Understandings? The most obvious historical application of the commerce clause was congressional authority over all tariffs and commercial transactions that crossed state or national lines. In addition, the commerce clause was originally understood to vest Congress with the power to regulate the country's navigable waters, even when those waters were located within a state.[17] These Application Understandings remain unchallenged in commerce clause doctrine today. More than this, Congress's power over navigable waters is closely related—although this relation is often missed—to the revolution in commerce clause doctrine that occurred in the last century.

There was a specific Application Understanding that exemplified Congress's power over navigable waters: the understanding that Congress could act to prevent obstructions to those waters. Even those who generally took a very limited view of Congress's powers agreed that Congress "may, under this power [the commerce power], declare that no bridge shall be built which shall be an obstruction to the use of a navigable water."[18] The building of bridges across navigable rivers will seem a trivial subject today, when the commerce power extends to manufacturing, agriculture, antidiscrimination law, and so much else. But if we look at this Application Understanding as a paradigm case, it goes a long way toward explaining and justifying the expansion of the commerce clause that occurred in the twentieth century.

Building a bridge over a navigable waterway need not itself be an act of interstate commerce. Bridge building can occur entirely within a state, without any commercial motivation. A bridge could in principle be built by volunteer labor simply to make it easier for people on one side of the river to visit their relations on the other side—all within a single state. Yet historically, the commerce clause authorized Congress to regulate or even prohibit such a bridge, provided that it obstructed interstate commerce.

From this Application Understanding, it may not be a small step, but neither is it an unbridgeable one, to the principle that drove the expansion of the commerce power throughout the last century. In *Wickard v. Fillburn*,[19] the case that broke the commerce clause bank, the Court held that Congress could regulate the amount of wheat grown by a farmer on his own land for his own use. The rationale for the Court's decision was that unlimited wheat growing by farmers all over the country could detrimentally lower the price of wheat, adversely affecting the interstate wheat market. *Wickard* held that the commerce clause empowered Congress to regulate activity that, "in the aggregate," threatened "substantial" harm to interstate commerce, even if the activity was "itself local" and hence not an instance of interstate commerce.[20]

To self-proclaimed originalists and textualists, *Wickard* has seemed an unspeakable distortion of the commerce power.[21] The obvious objection is that the growing of wheat on a farm located inside a state (for domestic consumption!) is not an act of interstate commerce. "Could anyone say with a straight face that the consumption of home-grown wheat is 'commerce among the several states?'"[22]

But this view neglects the Application Understanding of the commerce clause just discussed: the understanding that Congress always had power to regulate bridges built over navigable waters. What brought such a bridge within Congress's commerce power was, obviously, the fact that it might substantially harm interstate commerce. If we ask for a general rule governing the commerce power that captures, as a central instance of that rule, a law regulating in-state bridges that might obstruct interstate commerce, the rule cannot be that Congress may regulate only acts that themselves amount to interstate commerce. As just noted, building a bridge over a navigable river within a state is not itself "commerce among the several states." A rule that *would* capture the Application Understanding is the following: "The power to regulate interstate commerce embraces the power to protect that commerce from injury whatever may be the source of the dangers which threaten it, and to adopt any appropriate means to that end."[23]

This formulation, offered by Chief Justice Hughes in 1936 and essentially accepted by the Court in *Wickard,* is extraordinarily expansive, yet it can in fact be said to follow from the paradigm case. Yes, *Wickard* left in the dust a central, original *No-Application* Understanding. At the same time, however, the principle it embraced, and hence the revolution it heralded in commerce clause doctrine, is directly traceable to a paradigmatic Application Understanding.

Through the commerce clause, Congress was paradigmatically entrusted with a power to regulate at least some conduct threatening injury to interstate commerce even when this conduct occurred inside a state, and even when the conduct was not itself an act of interstate commerce. Those alive in 1789 might of course have said that this power was limited to the regulation of navigable waters. They might have said that this power had No Application on land. They almost certainly would have said that this power could not by any stretch be converted into a nearly plenary congressional authority to regulate agriculture, manufacturing, labor relations, and so on.

But the root power was there: the power of Congress to regulate in-state activity—activity not itself amounting to a transaction in or an instance of interstate commerce—in order to prevent injury to interstate commerce. The notion that this power stopped at the shores of navigable waters, however widespread this notion may have been in 1789, was a No-Application Understanding, which later interpretation was free to reject.

Separation of Powers

Separation of powers is another extremely important—but more difficult—field in which the Application/No-Application Understanding distinction can help untangle vexing doctrinal knots. A warning: only experts in this field may want to work their way through the complex arguments that follow.

A fundamental question in American separation-of-powers jurisprudence is whether or to what extent the powers granted to Congress, the President, and the courts are *exclusive*. On one view, the Constitution's legislative powers are granted to Congress alone, the executive powers in Article II to the President alone, and the judicial power to the courts alone. In other words, executive officers are constitutionally barred from legislating, judicial officers from executing, and so on. Call this the *strict separationist* view.

Strict separationism, advanced by some "textualist" scholars today and, in the past, occasionally supported by the Supreme Court, conflicts sharply with the realities of the contemporary federal government. In the modern administrative state, agencies routinely exercise lawmaking power, enacting regulations with the full force of law (enforceable both by fines and by incarceration) covering the workplace, food and drugs, product safety, consumer protection, environmental protection, and so on. Moreover, independent officers, commissions, and agencies routinely exercise executive powers even though they cannot be directly controlled by the President.

Looking to the constitutional text to resolve this problem immediately raises difficulties, because virtually every one of the Constitution's power-granting provisions is grammatically ambiguous, permitting exclusive and nonexclusive readings. The commander-in-chief clause, for example, does not say on its face that *only* the President may exercise the powers of commander in chief, but it can be read that way, and it always has been. On this view, Congress could not constitutionally appoint a designated general or bureaucrat to be commander in chief.

But the Constitution's powers can also be read as nonexclusive, meaning that the agent on whom power is conferred is not the only agent capable of exercising that power. Grammatically speaking, the commerce clause could be read as exclusive—only Congress may regulate interstate commerce—but it is not read that way today. Congress can criminalize the act of transporting cocaine into New York, but so can New York. While earlier case law accepted an exclusive-power reading of the commerce clause,[24] modern doctrine has rejected that reading, recognizing instead a zone of concurrent power, shared by the states and the federal government, to regulate interstate commerce. To be sure, Congress's power is superior to that of the states, so that Congress can preempt states from exercising their power to regulate interstate commerce, but the mere fact that Congress is granted the interstate commerce power does not by itself prohibit states from regulating interstate commerce.

In numerous older opinions, the Supreme Court adopted the view that the powers granted to each branch were exclusive. Thus, executive officers could not constitutionally legislate, because only Congress had the power to legislate. One body of law in which this strict-separationist position manifested itself was the (now repudiated) nondelegation doctrine, which held that Congress could not delegate legislative power to the President or other executive officers.[25] But the Court continued to adhere to the strict-separationist position long after the demise of the nondelegation doctrine—that is, long after it had stopped striking down Congress's creation of executive agencies charged with the power of making law.[26] In the 1980s, however, the Court began disclaiming the strict-separationist position, emphasizing that the three branches can share a great deal of overlapping, concurrent power, with no "hermetic" division between them.[27] Under the new case law, Congress's lawmaking powers became essentially nonexclusive, unlike its declaration-of-war power or the President's commander-in-chief power. In other words, even though a federal statute, signed by the President, could not delegate the President's commander-in-chief power to an independent administrative agency, federal statutes can and routinely do delegate Congress's legislative powers to administrative agencies. Similarly, while the Constitution vests the Article III judiciary with the "judicial Power of the United States," modern doctrine permits other federal actors (such as "administrative law judges") to adjudicate cases, interpret federal law, and otherwise exercise the judicial power. Or again, while the Constitution vests the President with the "executive Power," modern doctrine permits other actors, substantially independent of presidential control (special prosecutors, the Federal Reserve Board, judges in some cases), to take what are essentially executive actions.[28]

Some contemporary scholars do not like these results. They call for a renewed embrace of the exclusive-power reading of the Constitution's separation-of-powers provisions, so that only the President would have the power to execute, only Congress the power to legislate, and only the judiciary the power to adjudicate. These strict separationists argue, for example, that the Constitution should never have been read to permit an independent prosecutor (because prosecution is an "executive" power and hence only the President, or officers under his control, can be permitted to do it). They also argue for a return to some form of "nondelegation doctrine," under which courts would limit Congress's efforts to delegate its legislative power to administrative agencies.[29]

Now, how does the Application/No-Application distinction cut into this set of problems? The answer is complex, but if the problem is worked through, two conclusions emerge. First, current law has followed the paradigmatic pattern: it has retained the Application Understandings, while discarding No-Application Understandings. Second, the paradigm-case method helps clarify some of the doctrinal difficulties as yet unresolved.

Consider the situation where a power was originally understood to be exclusive. As noted, the declaration-of-war clause seems to have been so understood. Indeed, a core intention behind that clause appears to have been stopping the President from declaring war on his own, notwithstanding his commander-in-chief powers.

If this is so, the President's incapacity to declare war becomes a foundational paradigm case for the meaning of the declaration-of-war clause. That clause was understood to be not only *authorizing* (empowering Congress to declare war) but also *prohibitory* (preventing others from doing so), with at least one particular prohibitory Application Understanding—that the President could not declare war—central to its enactment. Thus this Application Understanding should be viewed (and has been viewed) as binding on subsequent interpretation.

To generalize, when a power was believed to be exclusive and was enacted with a core prohibitory Application Understanding—preventing some other actor, such as the President, from exercising the power in question—courts cannot later adopt a nonexclusive reading that would overturn this Application Understanding. If the Supreme Court today adopted a nonexclusive reading of the declaration-of-war clause, under which the clause no longer barred the President from declaring war, the Court would have surrendered a foundational paradigm case.

All this seems obvious enough, but this simple reasoning demonstrates the importance of ascertaining whether any core prohibitory Application Understandings can be identified in connection with a given constitutional power. For example, if there had been (counterfactually) a widespread understanding that the commerce clause would, by its own terms, bar states from imposing tariffs on imported goods, this Application Understanding would have to have been preserved as a paradigm case. This would mean that the current nonexclusive reading of the commerce clause (which rejects the idea that activity falling within Congress's commerce power cannot be regulated by the states) might have to be thrown out.

But there does not appear to have been any such understanding. On the contrary, just after the section in which Article I grants Congress the power to regulate interstate and international commerce, Article I goes on to add an express provision barring states from taxing imports or exports. (Most of the powers granted to Congress in Article I were probably understood to be nonexclusive. After Article I grants Congress the power to coin money, it goes on to bar states from coining money. This would have been quite unnecessary if the granting of the power to Congress had by its own terms been understood to be exclusive.) Undoubtedly, the Constitution was understood to stop states from imposing tariffs on interstate commerce, but the source of that paradigmatic prohibition was not the commerce clause. As a result, the contemporary nonexclusive reading of the commerce clause is consistent with paradigm-case interpretation.

Thus on the question of exclusivity (whether the power in question is an exclusive grant of power to the designated actor), contemporary understandings of both the commerce clause and the declaration-of-war clause confirm once again the power of paradigm cases and fall into line with the Application/No-Application pattern seen nearly everywhere else in constitutional law. With respect to the commerce clause, there was no foundational prohibitory Application Understanding that requires an exclusive reading of that clause, and sure enough, the clause is not read as exclusive today. By contrast, with respect to the declaration-of-war clause, there *was* a paradigmatic prohibitory Application Understanding (the clause prohibited the President from unilaterally declaring war), and American law still holds, if tenuously, to that core Application Understanding today.[30]

This allows us to specify how the paradigm-case method applies to the problem of deciding whether a particular constitutional power is exclusive or nonexclusive. If a grant of power to one actor was understood to have core prohibitory effects on other actors, courts ought to preserve these paradigm cases in subsequent interpretation. Ordinarily, they will do so by interpreting the power as exclusive. With these basic lines of analysis laid out, return now to the strict-separationist position that the powers granted to each branch are exclusive. Does the paradigm-case method support this position?

The answer is that some of the Constitution's powers will be properly viewed as exclusive, but they need not all be, and there is no basis for insisting that, as a matter of the original understanding, all the legislative powers must be exclusively exercised by Congress, all the executive powers exclusively exercised by the President, or all the judicial powers exclusively exercised by the Article III courts. Because the commerce clause, for example, was not originally understood to be exclusive, modern doctrine is perfectly defensible in allowing executive officers to regulate interstate commerce. By contrast, the commander-in-chief and declaration-of-war clauses were originally understood to have paradigmatic, prohibitory Application Understandings, and these Application Understandings remain binding today, sustaining an exclusive-power reading of these clauses.

But there is no basis for a categorical rule saying that executive officers may not legislate or that courts cannot execute. While there may well have been an original understanding that executive officers or judges would have no constitutional authority to make law, there was no constitutional commitment enacted prohibiting them from doing so.

The strict-separationist objection to this argument is that I have ignored the "vesting clauses." Each of the first three articles of the Constitution begins with a vesting clause. Article I provides that all the legislative powers granted therein "shall be vested in a Congress of the United States," Article II that the executive power is "vested in a President of the United States," and Article III that the judicial power is "vested in one supreme Court" and other, inferior courts that Congress may create. The strict separationist argues that these vesting clauses are exclusive and hence require a structural or categorical rule that only Congress can legislate, that only the President can wield the executive powers, and that only the Article III judiciary can exercise the judicial power of the United States. In my terminology, strict separationism asserts that the vesting clauses are prohibitory commitments, preventing each branch from exercising the powers granted to the others.

But the strict separationist has a problem. If the clause vesting the President with the executive power was originally intended to be exclusive, prohibiting all others from executing federal law, I would be very surprised to hear it, given that state officers, who are not under the President's control, were widely expected to have the power to execute federal law—to collect taxes, for example—if Congress chose to allow them to do so. Similarly, I would be very surprised to hear that the vesting clause of Article I, authorizing Congress to exercise "[a]ll legislative Powers granted herein," was originally intended to prohibit all other actors from exercising that power. As noted previously, at least some of the "legislative Powers" vested in Congress were pretty clearly understood not to be barred to the states merely by virtue of Congress's Article I, Section 8 authority. Congress had the power to regulate Indian commerce, but so did the states.

The strict-separationist reply to this point has always been to insist that the original understanding of the federal government's powers in relation to the states is irrelevant to the original understanding of each branch's power in relation to the other branches. We are asked to distinguish, in other words, between "vertical" and "horizontal" separation of powers. On the original understanding, it is said, the powers assigned to the various branches of the federal government may not have been *vertically* exclusive (prohibiting state actors from exercising the powers at issue), but they were *horizontally* exclusive (prohibiting members of other branches from exercising them). Aside from the President's role in signing legislation, neither the President nor any other actors in the executive branch were to have any power to pass laws. Conversely, within the federal government only the President—not Congress or the courts—was to exercise executive power.

As a claim about the original understanding, this assertion may well be largely correct. The modern administrative state might well have struck the framers or ratifiers as profoundly contradicting their intentions. Executive officers, they might have said, have no power to legislate.

But this understanding need not be binding on judges, from the point of view of the paradigm-case method. These understandings were No-Application Understandings. Modern courts are therefore free to disregard them.

The strict separationist will object that I am contradicting myself. By my own logic, an original understanding that Article I's vesting clause prohibited executive officers from legislating would be an Application Understanding, not a No-Application Understanding. Courts today could not, therefore, disregard it. But I have not conceded that Article I's vesting clause was originally understood to prohibit other actors from exercising Congress's legislative powers. I have conceded that there may well have been an original understanding that executive officers could not legislate; it does *not* follow, however, that there was an original understanding that Article I's vesting clause, by its own terms, effected that prohibition. On the contrary, this original understanding is easily traceable to the fact that, on the framers' view, Article II nowhere confers a general legislative power on the executive branch.

The framers very probably believed that the powers affirmatively granted to each branch were exhaustive. If Congress was not granted a particular power in Article I, it could not exercise that power. If the President was not granted a power to make law in Article II, he could not make law. If, by contrast, Article II had included some limited grant of lawmaking to the President—as it in fact does—this would not have been understood to contradict the vesting clause of Article I, even if it overlapped with the legislative power granted to Congress. In other words, the vesting clause of Article I—granting certain enumerated legislative powers to Congress—was not itself prohibitory. (I have warned readers that they would be getting a close analysis of these issues.) The treaty power provides a good example.

Treaties are of course law, so making a treaty is obviously a species of lawmaking. Article I grants to Congress, as we know, the power to regulate commerce with foreign nations. Was this grant of power understood to be exclusive, at least "horizontally"—prohibiting all other actors from exercising the power to regulate foreign commerce? If so, then it would seem to be in direct conflict with the power to make treaties with other countries, which Article II confides to the President (with the advice and consent of the Senate), and which clearly includes the power to make a treaty regulating commerce with a foreign state.

If the Article I grants of legislative power are really to be read as "horizontally" exclusive, as the strict separationist insists, then there are only two things that can logically be said about the President's power to make a treaty regulating commerce with a foreign state. First, the strict separationist could say that the President does not have this power. Such treaties are simply unconstitutional (or at the very least, that Congress would have to authorize such a treaty before it became valid). That view is perfectly intelligible, but it is not the law, and it is extremely unlikely that it was the original understanding either.

Second, he could say that such treaties are not unconstitutional, because the grant of the treaty power to the President in Article II is a narrow and express exception to the otherwise exclusive grant of legislative power to Congress in Article I. Again this view is perfectly logical, and it gets to the right result, but it gets there the wrong way. We are asked now to understand the vesting clause of Article I as if it said, "All legislative powers herein granted, *with such exceptions as may be stated hereafter,* shall be vested" in Congress. Or we are asked to read the treaty clause in Article II as if it said, "Notwithstanding the exclusive grant to Congress of the power to regulate Commerce with foreign Nations, the President shall have power to make Treaties." But neither clause says that. In other words, we are asked to understand the treaty clause of Article II as tacitly conflicting with, but overriding, a prohibition laid down in Article I. There is nothing logically incoherent about this view, but there is nothing compelling about it either. The treaty clause does not announce itself as being in direct conflict with Article I, and it is very unlikely it was so understood.

In other words, the right thing to say about the treaty power is this. It is *not* in conflict with Article I. Congress's power to regulate commerce with foreign states was *not* thought to be "horizontally" exclusive. Neither that specific grant of power to Congress nor Article I's vesting clause as such prohibits the President from making a law that regulates foreign commerce—as, indeed, he is specifically authorized to do under the treaty clause. To be sure, the President was not thought to have any general legislative power (outside of the treaty-making process). But that is *not* because the vesting clause of Article I, conferring the enumerated legislative powers on Congress, was exclusive. It is because no such power, apart from making treaties, is granted to the President in Article II.

At this point, someone will ask what possible difference it can make where we "locate" the understanding that the President would not have a general lawmaking power. This parsing of clauses, it will be objected, is hairsplitting and irrelevant. If the understanding was that the President would have no general lawmaking power, that's the end of it, regardless of whether that result is said to follow from the grant to Congress of the legislative power in Article I, or from the absence of a general legislative power in Article II.

This objection states the originalist viewpoint. An originalist has no reason to think carefully about these issues. The originalist will say that the Constitution "as a whole" bears out the "structural" understanding that the President was not to have a general lawmaking power. The modern administrative state, the strict originalist will say, cannot be squared with this understanding, regardless of where we locate it. And in saying all this, the originalist will be quite right.

But to take seriously the systematic importance of the distinction between Application and No-Application Understandings in constitutional law is precisely to see that constitutional law is not originalist in this way—and, for better or worse, to see that the analysis has to be much more careful. Article II's vesting clause confers the executive power on the President; another section of Article II goes on specifically to provide that the President shall take care that the nation's laws "be faithfully executed." Almost certainly, the original understanding of these provisions was that they did not authorize the President or other executive officers to make laws. Conceivably, the understanding may have been that executive officers would not be allowed to make laws even if Congress expressly tried to authorize them to do so. These understandings would have added up to something like strict separationism. But all these understandings are plainly No-Application Understandings. They are understandings of what certain authorizing provisions do not authorize. If, therefore, two centuries later, Congress begins creating administrative agencies and delegating certain lawmaking powers to them, courts are not bound to stick to these No-Application Understandings. Constitutional doctrine is free, in other words, to hold that executive officers may constitutionally exercise delegated legislative powers. On this view, the modern administrative state remains perfectly consistent with the paradigm-case method.

By contrast, if the vesting clause of Article I was itself understood to prohibit the President from making law, this would have been an Application Understanding, and it would remain binding. Having to think hard about the textual source of certain original understandings will undoubtedly be criticized as artificial, and it will be found highly objectionable by those originalists who like to read their preferred interpretations into the "Constitution as a whole" or its "structure," without having to bother to tell anyone where exactly the Constitution mandates the prohibition they insist is lurking in the interstices of its text. But once we see the importance of the Application/No-Application distinction in constitutional law, we cannot avoid this labor.

Constitutional law has utterly rejected originalism in its interpretation of the Constitution's powers just as it has in its interpretation of the Constitution's rights. Contemporary commerce clause doctrine rejects numerous important historical No-Application Understandings, but it has adhered to the foundational Application Understandings. Hence from the point of view of paradigm-case interpretation, the strict separationists have to show more than that the original understanding was separationist. To make their case, they would have to show that our contemporary, more flexible separation-of-powers doctrine violates a foundational Application Understanding.

This is a burden they have yet to shoulder. One can hardly blame them for this, since no one has previously demanded it of them. But the distinction between Application and No-Application Understandings requires just this sort of analysis.

I will be accused of being "clause-bound" here. It will be said that I am rejecting a "holistic" approach to constitutional interpretation in favor of an approach that calls on interpreters to focus with tunnel vision on one clause at a time, without taking into account the importance of reading the various clauses in conjunction with one another to produce a coherent whole. This is not so.

I said a moment ago that one of the reasons not to read the vesting clause of Article I as prohibitory was that this reading would require us to see a conflict between Article I's commerce clause (granting power to Congress to regulate foreign commerce) and Article II's treaty clause (granting the President the power to make treaties). I said that, on this view, we would be obliged either to hold that the President's treaty power did not include the power to make treaties dealing with commerce or else to hold that the treaty clause of Article II flatly—but tacitly—contradicts and overrules the earlier clauses of Article I. I said that neither of these readings was appealing. I suggested that we ought instead to read Article I's vesting clause as nonexclusive, thus eliminating the supposed conflict. This was a holistic argument, taking advantage of familiar premises directing interpreters not to read one provision in a legal text as contradicting another, unless the text requires this reading.

Similarly, I said that Article I's grant of power to Congress to coin money should not be seen as exclusive because the Constitution goes on to add a provision barring states from coining money, which would be superfluous on an exclusive-power reading. There is nothing clause-bound in insisting on painstaking attention to whether the vesting clauses of Articles I, II, and III were, of their own terms, understood to prohibit other actors from exercising the powers respectively granted by those articles. Paradigm-case reasoning is deeply interested in overall textual coherence; it merely rejects the simple, originalist understanding of the "holistic" approach, in which, once the text "as a whole" is said to bear out a certain original understanding, that understanding is supposed to bind subsequent interpretation. The question that the latter approach does not answer is whether we are dealing with an Application or a No-Application Understanding.

I do not think strict separationists have made the case that contemporary, flexible separation-of-powers doctrine violates foundational Application Understandings, as opposed to mere No-Application Understandings. But in resolving this question, arguments from overall textual coherence are certainly relevant. Legislative history would also be relevant here, of course, but it is unlikely that historical evidence will resolve the matter. (Where the question is whether a particular understanding was "attached" to one particular clause or another, both of which could sustain it, the legislative history is likely to be suggestive but not conclusive.) It is appropriate, therefore, to have recourse to other considerations too. For example, one important consideration might be that a strict-separationist view would undermine the modern administrative state.

Thus from the point of view of paradigm-case reasoning, there is no categorical unconstitutionality in administrative agencies passing laws or adjudicating cases. Nor is there any categorical unconstitutionality in an independent prosecutor, who exercises executive authority even though Article II vests the President with the executive power. Nor is there any fundamental problem with judges participating on commissions that promulgate sentencing guidelines. These pieces of modern separation-of-powers doctrine are very difficult to reconcile with originalism, but not with paradigm-case interpretation. The jettisoned historical understandings are No-Application Understandings, which are not binding.

But if legislative powers can be conferred on executive officers, and if judicial officers can execute, does this mean that separation of powers has become a constitutional nullity? Does it mean that, in reality, there is no more separation-of-powers doctrine in American constitutional law?

No. It means only that separation-of-powers law need not be worked out through a set of strict-separationist rules, purportedly confining each branch to the right kind of power. Instead, separation-of-powers law properly addresses itself to the checks and balances on each branch that the Constitution demands. The fundamental question in any given case is not whether executive officers are "making law"—they are not constitutionally prohibited from doing so—but whether they needed Congress's approval to take the challenged action and whether they had that approval. Separation-of-powers doctrine is not concerned with confining each branch to the "right" kind of power, but rather with ensuring that each branch of government is checked in the appropriate way by the other branches. The idea that different branches of the federal government can have *concurrent* powers—that their respective powers are not strictly exclusive—is not in the least inconsistent with achieving this goal. On the contrary, as Justice Jackson recognized in the *Steel Seizure Case*, the existence of concurrent, overlapping jurisdictions among the branches makes it easier for one branch to check the other.[31]

Counterexamples

There are, to my knowledge, only two areas of constitutional doctrine where a foundational Application Understanding could arguably be said to have been rejected. The first concerns the contracts clause, the second the declaration-of-war clause.

The contracts clause, nearly everyone agrees, "was designed above all to prevent states from enacting debtor relief and similar laws."[32] In the 1780s, a number of states had enacted measures canceling or postponing debts that private parties owed to private creditors. These debtor-relief measures seemed justifiable or necessary to many at the time, because they were enacted during a period of serious economic distress. But the Constitution prohibited them. The central point of the contracts clause, which prevents the states from "impairing the obligations of contracts," was to make such debtor-relief measures unconstitutional.

Nevertheless, in *Home Building & Loan Assn. v. Blaisdell*,[33] the Supreme Court seems to have upheld a debtor-relief law of exactly this kind. As a result, the contracts clause may be the one guarantee in the American Constitution whose foundational paradigm case has been repudiated.

Blaisdell is a widely admired decision. Many believe the debtor-relief measure in *Blaisdell* was justifiable because of the serious economic distress facing the nation in the 1930s. But as just noted, the Constitution was enacted at a time of very serious economic distress, and the contracts clause appears to have embodied a clear commitment to the unconstitutionality of such measures. If *Blaisdell* does indeed represent a repudiation of a foundational paradigm case, and the argument made in the rest of this book is accepted, then, however justifiable, the case is wrong and should be overturned.[34]

The second arguable counterexample is the power that today seems to be enjoyed by the President to commit the nation's armed forces to battle without a declaration of war by Congress and in the absence of an imminent armed threat to the United States. Prohibiting this precise outcome may have been a paradigmatic object of the declaration-of-war clause. That clause vests Congress with the power to declare war. If the core Application Understanding of this provision was that it stopped the President from making war unilaterally, then arguably this understanding has been violated today.

It is important to remember, however, that American courts have never officially retreated from the principle that the President may not unilaterally declare war. On the contrary, they have on many occasions reaffirmed this principle. As a result, the declaration-of-war clause does not really present a counterexample to the core thesis pursued for the last fifty pages—that American constitutional law has adhered to and built on foundational Application Understandings, even while running roughshod over No-Application Understandings. But paradigm cases are not to be respected only in principle; they have to be respected in fact. And in fact, the actual practice that developed over the twentieth century seemed to allow the President effectively to make war without express congressional authorization. The wars of the early twenty-first century have not continued this pattern; for both the Afghani and Iraqi wars, the President secured congressional authorization before sending the army into battle. But if a President in future should attempt in essence to declare war without congressional approval and in the absence of an imminent attack or threat, courts should be prepared to hold this presidential power unconstitutional.

Thus in the law of speech, religion, searches and seizures, self-incrimination, takings, equal protection, spending, commerce, and separation of powers, American constitutional law reveals a peculiar but repeated asymmetry in its relationship to history. Much that was important to the original understanding of the Constitution is gone; early No-Application Understandings have repeatedly fallen away. But the Application Understandings have remained intact, and they have been central to the radically new doctrinal paradigms that developed in the twentieth century.

II

Commitment, Intention, and Self-Government

4

The Paradox of Commitment

So: in field after field, constitutional law has rejected important original No-Application Understandings, while adhering to and building on the Application Understandings. Why?

It is true that, as compared to many asserted original intentions, the foundational Application Understandings are better established by the historical evidence and were more widely shared at the time of enactment. These criteria alone, however, cannot explain the asymmetry, because some discarded No-Application Understandings satisfy them just as well. The understanding that the Fourteenth Amendment did not forbid states to keep women off juries, or to segregate on the basis of race, was as widely shared, and is as well established, as an originalist could like. But it has gone the way of so many other No-Application Understandings.

What, then, are we to make of the distinction between Application and No-Application Understandings? The key to understanding it, I will argue in the chapters that follow, lies in distinguishing between *commitments* and *intentions*.

Road Map

This argument will require three showings. First, I need to distinguish between commitments and intentions and to say why agents have a special reason to adhere to their commitments that they do not have in the case of mere intentions. Second, I have to show that it makes sense to see American constitutional law as concerned in a special way with historical commitments, as opposed to mere intentions. Third, I have to show that when constitutionalism is seen this way, the asymmetric treatment of Application and No-Application Understandings becomes intelligible. This chapter attempts to discharge the first two tasks.

Chapter 5 deals with the third, and Chapter 6 addresses some important objections.

Three warnings. First, the arguments of this part of the book will not be like those of the last. Part I concerned constitutional doctrine. Its arguments were of a sort entirely familiar to lawyers and legal scholars. Part II is different. I will be offering arguments here about the basic meaning of commitment, of freedom, and of American constitutionalism. This will not be jurisprudence, but philosophy—and it will be philosophy in the analytic mode, despite the galling grandiosity of some of the claims.

Second, the argument to follow is nothing like a proof. I am *not* saying: here is the *only* possible or acceptable account of our commitments, our freedom, our Constitution. All I am saying is this: here is *one* way we could plausibly understand those things, and if we do, we will have a theory of constitutional law that explains why Application Understandings should have so much more purchase than No-Application Understandings. So the grandiosity will not be quite so grandiose as it sometimes sounds.

Third warning: my arguments will be jarring to many readers. In the first place, distinguishing between commitments and intentions is unfamiliar in constitutional law, and while the distinction is better known among philosophers, the distinction between Application and No-Application Understandings is familiar to nearly no one. Moreover, I will spend a considerable amount of time trying to explain why people who give themselves commitments have reason to follow them—a problem that does not even seem problematic at first blush to most people, but that nonetheless poses a puzzle with which philosophers have long grappled. Finally, in offering a solution to this puzzle—a solution on which everything else in the argument depends—I will make repeated reference to the experience we have of making and following commitments in our individual lives. So the entire argument that follows will be vulnerable to the charge that it assumes, without ever proving, that what is true of individual commitments is true, mutatis mutandis, of constitutional commitments—that political self-government may be profitably understood by analogy to individual self-government. To this charge, I simply plead guilty, but I will say more about it in Chapter 6.

Commitments and Intentions

Most of us are familiar with the difference between intending and committing. The distinction, as a phenomenological matter, is straightforward. Commitments create—or seem to create—obligation. Mere intentions do not.

Say it was my intention this morning to leave the office at 5:00 this evening. I often leave the office at 5:00; I expected and intended to do so again today. But now that 5:00 has come, I don't feel like leaving. Something interesting has come up. So I stay on without compunction. My preference has changed, and that's all there is to it. Intentions do not, without more, create obligations demanding some kind of special justification, rather than a mere change in preference, before we depart from them.

If, however, I *committed* myself to leaving at 5:00, the situation is different. Now I will feel that I have an additional and imposing reason for leaving: namely, that I committed myself to it. I will feel that I *ought* to leave, despite my changed preference. In fact, I probably made the commitment because I suspected that when 5:00 arrived, I would want to stay on. An agent makes a commitment precisely in order to lay an obligation on himself, and this obligation is supposed to govern his future conduct even in the face of a later contrary preference.

By "commitment," I am not referring only to assurances I have made to others; indeed, I am not referring to such assurances at all, except in a derivative sense. I refer primarily to commitments I have made to and for myself. My commitment to leave the office at 5:00 may have been made without a word to anyone else.

The obligations created by commitments are not indefeasible. If I were a doctor, and someone's life turned out to depend on my staying on past 5:00, then presumably I should stay on, despite my commitment to leave. But while a commitment need not be absolute, a special justification of some kind seems necessary to overcome it. Definitively, a mere change in preference will not do. If at 5:00, having committed myself to leave, I simply "feel like" staying on, and do stay on, then I have failed to live up to my commitment.

Commitments can be self-interested or moral or both at once. There can be commitments to eat no dessert, to finish a job, to honor a principle, to fight to the death. There can be commitments of the New Year's resolution variety, but there can also be much more subtle, less articulate commitments, which we form only gradually, as for example the commitment we might have to an institution, to a relationship, or even to a particular kind of life. Doubtless we do not always keep them, but the experience of making commitments and of feeling their obligation-creating, reason-giving force is, I think, wholly familiar.

The Irrationality of Commitments

Sadly, the reasons for action our commitments give us seem to be illusory. If, at 5:00, leaving work is the action rationally dictated by my beliefs and preferences, I ought to leave—but not because of my commitment. I ought to leave because it is the rational thing to do. If, on the other hand, staying on is the rational thing to do, I ought to stay on, notwithstanding my commitment. In neither case does the commitment supply a reason to act. It may happen that I have reason to act consistently with my commitment, but I have no reason to *follow* it—to act *because* of it.

To be sure, I may have had a very good reason this morning to make a commitment to leave the office at 5:00. In the morning, my preference was that I should leave at 5:00. If I suspected that I would feel differently at 5:00, it was rational for me to try to give myself a new, additional reason for leaving at 5:00—a new reason with sufficient force to get me out of the office despite my 5:00 preference to stay on. The only difficulty lies in thinking that I could achieve this result by "committing" myself to leave at 5:00.

In the morning, given my then-present preferences, I thought that leaving at 5:00 was the best thing for me to do. But when 5:00 comes, rationality requires me to consult my beliefs and aims at that time. I have no reason to do something now just because I made a commitment to do it some time in the past, especially if that commitment was based on preferences I no longer hold. How could this morning's commitment, absent some kind of bootstrapping, have altered whatever reasons I actually have for staying or going at 5:00?

To be sure, there will be situations in which we know that our present cognitive faculties are untrustworthy. In these situations, we might rationally choose to defer to what we thought best earlier. But these circumstances will not obtain for all the commitments we make, and even when they do, they do not make the idea of following a commitment clearer. If present confusion gives me reason to defer to my past judgment, that will be true whether or not, at the earlier moment, I committed myself to anything. An earlier *intention* would have been just as good. The picture of a self-consciously discombobulated but rational agent choosing to defer to his earlier, cooler thinking does not make sense of the idea that something different occurs when we *commit* ourselves to *x* (rather than merely forming an *intention* to *x*), nor of the concomitant idea that we have special reason to *keep* our commitments—to do what we committed ourselves to do *because* we committed ourselves to it.

Hence a paradox. We seem to have reason to make commitments; we do in fact make them; and we feel the obligations they seem to create. But we apparently have no reason to keep them.

As a number of philosophers have pointed out, underlying this puzzle is the particular temporal orientation characteristic of standard contemporary conceptions of rationality. The "standard account of rational action" measures an action's rationality by reference to the agent's *present* beliefs and preferences (including his present preferences about how things should go for him in future). By tying rationality to the agent's preferences "at the time of action," the "standard account" has "no resources" through which to capture the phenomenon of following through on a commitment "counter-preferentially."[1] In Michael Bratman's words, the "standard . . . model of rational action does not seem to have clear room for . . . a commitment to future action."[2]

From this point of view, the whole practice of making commitments—again, I mean commitments made to oneself—tends to look like a plunge into mysticism. Such commitments, it might be said, are like vows sworn to God. Or they are like promises made to oneself, in which case they still make no sense. The recipient of a promise (it is said) is always free to release the promisor. Thus if the same agent is both promisor and promisee, the promise cannot bind, because the agent can always release himself from the obligation. As Thomas Hobbes put it, a person cannot be "bound to himself."[3] People may feel some sense of obligation from "committing themselves," but these feelings cannot rationally be cashed out.

Thus commitment and rationality seem at loggerheads. If we are wholly rational, we cannot recognize obligations flowing from past commitments we have made to ourselves. If, nevertheless, we feel the normative pull of our commitments, we are (to that extent) irrational.

Commitments and Precommitments

To understand the difficulty at issue here, it is essential to distinguish commitments from precommitments. Standard accounts of rationality have no trouble with precommitments. Their problem is with commitments.

A precommitment is any kind of "external mechanism" that a person might deploy at time 1 to tie his hands at time 2, such as entering into a contract or locking the liquor cabinet and giving away the key. Precommitments alter the costs, benefits, or feasibility of the agent's future options in order to make it rational for the agent to follow a certain course of action at time 2. Ulysses, tying himself to the mast of his ship in order to hear the Sirens, is the classic figure of precommitment.

Precommitments can be unproblematically rational because they can maximize the agent's expected welfare (as measured, at any rate, by his preferences at time 1), and they do not involve the agent in counter-preferential action. Ulysses at time 1 orders his men to bind him to the mast. This order conforms with Ulysses's then-present preferences. To be sure, at time 2, Ulysses would like to yield to the Sirens' song and does not do so. But that is not counter-preferential action either; at time 2, Ulysses is physically prevented from acting on his then-present preferences.

A *commitment*, by contrast, as I will use the term, works in the absence of any external mechanisms altering the costs, benefits, or feasibility of the agent's time-2 options. A commitment contemplates counter-preferential action. The practice of making and following commitments specifically contemplates an agent resolving at time 1 to perform at time 2 an action that may run contrary to his time-2 preferences—and then sticking to that resolution in the face of his time-2 preferences. That is why Bratman correctly says that the standard, presentist account of rationality "does not seem to have clear room for . . . a commitment to future action."[4]

There is a black cup on my desk. It held coffee; it is empty now. I resolve to pick it up in one minute. I do not merely intend to pick it up; I commit myself to picking it up. I will think of nothing else for the next 60 seconds. I will be sure to pick it up, however foolish I may feel lifting up an empty mug, alone in my office, for no reason. I will have no reason to do it, except one: I committed myself to it. And for that reason, I will in fact—I do in fact—pick it up.

No: this is impossible. At least it is impossible if I am rational. I cannot commit myself, by myself, to anything—because there is no such thing as a person being bound to himself. As a rational agent, I cannot act *on*, I cannot act *because of*, my resolution. Yet it seems to me that I can, and it feels to me, now I have committed myself, that I should.

I have no reason to pick up the cup; I pick up the cup. What have I proved? That I am prey to cant, to mysticism, to magical thinking?

Constitutional Commitments—and Their Denial

Consider now how this difficulty applies to constitutional law. There is a seeming paradox of constitutional democracy, similar to the paradox of commitment just described. In fact, the paradox of constitutional democracy *is* a paradox of commitment.

In democracies with a written constitution, constitutional provisions are supposed to be obligatory, requiring special justification before contrary action is allowed, if such action is allowed at all. In other words, certain fundamental rules or principles are supposed to be followed *because* the constitution sets them down. This means that they are supposed to be followed even in the face of contrary political will. Although in well-functioning constitutional democracies, at any particular moment, a present majority of a nation's citizens may support most or all of that nation's constitutional law, one of the primary purposes of constitutional law is to bind even in the face of contrary popular will. Or at least so constitutional law is understood; such is the phenomenology of the practice.

Unfortunately, just as individuals have no good reason to act *because* they committed themselves to doing so, democratic societies have no good reason to act on their constitution's fundamental principles *because* their constitution sets them down. It would be undemocratic for them to do so. Democratic citizens ought to follow those principles they prefer, or believe to be best, in the here and now.

This argument, which pits constitutional law against democracy, has long been a staple of American constitutional thought. It was the basis, for example, of Alexander Bickel's famous "counter-majoritarian difficulty." "[W]henever the Supreme Court declares unconstitutional a legislative act," Bickel wrote, "it thwarts the will of representatives of the actual people of the here and now; it exercises control, not in behalf of the prevailing majority, but against it. That, without mystic overtones, is what actually happens."[5] And that is why constitutional law, Bickel added, can be called "anti-democratic."

Thus the paradox of commitment reappears in constitutional law: democratic peoples, like rational persons, should never follow their commitments. Underlying this problem is a presentist conception of democracy, just as a presentist conception of rationality underlies the problem of individual commitments. Democracy, on this view, in principle requires governance in accordance with present (popular) beliefs and preferences, just as rationality is supposed in principle to require action in accordance with present (individual) beliefs and preferences.

The presentist conception of democracy is often explicit in works of constitutional theory. Bickel himself provides an example. "[A]lthough democracy does not mean constant reconsideration of decisions once made," Bickel wrote, "it does mean that a representative majority has the power to accomplish a reversal." This power—belonging to a representative majority "of the actual people of the here and now"—is "the essence" of democracy, "and no less so because it is often merely held in reserve."[6]

But the presentist conception of self-government is hardly a creation of American constitutional theorists. It dates back at least two-and-a-half centuries. Rousseau, for example, held it self-evident that "the general will that should direct the State is not that of a past time but of the present moment."[7] As a result, Rousseau found constitutionalism "absurd," at least for a self-governing polity; a constitution could not be binding against the people, because (present) popular will was the sole touchstone of legal validity.[8] Jefferson had a similar objection to entrenched constitutions: "The earth," he wrote, "belongs to the living."[9]

Without Rousseau's or Jefferson's radicalism, the same presentist understanding of democracy remains prevalent in political thought today, both in rational-choice accounts of democracy and in more philosophically oriented accounts.[10] From the presentist point of view, constitutionalism looks almost irremediably undemocratic.[11] It looks like governance by "the dead hand" of the past. And for over a hundred years, some of the most influential American constitutionalists have been trying to bury this dead hand.

"The intentions of our ancestors," wrote Christopher Tiedeman in 1890 in one of the first books on constitutional theory written in America, "cannot be permitted to control the present activity of the government."[12] Thayer's *American Doctrine of Constitutional Law*, highly influential throughout the first half of the twentieth century, argued for judicial restraint out of respect for the need and ability of the living to govern themselves.[13] In 1962, Bickel urged judges to find a way to express "current . . . popular will" in their "constitutional adjudication."[14] Twenty years later, John Hart Ely would argue that the fundamental purpose—and only fully legitimate purpose—of constitutional law was not to impose on today's citizens "substantive" value judgments laid down in the past, but rather to protect the representative processes through which today's citizens govern themselves.[15]

These important figures in American constitutional thought differ considerably one from another, but they pursue a common project. Every one of them fights the past. Constitutional law, if it is to be squared with democracy—and every one of these authors means to do just that—must somehow find a way to suppress its own historicity. It must deny that it carries forward, into the present and future, the force and authority of past judgments about justice, power, and liberty. In a word, constitutional law must deny its own *commitments*. Why? Because there is no reason for people today to follow commitments made in the past.

Constitutional law, if it is not to deny its own commitments, needs to solve the paradox of commitment. It needs an account of commitment overcoming the apparent paradox that seems to confront agents who make commitments and feel their force. But there is a further, complicating problem in the case of old constitutions. The persons who originally enacted the American Constitution are dead. In what possible way, it might be asked, could any commitments they made bind us today? It makes no difference, someone might say, whether the general paradox of commitment can be solved in the case of individuals. For even if it could, we would still be left with the fact that in the case of the Constitution, those who made the commitments are gone, which means that their commitments could not possibly be authoritative for us anyway. So unless there is some answer to this latter problem, there is no point wasting our time with the former.

But this way of thinking turns out to put the cart before the horse. At first it may seem that the problem with constitutional commitments lies conclusively in the fact that the framers are dead. But those who make this argument turn out, on close inspection, to be operating with a confused or unintelligible way of thinking about how commitments could bind an agent in the first place, even when there is no question about whether the agent who made the commitment is the same agent who is called on to follow it. If we can come to a satisfactory account of commitment—if, that is, we solve the more general paradox of commitment—we will see that the problem of the framers' death no longer seems so difficult to answer.

Ulysses Bound and Unbound

The work of Jon Elster provides an illustration. Two decades ago, Elster's *Ulysses and the Sirens* offered an analysis of rational precommitment and suggested that constitutions might be profitably understood in these terms.[16] A constitution, Elster suggested, is a Ulysses-like act of self-binding, undertaken by "sober" citizens in anticipation of their own self-destructive passions. *Ulysses and the Sirens* was therefore a counterexample to the phenomenon described previously: it was an attempt to acknowledge and to justify the idea of constitutional law as an institution designed to hold a nation to its own past commitments.

More recently, however, in *Ulysses Unbound*,[17] Elster has revised his earlier position. In essence, Elster now says, his earlier book indulged in some cant, which he wants to recant now.

The truth about politics, says Elster in *Unbound*, is that people do not really "try to bind themselves"; they try "to bind others."[18] This is particularly true, he says, of constitutions. Constitutions may present themselves as acts of collective self-binding, but in truth they are almost always efforts by some individuals "to bind others," and "that's all there is to it."[19] "To speak of *self*-binding in such cases," says Elster, "is cant."[20]

Consider, says Elster, the "Future-Generation Problem."[21] "When the constitution imposes substantive rights and duties" on future generations, "combined with stringent supermajority requirements for amendment," there can be no legitimate talk of self-binding:

> It is arbitrary to let one generation impose a virtual ban on abortion or a right to abortion, a ban on income taxes or a right to bear weapons, unrestrained freedom of contract or a right to an adequate income, on its successors. There is no cant-free way in which these procedures can be referred to as *self*-binding. The fact that a later generation may welcome being bound is neither here nor there, since founding generations will rarely be in a position to anticipate this preference.[22]

In short, those who frame a constitution are mortal. In many cases, they are better than mortal; they are dead. The notion that "we" Americans gave "ourselves" the Constitution is nonsense. To say otherwise is "cant."

Elster's "cant-free" is the equivalent of Bickel's "without mystic overtones." If we are to think clearly (we are told), without "mysticism" or "cant," we have to acknowledge that, with regard to "future generations," a constitution is not an act of self-binding at all, but an attempt by some people to "to bind others." "That's all there is to it."

So we seem to have a clean, hardheaded position: what undermines the idea of constitutional commitments is the simple fact that those who made these commitments are dead. Strangely, however, *Ulysses Unbound* cannot quite keep itself to this clean argument. Another idea intrudes, muddying the picture.

Recall that after saying there is no "cant-free" way to describe a constitution as an act of "self-binding" vis-à-vis future generations, Elster adds: "The fact that a later generation may welcome being bound is neither here nor there, *since founding generations will rarely be in a position to anticipate this preference.*" This sentence is peculiar. Or rather: its first half seems obvious, but the second, italicized half is odd.

Could Elster be implying that a constitution can, without cant, be regarded as an act of self-binding when the later generation *does* "welcome being bound" and the long-dead framers *were* "in a position to anticipate" this preference? The answer is—yes, he is. With respect to certain kinds of constitutional constraints, which he calls "delaying and stabilizing" devices, Elster maintains that a constitution "can be seen as an act of self-binding," although, he adds, "in a looser sense."[23]

What are these "delaying and stabilizing" devices? They are not "substantive rights or duties." They are procedural. An example of a "delaying device" would be a provision stipulating that certain laws (for example, an increase in legislators' pay or in deficit spending) cannot take effect until a certain period of years has passed after enactment. These provisions, as Elster describes them, do not entrench any particular, "substantive" preferences, but only help out future generations with their own problems of rationality—problems caused by hyperbolic time discounting or shortened time horizons.[24] At any present moment, agents face the danger that their own hyperbolic time-discounting functions—that is, their preference for present satisfaction as compared with future satisfaction—will lead them into behavior destructive to their own welfare. Elster's "delaying and stabilizing" rules are rules designed to assist future generations in avoiding this danger.

But how can these procedural constraints be seen as acts of self-binding, even "in a looser sense," when the framers are dead? What makes "loose" talk of intergenerational self-binding legitimate, rather than cant, in the case of these "delaying and stabilizing" devices?

The difference, according to Elster, is supposed to turn on the fact that the framers can plausibly expect future generations to "welcome being bound," or at least "to have reasons" for wanting to be bound, by these "delaying and stabilizing precommitments." All rational agents can be expected to welcome being bound by devices that stop their own hyperbolic time-discounting functions from leading them into self-destructive behavior. And if, Elster writes, "future agents are expected to have the same reasons for wanting to be restricted as the founding generation," then the constitution "*can* be seen as an act of *self*-binding."[25] "If the problems to which the constitution is offered as a solution can be expected to persist indefinitely, the framers can say with some justification that they are acting on behalf of a temporally extended 'self' that also includes future generations."[26]

Given these premises, the peculiar way that Elster finished the passage quoted previously now makes sense. Hyperbolic time-discounting problems are "perennial," Elster says, and a constitution's framers know that. Hence a delaying precommitment enacted in 1789 remains an act of self-binding in 2004. By contrast, a constitution's framers "are not in a position to anticipate" future generations' "substantive" preferences—for example, whether they will or will not support abortion rights—and hence constitutional commitments to such "substantive rights or duties" are *not* instances of self-binding.

This line of argument is mysterious.

If A ties B's hands while B is asleep, we would not ordinarily say that this counted as an act of self-binding just because A reasonably believes that B will in fact "welcome being bound" when she wakes. Whether she does or not, if B demands to know what A thinks he is doing by tying her hands, it hardly makes sense for him to answer, "Why, you tied them yourself." Certainly we would not be tempted to describe A's tying of B's hands as an act of self-binding by B, not even "in a looser sense," if all A could say was that he wanted his *own* hands tied and he "expected" B "to have the same reasons for wanting to be restricted" as he.

It seems, then, that, perhaps despite himself, Elster's understanding of the relationship between a nation's past and future generations must be more complicated than one might at first have thought. For if the founding generation and the future generations were really independent agents, like A and B, the founders' knowledge that future generations will "welcome being bound" would not turn the former's tying of the latter's hands into an act of self-binding by the latter. In other words, if the founders are dead, and "that's all there is to it," then the founders' ability to anticipate our preferences, no matter how accurate, could not turn the Constitution into an act of self-binding. Instead, it seems there must, after all, be some notion of a "temporally extended self" behind the scene, able to bind itself through a constitution, at least with respect to some kinds of restraints.

But even on this assumption, it remains mysterious for Elster to say that the founders' ability to anticipate our preferences is the decisive criterion by which to decide whether a constitutional constraint counts as a legitimate act of self-binding.

When we think about a single temporally extended agent acting to bind himself in future, what is the significance of the agent's "being in a position to anticipate" that he will "welcome being bound"? This fact may be important in many respects, but it will not be important to the issue of whether the agent has engaged in an act of self-binding. Say that you call the firemen's fund and bindingly pledge to make a substantial charitable donation. You have bound yourself, regardless of whether you expect yourself to welcome this pledge when it's time to pay up. Even if you correctly expect yourself *not* to welcome it, you were still the one who made the call, and "that's all there is to it." The question of whether an agent has bound himself does not ordinarily depend on whether he justifiably expects himself to welcome this particular constraint in future.

But the story of Ulysses and the Sirens already makes this clear. If that story counts as an instance of self-binding, it is not because Ulysses correctly anticipates that he will "welcome being bound" when he hears the Sirens call. On the contrary, he knows that his bonds will then infuriate him. To be sure, Ulysses at time 1 can justifiably say that he will, even at time 2, "have the same *reasons* for wanting to be restricted"—Elster's other formulation of the condition under which an act can be regarded as an act of self-binding. In other words, at time 1, Ulysses justifiably believes that being bound at time 2 will be in his own best interests, regardless of what he himself thinks at that moment. This belief, however, is an explanation of why Ulysses's act of self-binding can be said to be *rational*. It does not explain why his act is an act of *self-binding*.

In other words, Elster's argument has run together the question of a constitution's *rationality* with that of its authority as *self-given*—its status as an act of self-binding.

So the clear, hardheaded argument against the idea of constitutional commitments that we first thought we had before us in *Ulysses Unbound* is not the one we have at the end. Ultimately, *Unbound* seems conspicuously unclear on the issue of the legitimate bindingness of constitutional commitments. This is so for two reasons.

First, the hardheaded perspective, according to which people who have been dead for a century or two are just that—dead—and their consent to a law in their own time cannot be viewed as the consent of the living to that law, which seems so "cant-free," so "un-mystical," is not in fact the perspective with which Elster ends in *Unbound*. Perhaps he meant to adopt this perspective but could not quite bring himself to do so all the way, because it would have required him to reject constitutionalism altogether. Like nearly every political scientist and theorist today, Elster wants to preserve a space for some temporally extended, self-binding constitutional commitments, which is not surprising, given the ubiquity of constitutionalism in contemporary democratic societies. Unfortunately, the conceptual resources for doing so are not at hand.

Second, in trying to explain the bindingness of at least some constitutional commitments, Elster invokes what is ultimately a criterion of *rationality*— whether the framers at time 1, when making a constitutional commitment, can justifiably believe that they are acting to satisfy the preferences or maximize the welfare of future generations—when what he claims to be providing, and needs to be providing, is an account of *self-government*. Elster raises the question of whether a constitution can claim the legitimate authority of an act of collective self-binding. But the answer he gives responds to a quite different question. He says that constitutional constraints are justifiable when they impose a constraint on future generations that the founding generation could justifiably expect future generations to welcome. That consideration might make a constitutional commitment *rational*—assuming that law's rationality is to be tested by its probable effects on expected future social welfare—but it has little to do with the Constitution's status as an act of *self-binding*.

In other words, a tenable account of constitutional commitments would have to sound not in rationality, but in self-government. Or more precisely: it would have to explain the rationality of constitutionalism by reference to the demands of self-government.

The Constitution's commitments were made in the past. We had no opportunity to draft them, to ratify them, or to reconfirm them today. And yet most Americans feel they remain binding, remain obligation-creating, even today. What does this prove? That we are irrational—prey to magical thinking, to "mysticism," to "cant"?

Saving the Rationality of Commitments

Return now to the more general paradox. I will try to solve this paradox in the case of individuals' commitments. Then I will come back to constitutional law.

Philosophers have advanced a number of arguments to show how individuals' commitments can at least under some circumstances be reconciled with the demands of present-oriented rationality. Three of these arguments are particularly well known. Each succeeds on its own terms, but each leaves something decisive out. Seeing what they leave out will point the way to a different solution.

The first argument maintains that successful acts of commitment cause psychological effects on the agent such that, at time 2, it becomes rational for him to do as his commitment bids. One version of this causal-psychology solution says that making a commitment can cause the agent's time-2 preferences to change: he comes to prefer to do what the commitment calls on him to do, because he has a "taste for being resolute." A second version holds that by making a commitment not to x, an agent causes himself to regard x as "infeasible,"[27] even though x remains physically possible. Once again, it then follows that the agent's refraining from x at time 2 is rational, because a rational agent always chooses only among the options he regards as feasible.

The obvious difficulty with these arguments is the danger of bootstrapping. A "taste for stick-to-itiveness" looks (when the agent is sticking to a decision he knows is not otherwise preference maximizing) rather like a preference for irrationality, and believing that x is "infeasible" (when the agent knows x is possible) looks rather like holding a belief known to be unreasonable. It is hardly appealing to explain the rationality of seemingly irrational conduct by imputing to agents a "preference for irrationality" (which they may "rationally satisfy") or beliefs they know to be unreasonable (which they may "rationally act on").

But it may be insisted that the psychological mechanisms of commitment-making are ultimately matters of fact, and that if agents really do have a taste for resoluteness or really do come to view x as "simply not an option" after having committed themselves not to x, an account of the rationality of their actions may legitimately take these attitudes into account. It might be added that these attitudes can be instrumentally valuable to an agent in the long run. Hence a rational agent may have reason to cultivate these attitudes in himself, and then to take advantage of them in regulating his future conduct.

Granting all these claims, this picture of commitment-making remains deeply unsatisfying. We are told that an agent who successfully commits himself not to x will, at time 2, no longer prefer x or no longer regard x as something open to him to do. This argument offers an account of the psychology of commitment, but it gets the psychology wrong. To feel the bite of a commitment against a course of action is to feel that we *should* not do something we *could* do and *would like* to do. Rather than seeing the forbidden action as no longer preferred or no longer feasible, we feel we ought not to do it, despite our preferences and despite its feasibility.

The flaw here is that the causal-psychology account "explains" commitments only by turning them into precommitments. A precommitment, as we have seen, is a device for altering the costs, benefits, or feasibility of the agent's time-2 options in such a way as to make it rational for him at time 2 to follow his time-1 commitment. That is just how a commitment works, according to the causal-psychology solutions. When assimilated to precommitment, a commitment's normative and phenomenological distinctiveness—the sense an agent has that he *could* do *x* and that he would *prefer* to do *x*, but that he *should* not do it, having committed himself against it—is not explained. It is explained away.

A second solution to the paradox of commitment is more straightforward. Here the idea is that we stand to gain, overall, if we can successfully organize our conduct over time into coordinated, systematic plans. One way an agent can coordinate his conduct in this fashion, and save on unnecessary "deliberation costs," is by adopting the practice of forming future-directed intentions and following through on those intentions without necessarily reexamining them later. Among others, Bratman has made careful arguments for the welfare-maximizing potential of this kind of "planning agency."[28]

This account may be sufficient to cover a good deal of the real-life phenomena of commitment-making and commitment-following that we actually observe. Nevertheless, a story of welfare-enhancing coordinated conduct, accomplished through systematic planning activity, seems quite inadequate as a complete account of commitment.

The dissatisfying element is that, on this account, there is little if any difference between *intentions* and *commitments*. The welfare-maximizing argument attempts to show (quite plausibly) that forming and following through on future-directed intentions provides demonstrable benefits to the agent that would be unavailable otherwise. But in this story, an intention is all that is needed. There is no particular place for any distinctive normative operation of commitment. Indeed, Bratman explicitly merges the two concepts. In Bratman's account of "planning agency," the agent need only arrive at a well-considered future-directed intention in order to be making a "plan." Every such intention exerts normative force in future, because of the instrumental value of engaging in "planning agency." It follows, for Bratman, that every "intention is a kind of commitment."[29]

Yet to repeat, in everyday experience, there is a world of difference between my merely *intending* to leave the office today at 5:00 and my *committing* myself to do so. The commitment creates a sense of obligation that the intention does not. Once again, the distinctive normative and phenomenological dimensions of commitment disappear in this account. The sense of an agent's imposing an *obligation* on himself has little or no place in the coordination account.

A third solution to the paradox of commitment proceeds in a very different way. It conceives the commitment-making agent as a series of time-sliced "selves" strategically negotiating with one another to reach agreement on a Pareto-superior course of action. Edward McClennen argues along these lines.[30] So does George Ainslie. Modeling the agent as a succession of independent "selves" or "states," Ainslie argues that all the puzzles in which an agent's rationality at each moment leads to irrationality over time can be reconceived in terms of collective-action problems solvable through the familiar analytics of multiple-agent bargaining games.[31]

The obvious objection to multiple-self-bargaining models of commitment is that a time-sliced "self" or "state" would have no reason to take an interest in these bargaining strategies. In ordinary repeat-play bargaining games with A and B as the players, it is understood that A and B will continue to exist over the course of the game—and, presumably, thereafter. This assumption is necessary. If A is going to cease to exist right after he makes his move at time 1, it becomes hard to think of him devising complex, self-denying bargaining strategies to influence B's move at time 2, given that A will no longer be around to enjoy the fruits of his efforts. But if an individual is divided into a "time-1 self," "time-2 self," and so on, these "selves" will precisely cease to exist after their moment in the limelight.[32]

Ainslie's account, however, offers a response to this objection. On Ainslie's assumptions, each time-sliced "state" supposedly has a decided preference that its future selves do well (one might wonder why this is so). As a result, each will be best off, as measured by its own present preferences, if it can successfully induce its future selves to refrain from indulging in pleasures that are self-destructive in the long run. If the time-1 self's decision to refrain from such pleasures serves as a "precedent"[33] that the others follow, then the time-1 self will actually do better by refraining, despite the fact that it will have ceased to exist by the time the others have their turn.

This picture may be peculiar, but it is, I suppose, intelligible. If a person with a day to live has a strong enough preference that his children should be self-denying in future, and can best hope to bring about that result by denying to himself the pleasure of gratifying the same desire he wants them to resist, then it would seem rational for the expiring person to be self-denying.

Granting this reply, the multiple-self picture of an agent making a commitment remains unsatisfying. Yet again, the multiple-self solution does not so much explain, as explain away, the definitive element of commitment that stands in need of explanation: the sense of *resolving* to act a certain way in future and of feeling *bound* by this resolution. Ainslie's time-sliced agents hold themselves out as *precedents;* they do not resolve to do anything. They cannot resolve to do anything in future, because they will not exist in future. If the practice of commitment has here been rationalized, rationality has been purchased at the expense of the phenomenon itself. The agent in this story does not make a commitment at all; he merely sets an example, which he hopes others will follow.

Why does each of these three solutions to the paradox of commitment fail to capture the definitive features of commitment? The reason, I think, is that they are all attempting to answer the wrong question. They are falling into the same trap that we saw previously in Elster: trying to give an account of commitment that sounds in *rationality,* when they need to be giving an account that sounds in autonomy or *self-government.* The obligation-creating and hence reason-giving force of commitments can be understood only when they are situated within an account of self-government.

Self-Government over Time

The capacity for self-government over time—for autonomy, not rationality—holds the key to the riddle of commitment. It is not that commitments are irrational. But their reason-giving force becomes intelligible only when they are seen as efforts at self-government. And this can be done only when it is recognized that self-government is not an affair of the present moment, but has a temporally extended dimension.

Distinguish between two pictures of freedom or self-governance. On one picture, free agents "live in the present," following nothing but their own "voice" in the here and now, acting solely on their own present preferences. This picture of freedom may or may not be intelligible. But even if it is, it is not the only one.

In the second picture of freedom, self-governing agents attempt to give their lives purpose and meaning *over time*. On this view, agents commit themselves to various courses of action, to relationships, to institutions, to principles, and so on, and hold themselves to these commitments for substantial periods of time. Much of the time, when considering what to do, they do not ask themselves, "What is my present preference?" or even, "What is my best present all-things-considered judgment?" Rather, they ask themselves what they ought to do *given* the purposes and undertakings in which they are already engaged—purposes and undertakings to which they committed themselves earlier.

It seems to me most of us live a good deal of our lives this way. We live committed lives. It is possible to think of this kind of life as reflecting a failure of nerve, a cowardly passivity, or a lazy inclination to habituality. All these things could be true; these are the moral dangers of commitment. To avoid these dangers, the agent must be prepared to reexamine his commitments from time to time, and to break from them if he can no longer recognize them as his own. But on this second picture of freedom, the pivotal mistake would be to think of such moments of repudiation, of breaking from the past, as moments of true freedom.

Emancipation is not freedom. On the second picture, true freedom can never be attained merely by repudiation. One who walked away from all his old commitments would have to give himself new ones. Only thus could he be self-governing. Self-government, on this view, requires a practice of making and keeping commitments.

The idea of freedom as incorporating adherence to enduring commitments, rather than merely acting on present beliefs and preferences, is an old one, expressed by many people in many fields in many different forms. In philosophy, the obvious reference is to Kant. In legal circles, Laurence Tribe gave the idea powerful articulation thirty years ago:

> To be free is not simply to follow our ever-changing wants wherever they might lead. To be free is to choose what we shall want, what we shall value, and therefore what we shall be. But to make such choices without losing the thread of continuity that integrates us over time and imparts a sense of our wholeness in history, we must be able to . . . choose in terms of commitments we have made.[34]

In my terminology, Tribe is making the point that human selfhood and freedom are temporally extended things, and that freedom, as a result, involves the practice of making and following commitments over time.[35] This picture of self-government breaks resolutely from the presentism that makes commitments, both individual and constitutional, seem so paradoxical.

I have used (and will use) the term "self-government" to refer to both individual and political freedom, even though we often reserve the terms "governance," "government," and "self-government" for polities, using "freedom" or "free will" for individuals. I use "self-government" even in the case of individuals because the capacity for self-government may not be quite the same thing as the capacity for free will. At least, as we normally use these terms, self-government has a different valence.

Governance implies rule. All government, including self-government, implies that people are governed, that they are ruled. In self-government, whether we are speaking of individuals or polities, the governed are also supposed to be the governors, the ruled the rulers.

The concept of free will is certainly capacious enough to accommodate the thought of an agent constraining himself in future (as, for example, in free-will accounts of promising), but it does not demand that this thought be accommodated. A perfectly free will, it might be supposed, would be absolutely ungoverned. A will that aspires to perfect freedom, we might say, aspires to a state of no constraint, and hence a state of pure present ungovernedness. Insofar as present will is constrained, we might say, it is not free.

But the self that aspires to self-government does not aspire, even notionally, to be ungoverned. The self-governing self is always as much governed as governing. The self-governed agent cannot be adequately understood through an ideal of pure ungovernedness. An agent who has perfect freedom to act—and who does act—on his present preferences is not yet self-governing. Such an agent is rational (according to the standard account), but this rationality does not imply self-governance.

We can imagine a rational slave. A rational slave would be one who acts systematically and strategically to maximize his welfare, given the limited options available to him. We can even imagine a slave who takes pleasure in being a slave, although this presumably is harder to find. But we cannot imagine a self-governing slave, for that is a contradiction in terms. A slave's rationality does not make him free.

An animal can act rationally. A cat trying to open the cabinet where its owner keeps the cat food is acting in a rational, goal-oriented fashion. An animal achieves perfect freedom when it is able to act without constraint on its present preferences. The freedom proper to animals consists in the absence of present constraint. It is the freedom of being stray.

What animals, other than persons, cannot do is to give themselves commitments and hold themselves to those commitments over time even at moments when their commitments run contrary to their then-present preferences. Giving himself his own ends and living them out over time is also foreclosed to the slave, not because he has no capacity for it, but because his master has the power to assign ends to him and to make him pursue those ends over time. The master is in this exact sense the slave's governor. If the slave had this power over himself, he would be his own master—his own governor.

Thus a person's freedom—as opposed to an animal's—is bound up with his capacity to give his life purposes of his own making and to pursue those purposes over time. This freedom is called autonomy or self-governance. A self-governing agent does not act merely on his present preferences. He will have given himself his own ends and held himself to those ends over time.

Commitments enter the picture just here. An agent who understands his own freedom as depending on his capacity not merely to act on present preference, but to hold himself to his own self-given purposes over time, will seek to hold himself to these purposes even when they run contrary to his present preferences. To be free in the human sense, therefore, is, just as Kant said it was, to be self-law-giving—*autonomous*. And to commit oneself is, precisely, to give oneself law.

Kant's autonomy, however, is not the autonomy I am describing. This is because, for Kant, the great run of human motivation is "heteronomous" and therefore inimical to true autonomy. The practice of commitment that I am calling fundamental to a person's autonomy is indifferent to Kant's version of the autonomy-heteronomy distinction. It makes no difference whether a person is committing himself to the dictates of pure reason or the dictates of the Atkins diet. The concept of commitment that I am describing is, to this extent, decidedly un-Kantian.

In other words, to get to the idea of freedom I mean to be describing, it is a question of taking a Kantian view of freedom as self-law-giving, and then adding to this view the thought that the practice of making and following commitments over time—both large and small, whether these commitments are attempts to hold oneself to "reason" or "morality" or the most mundane materially motivated courses of action—is the fundamental way that we exercise our distinctive capacity to give ourselves law.

Precommitment devices do not answer to this ideal of freedom. When an agent at time 1 precommits himself to x at time 2 (for example, by tying himself to a mast), he takes action at time 1 intended to change the costs, benefits, or feasibility of his time-2 options in such a way that x becomes the rational (or in some cases only) thing to do. If the precommitment succeeds, the precommitment causes him to x, but it lays no *obligation* on him to x and does not count for him as a *reason* to x. In this respect, he does not regard his past agency as bearing any authority over his own actions in the present. At time 1, he sees his time-2 self as a kind of "patient" requiring supervision and discipline. At time 2, he looks back on his time-1 self, whether gratefully or resentfully, as a source not of authority but of causal constraint. At an extreme, the precommitting agent may view his life in *multiple-self* terms, as a thing peopled by a series of separate, successive selves or states in competition with one another, each of whom has the goal of seeing to it that his own present preferences win out over the others'. In all these ways, the precommitting agent need not see himself as a temporally extended subject engaged in a temporally extended project of self-governance, giving himself and holding himself to his own law over time.

By contrast, the agent who makes a *commitment* at time 1 does not attempt merely to exert a causal influence on himself at time 2. He asks himself at time 2 to see the commitment he has made as laying an obligation on himself, and therefore giving him a reason to act, even though the costs, benefits, and feasibility of his time-2 options remain just as they would have been without the commitment. If a commitment succeeds, the agent at time 2 takes action because he regards his commitment as authoritative, as a law he has imposed on himself. The commitment becomes for him an exclusionary reason, in Raz's sense, preempting calculation at time 2 of what would otherwise be the right thing to do. He takes the commitment as a law he has given himself, and therefore he necessarily regards himself as a temporally extended subject engaged in a temporally extended project of self-governance.

In short, an autonomous self is one that can give itself, and act on, a certain kind of exclusionary reason.[36] Autonomous agents are those able to give themselves, and to act on, reasons of the kind we create when we make a commitment.

But why is it rational for an agent to give himself or to hold himself to an exclusionary reason of this kind, preempting his own present all-things-considered judgment in future? The answer is not (1) because the agent will in this way save on "deliberation costs" and reap "coordination benefits," thereby maximizing utility; or (2) because the agent has reason to fear that his reasoning faculties will be defective at time 2. These answers sound, once again, merely in instrumental rationality.

The picture to bear in mind here is not Ulysses tied to the mast. He exemplifies precommitment. We deal rather with an agent who would make and follow a commitment. This agent means to be self-governing; he means to be the author of his own life. He is aware that giving himself and holding himself to his own purposes over time is a fundamental aspect of the distinctive freedom of which he, as a person, is capable. He has, moreover, decided that some course of action is important enough that it is worth devoting some portion of his life to it, important enough to overcome the call to act on present preference. He does not claim that his time-2 self will suffer from addled faculties or otherwise be in danger of acting irrationally. On the contrary, he may see his time-2 self as all too rational, pursuing present preferences all too well, while losing sight of the larger temporally extended purposes that he means to pursue.

Those who commit themselves attempt the reins of time. They seek to be their own master, rather than a slave to rationality, over time. They seek to give their lives purposes and meaning of their own choosing. They call on themselves to hold to this or that course of action, relationship, job, or principle for some period of time, even in the face of contrary present preferences. They regard these past acts of commitment-making as a legitimate source of authority over themselves in future. And they do so just because they mean to be self-governing.

The obligation-creating force of a commitment flows ultimately from the role that commitments play in autonomy itself. Autonomous agents are precisely those agents who can give themselves temporally extended obligations in the form of commitments and follow through on those commitments over time. They govern themselves by living out these self-given commitments over time. If a person does not engage in the practice of making and following commitments, he will not be self-governing. He will be—the idiom is precise—less of a person. He might achieve the rationality of which a slave is capable. He might attain the kind of freedom of which an animal is capable—the freedom of a stray dog. He will not, however, attain the distinctive kind of temporally extended freedom available to persons.

On the standard account of rationality, following a commitment is irrational; one may have reason to act *as* the commitment requires, but not to act *because* the commitment so requires. This is to say: the precise capacity that most centrally defines self-governance in the human sense—

the capacity that distinguishes a person's autonomy from an animal's freedom, the capacity to give oneself commitments and hold oneself to them over time, giving one's life meaning and purpose, even if these commitments happen to run contrary to one's present preferences at particular moments—cannot be captured within the standard account of rationality. On the standard account, self-government is irrational.

Nor can this capacity be captured within the prevailing present-oriented conception of democracy. A perfectly democratic nation, on the prevailing view, would act solely on its own present deliberation and preferences. In other words, on the prevailing view, which underlies so much contemporary constitutional theory, self-government is undemocratic.

These paradoxes are resolved only when the dimension of time is restored to the idea of self-government and when the value of self-government is put into proper relation with the value of rationality. Rationality is instrumentally valuable. Autonomy is an end in itself, superseding the claims of present-oriented rationality.

A person wants autonomy first, rationality second. The sense, however, in which a person "wants" autonomy, and hence has an "interest" in following his commitments, is not that of a preference to be balanced against other preferences in a rational calculus. Kant made the same point about the "interest" we have in following the dictates of morality. He referred to the

> impossibility of discovering and explaining an interest which [a person] can take in moral laws. Nevertheless, he does indeed take such an interest, the basis of which in us is called moral feeling. Some people have falsely construed this feeling to be the standard of our moral judgment, whereas it must rather be regarded as the subjective effect that the law exercises upon the will.[37]

For "moral laws" in this passage, substitute "laws we have given ourselves." Most of us probably do derive "a feeling of pleasure or satisfaction in the fulfillment" of our commitments, but this feeling of pleasure or satisfaction is not to be equated with our true interest in fulfilling our commitments. It is not that people have a "taste" or "preference" for autonomy—a "preference for stick-to-itiveness"—that ought rationally to be balanced against their other tastes and preferences. Autonomy has priority over rationality.

There is more than one way to conceptualize the priority of autonomy over rationality. For example, the capacity for autonomy could be figured as a constitutive condition of an individual's selfhood—of his being the same person over time—which his capacity for instrumental rationality, it might be said, necessarily presupposes. Or autonomy, understood in the commitment-based terms I have suggested, could be said to follow from our having the authority over ourselves that is logically necessary to our ability to make, in Frankfurtian terms, the higher-order decisions determining which of our preferences we will rationally pursue—an ability necessary to make sense of instrumental rationality itself. Or autonomy could be figured as a moral value superseding mere rational preference satisfaction, a thought that may be implied when people condemn as immoral an individual's selling himself into slavery.

Kant, in whose terms this question is not easy to pose (because he fuses the concepts of rationality and autonomy), suggests that philosophy hits a "limit"—an "extreme limit," he says—in the "idea of freedom." The idea and priority of autonomy must be presupposed, Kant writes, but can never be fully explained.[38] Perhaps so. I mean to be agnostic here, to the extent possible, about the best way to understand autonomy's priority.

The point, however, is that the rationality of commitment takes on its intelligibility only when autonomy has been acknowledged to be an end in itself, prior to the demands of instrumental rationality. An agent is autonomous if he can make his own commitments and follow through on them, even when doing so runs contrary to his present preferences. This means that he would not have reason to follow his commitments if autonomy were not, for him, an end in itself, prior to and structuring his concern for instrumental rationality.

We have reason, then, to follow our commitments, but not the kind of reason that sounds in standard, present-oriented accounts of instrumental rationality. The practice of making and following commitments is a central piece of our autonomy. It is what makes us self-governing. Ignoring our commitments may make us rational, in the standard sense, but it cannot make us free.

In other words, the reason we spend much of our time living and reasoning within commitments we have given ourselves is not only instrumental. It is not only because deliberation is costly, nor because we cannot always be reevaluating our options, nor because we stand to gain more utility overall by coordinating our conduct in systematic plans. We live out our self-given commitments for a more fundamental reason. By doing so, we exercise the distinctive form of autonomy of which humans are capable—giving our lives shape, meaning, and purpose over time.

American Constitutionalism and Democracy

From the account of self-government over time just outlined, it is a short step to solving the paradox of constitutional democracy described earlier. The seeming paradox of constitutional democracy is generated by the confrontation between constitutional commitments, laid down in the past, and the ideal of democratic self-government as government by present popular will. But if self-government is itself a matter of making and following temporally extended commitments, then this paradox disappears.

Human self-government consists in fundamental part of laying down and living out self-given commitments over time. This is as true of political self-government as it is of individual self-government. As a result, there is no fundamental opposition between constitutionalism and democracy. There is no "counter-majoritarian difficulty" of the kind Bickel described. Constitutionalism, although counter-majoritarian, is not counter-democratic. On the contrary, constitutionalism *is* democracy—or at any rate, it ought to be democracy, it aspires to be democracy—over time.

American constitutionalism is not a "check on democracy." Nor does it serve, as Ely would have it, merely as a vehicle for governance by present, deliberate majority will. Nor does it serve, as rational-choice thinking would have it, as a vehicle for maximal satisfaction of the present voters' preferences. On the contrary, American constitutionalism is a practice through which a democratic nation seeks to govern itself by making and living up to its own enduring commitments, even in the face of contrary majority preferences at one moment or another. Our constitutionalism, in other words, stands for a form of democracy that rejects presentism. In American democratic constitutionalism, self-government is understood to consist in fundamental part of governance by self-given commitments laid down in the past as law for the future.[39]

I have not argued here that the ideal of government by present popular will is incoherent, untenable, or morally unacceptable.[40] Perhaps there are two intelligible conceptions of democratic self-government, one presentist and will-based, the other temporally extended and commitment-based. American constitutionalism is best understood as embracing the latter.

From its inception, American constitutionalism has aspired to the revolutionary image of a citizenry giving itself, through a special, democratic, constitutional politics, its own fundamental principles and framework of government. Indeed this ambition was the one world-historical innovation of the American constitutional revolution. There had been democratic societies before late-eighteenth-century America. The Bill of Rights largely tracked English precedents. Even the idea of a democratic constitution preexisted the American Revolution.

But prior to the American Revolution, the concept of a democratic constitution meant only a constitution that established a democratic form of government. A democratic constitution did not itself have to be democratically made. Late-eighteenth-century Americans did not invent constitutional democracy, but they did invent democratic constitutionalism—where that phrase means that the constitution not only had to establish a democratic (or "republican," in the eighteenth-century vocabulary) form of government, but also had itself to be democratically enacted. Through this new form of constitutionalism, Americans would attempt democratically to lay down their own fundamental political commitments and hold themselves to these commitments over time—not as a *restraint* on self-government, but as an *act* of self-government.

Constitutional commitments can of course be repudiated, but if self-government is to be achieved, they cannot be repudiated whenever a majority wills something that conflicts with them. Rather, a new exercise of special, democratic, constitutional politics is necessary to amend. Unless and until the Constitution's commitments are altered or abolished, they remain binding—again, not as a constraint on democracy "in the here and now," but in the service of democracy over time.

When self-government is understood in present-tense terms, the authority of the Constitution is deeply problematic. If democracy means governance by the present will of the governed, then, to claim legitimate authority, constitutional law is obliged to make one of two claims. Neither can succeed.

First, constitutional law can invoke a proceduralist account of itself, in which the Constitution's requirements are supposed to be the necessary conditions of a presentist democratic process. The problem with this account is that it is false to our law. The Constitution's greatest rights are substantive, not procedural. Second, constitutional law can claim authority by adopting a universalist account of itself, in which its rights are said to be prior and superior, as a matter of justice, to the claims of self-government. The problem with this account is that it is false to our history.

To be sure, many Americans have believed in universal rights, "human rights," natural law, or other fundamental moral truths. The Declaration of Independence is an eloquent expression of this view. But the reality is that natural law and foundational truths cannot govern—not by themselves. If there were such a thing as natural law, its rights would still have to be incorporated into real law by real human beings in order to govern. And these human beings would differ as to what the right rights were. In the face of such disputes, the American answer has always been that such disagreements have to be resolved democratically—by laws, and ultimately by a constitution, enacted through deliberation and consent. The Constitution, on the American view, must be law the people has given itself. Its claim to authority is not a claim to expressing universal truths, binding on all societies everywhere, but a claim to being this nation's self-given law.

This is why American constitutional law must always answer to democracy and must resolve its seeming antithesis with democratic self-government. The commitment-based account solves that seeming antithesis. Constitutional law can continue to claim legitimate democratic authority today because democratic self-government consists in important part of a nation's laying down and living up to its fundamental commitments over time. Only this account makes good on the Constitution's claim to supreme political authority.

"But the framers are dead," someone may say. "Their commitments are not ours. All this talk of constitutionalism as self-government over time really is 'cant,' just as Elster says."

I promise to answer this objection later. I hereby commit myself to doing so. But first let me complete the principal argument. The immediate task is to show that, if constitutional law is understood in commitment-based terms, then judges have a very good reason to distinguish, as they have, between Application and No-Application Understandings.

5

Commitments and Original Understandings

Commitments differ from mere intentions. Commitments create obligations. Mere intentions do not. To commit oneself is to engage in a special normative operation that goes beyond intending, through which one imposes obligations on oneself over time.

Originalism never grasped the significance of this distinction. Originalism is intention-based, holding that all the intentions formed by the relevant agents at the relevant time have equal normative status. But if constitutional law is concerned with honoring commitments, then judges have to distinguish among the historical understandings, separating those representing only intentions from those representing commitments. And No-Application Understandings, it turns out, are never commitments.

No-Application Understandings

Consider an individual case, to make the concepts clear. Say I commit myself never again to smuggle heroin into the country, no matter how much they pay me. I understand that there are many actions this commitment does *not* enjoin. Here is one: my commitment, as I understand it, does *not* forbid me to torture small animals. I can torture as many of them as I like, as far as this commitment is concerned. This is a No-Application Understanding.

From this original No-Application Understanding, does it follow that I have committed myself *to* torturing small animals?

Obviously not. If someone said, "But you understood your heroin commitment not to prohibit the torturing of small animals; therefore you have an obligation to torture them," we would regard this person as confused. I can go through my entire life never torturing a single small animal without having somehow violated my heroin commitment. The original No-Application Understanding puts me under no *obligation* to torture small animals, and where there is no obligation, there is no commitment.

So: when I commit myself against *x*, believing that this commitment does *not* prohibit *y*, I do not thereby commit myself to *y*. Suppose, then, that every single framer and ratifier understood the Fourteenth Amendment *not* to prohibit states from segregating blacks and whites in schools, on trains, or anywhere else. Would that No-Application Understanding mean that the Fourteenth Amendment made a commitment to segregation?

Obviously not. If, after enactment of the Fourteenth Amendment, every state had passed laws integrating their schools and all other public facilities, plainly there would have been no violation of any commitment embodied in the Fourteenth Amendment. The original No-Application Understanding that segregation was not prohibited would imply no commitment to segregate. In this simple sense, then, it is clear that No-Application Understandings do not represent commitments.

But this conclusion does not end the matter. There is another possibility to be considered. Did the Fourteenth Amendment create a commitment to the *permissibility* of state laws segregating the races? The real question, an originalist might say, is not whether the Fourteenth Amendment *obliged* the states to segregate (no one has ever supposed it did), but whether the Fourteenth Amendment *permitted* them to segregate.

Certainly the Fourteenth Amendment was originally intended to permit segregation. But from a commitment-based point of view, an intention is insufficient. The question is whether the Fourteenth Amendment *committed* the nation to the permissibility of segregation.

In other words, we have seen that a prohibition against *x*, understood not to apply to *y*, implies no commitment to *doing y*. But the question now is different. The question is whether a prohibition against *x*, understood not to apply to *y*, at least implies a commitment to the *permissibility* of *y*. If the Fourteenth Amendment committed the nation to the permissibility of state segregation laws, then judges (on a commitment-based account of constitutional interpretation) would be required to honor that commitment. The No-Application Understanding would represent a commitment—a commitment to permissibility.

But No-Application Understandings do not represent commitments of this kind. When I committed myself never to smuggle any more heroin into the country, with the understanding that this commitment had No

Application to torturing small animals, could it be plausibly said that I thereby committed myself to the *permissibility* of torturing them? No. I may well have thought that torturing animals was grotesque. My No-Application Understanding implies no obligation to regard the torturing of animals as permissible; it is an understanding only that *this* commitment (the heroin commitment) does not prohibit it. A commitment not to *x*, understood not to prohibit *y*, implies neither a commitment to doing *y* nor a commitment to *y*'s permissibility.

But wait: suppose at the time I made the heroin commitment, I didn't think torturing small animals was grotesque. Suppose I thought it was just fine. And suppose, on top of that, I would never have made my heroin commitment if I had believed that it would bar me from torturing small animals whenever I liked. In these circumstances, is it now the case that my heroin commitment was also a commitment to the permissibility of torturing small animals?

The answer is still no. Say that the day after I made my heroin commitment, I changed my mind about the permissibility of torturing animals and decided to enter into an international convention banning their torture. If the heroin resolution implied a *commitment* to the permissibility of torturing small animals (rather than a mere *understanding* that such torture remained permissible), I would not be able to enter into this international convention without violating or in part repealing my heroin commitment. But no one would say that my entering into the international convention against the torture of small animals violated or repealed my earlier commitment in any way. The heroin commitment says nothing against my entering into a convention banning the torture of animals, no matter how clear and strong was my understanding that the heroin commitment did not apply to (did not prohibit) torturing them.

From the fact that I understood my heroin commitment to have No Application to torturing small animals, there can be no inference that I somehow committed myself to the permissibility of torturing them. The heroin commitment may have been enacted on the *understanding* that I would remain permitted to torture animals, but it imposed on me no *obligation* to keep that act permissible. And where there is no obligation, there is no commitment.

In short, No-Application Understandings, even of commitments, are not themselves commitments. They are, precisely, understandings of what the agent has *not* committed himself to, so far as *this* commitment is concerned. They reflect, therefore, at most, an intention not to be committed.[1]

To say that my heroin commitment does not, as I originally understand it, prohibit torturing small animals means precisely that this commitment does not commit me one way or the other on this matter—neither in favor of it, nor against it, nor to its permissibility.

Needless to say, I *could* have committed myself to the permissibility of torturing small animals, if I had wanted to. It is easy to make commitments to permissibility. A person committing himself against *x* can always *also* commit himself to *y*'s permissibility.

Say that on the day I made the heroin commitment, I feared that someday soon I might experience an overwhelming temptation to enter into an international convention prohibiting the torture of animals. Perhaps I wanted to commit myself against succumbing to this temptation. So I might have made the following commitments: "Not only will I never again smuggle heroin into the country, no matter how much they pay me; I hereby further commit myself to the permissibility of torturing small animals."

But this is only to say that I could have made *another* commitment, different from and independent of the first. A commitment to the permissibility of torturing small animals, if I had made one, would have had to supplement my heroin commitment. When an agent commits himself against *x,* no matter how clearly he understands this commitment not to apply to *y,* he has not thereby committed himself to *y*'s permissibility. An additional, independent commitment is required in order to create a commitment to *y* or to *y*'s permissibility.

Thus, to return to a constitutional example, the Fourteenth Amendment was almost certainly understood at the time of its enactment not to prohibit racially segregated schools. But this No-Application Understanding was not a commitment: it was neither a commitment *to* segregate the schools nor a commitment to the *permissibility* of segregated schools. Hence judges who were concerned with adhering to constitutional commitments, but not with adhering to mere understandings or intentions, would be free to disregard this original understanding.

I want to emphasize it: I am not saying that it is somehow impossible or specially difficult to constitutionalize a commitment to the permissibility of certain laws. The First Amendment prohibited Congress from interfering with state ecclesiastical laws, thereby enacting a commitment to the permissibility of state laws that we today would regard (and many in 1789 would have regarded) as establishments of religion. But the Fourteenth Amendment contains no commitments to the permissibility of any particular state laws.

The Fourteenth Amendment could easily have contained a Section 6 committing to the states a power to segregate their schools. Such a commitment could have taken a variety of forms. It could have said, "Notwithstanding any other provision of this Amendment, neither Congress nor the courts of the United States shall make any law or decide any case respecting the segregation of the races." Or, "The states shall retain sole power to regulate the terms on which individuals of different races may commingle, whether in public or private." Or, "Nothing in this Amendment shall be construed to prohibit the segregation of individuals on the basis of their race or color." Any of these provisions would have created a constitutional commitment, of one kind or another, to the permissibility of state segregation laws.

But no such commitment was enacted. We will never know why; perhaps no such commitment could have received the requisite number of votes. The reason, however, is irrelevant. In their hearts, many of the Fourteenth Amendment's framers or ratifiers may have been personally committed to the permissibility of state segregation laws. But if these personal commitments existed, they were never enacted into the Constitution. They were never made into constitutional commitments. The permissibility of state segregation laws remained only a No-Application Understanding of other provisions of the Fourteenth Amendment, and No-Application Understandings are merely understandings of what has *not* been committed to. They are not themselves commitments.

No-Application Understandings on Matters "Very Close" to Those That Were Prohibited

Someone might say, however, that I rigged my heroin example to make the previous arguments too easy. To show the noncommittal status of No-Application Understandings, I discussed a No-Application Understanding that concerned a subject matter (torturing small animals) absolutely irrelevant to the subject matter of the commitment (smuggling heroin into the country). The situation is different, it might be objected, if the agents' No-Application Understanding reflects a deliberate, conscious decision not to prohibit something very close in subject matter to what was prohibited. In that event, their act of commitment against x took, consciously and clearly, a stand in favor of the permissibility of y. Thus they implicitly committed themselves to y's permissibility.

For example, the framers of the Fourteenth Amendment were well aware of the women's rights movement, which included demands for the suffrage and for other forms of sex equality. But the framers deliberately chose not to vindicate those demands.[2] In these circumstances, someone might say, there was clearly an express, deliberate decision to leave states free to pass laws denying women important rights and privileges granted to men. That puts things (it might be said) in an altogether different light from my heroin story.

Assume that in fact the makers of the Fourteenth Amendment made a clear, deliberate decision to leave states free to discriminate against women. It would still be the case that the Fourteenth Amendment makes no commitment to this state freedom. It makes no difference that the framers of that amendment consciously decided not to prohibit something "close" in subject matter to what they were prohibiting.

We would see this right away in an individual's case.

Suppose Odette commits herself never again to deceive the well-meaning but dense Swann, who is in love with her. She even writes it down in a diary: "Resolved: no more deceiving Swann." At the time Odette makes this commitment, she specifically thinks about the difference between outright lies and mere omissions—the latter referring, as Odette understands it, to situations where Swann mistakenly believes something, but where she has not affirmatively misrepresented anything. She intends, clearly and in advance, that her commitment will not prohibit such omissions. It will prohibit her from lying to Swann, but it will not require her to correct Swann's misimpressions so long as she herself has not lied to him. Here, Odette has consciously decided not to prohibit something "close" in subject matter to what she has committed herself against. But this does not make Odette's No-Application Understanding a commitment.

Say that a few months have passed. Because of some ambiguous words and actions on Odette's part, Swann comes to believe that she loves him. In fact, however, she does not. Rather, she loves and hopes to marry the handsome Duke, who happens to be Swann's best friend. One day, Swann reveals his mistaken belief to Odette: he is so happy to know that his love for her is now requited. Swann is sufficiently obtuse that, if Odette does not disabuse him, he will take her silence as confirmation of his false belief. And Odette knows this.

Now, suppose Odette means to honor her commitment not to deceive Swann. She doesn't have to. She might have forgotten all about her commitment, or she might decide to repudiate it. But suppose she means to honor it. Odette asks herself whether her commitment against deceiving Swann requires her to speak up and disabuse him.

As it happens, Odette would much prefer to remain silent. It will be most unpleasant to tell Swann the truth, and as it happens, she stands to profit substantially if Swann persists in his misconception. So Odette would prefer to keep her mouth shut. But she reflects nonetheless on whether her commitment obliges her to tell Swann the truth.

She remembers her original understanding. She knows that at the time she made the commitment, she was clear that it would not apply to this kind of case. This is not "deception," as she originally understood it. Rather, this case involves an "omission," which, she clearly recalls, was not supposed to count. Does this original understanding dispose of the interpretive question?

If Odette's approach to interpretation were intentionalist—in the way that originalism is intentionalist—the answer would be yes, and the interpretive question would be easy to answer. She would say, "I specifically intended that remaining silent would be permissible under my no-deceiving-Swann commitment, so I am free to remain silent." Case closed.

But if Odette were to take a commitment-based stance toward interpretation, her original understanding would not be dispositive. The only commitment Odette made in this story is a commitment not to deceive Swann. She certainly did not commit herself *to* misleading him through silence. Nor did she commit herself to the *permissibility* of misleading him through silence. She made a commitment *against* something—deceiving Swann—not to the permissibility of anything.

True, as she originally understood it, her commitment had No Application to omissions. She intended her commitment not to prohibit omissions. But a mere intention is not a commitment. She made no *commitment* whatever about misleading Swann through silence—neither to it, nor against it, nor to its permissibility. Odette may certainly choose to stick to her original understanding; she may say, "On reflection, I believe my original understanding was right." But if she means to honor her commitment against deceiving Swann, her job is to interpret that commitment—to think through, in good faith, what it means to deceive him. In answering this question, her original intention is not conclusive.

In other words, if Odette adopts what I will call a *commitmentarian* perspective, rather than an originalist perspective, she may decide that her commitment *does* require her to speak up. She is free, as an interpretive matter, to come to the realization that, despite her original understanding, silence can in some cases be deceiving. In short, she is free to conclude that her original No-Application Understanding was wrong.

The point is not that Odette *must* reject her original No-Application Understanding. The point is only that the question is an open one. It is not precluded by her earlier intention. The intention does not oblige. Only the commitment does.

This is the central difference between originalist and commitmentarian interpretation. Originalism requires adherence, to the greatest possible extent, to all the "founding" intentions. Commitment-based interpretation, by contrast, has no special regard for the original No-Application intentions, which were not commitments. Thus if Odette regards her undertaking as a commitment, her original No-Application Understandings are not dispositive.

There should be nothing surprising about this conclusion. Our commitments frequently demand more of us than we originally suppose. We interpret them to do so all the time.

Perhaps when deciding whether to have a child, my (stupid) original understanding was that parenthood would not require me to give up much of my free time. Perhaps I would never have agreed to have a child had I known how much of my time it would take. In fact, let's say that, before agreeing to have a child, I specifically decided that I would not give up much of my free time.

But having become a parent, I undertook certain commitments, and honoring these commitments may well exact much more time than I understood or intended. Thus originalism is not an adequate interpretive methodology for me if I want to live up, in good faith, to the commitments I have undertaken by becoming a parent.

Commitments launch our lives down certain paths, enmeshing us in networks of goals, relationships, and obligations. Commitments always have an "objective" as well as a "subjective" component; through a commitment, we engage ourselves to something we think of as existing at least in part outside ourselves. Thus honoring a commitment—which we are not absolutely required to do; we can always walk away from our commitments, even from our child-rearing commitments—is never reducible solely to figuring out what exactly our initial intentions were.[3]

A No-Application Understanding may reflect an intention to remain uncommitted. But an *intention* to remain uncommitted is not a *commitment* to remain uncommitted. It is merely an intention, which in commitmentarian interpretation exerts no binding force. A parent may well discover that her commitments require much more from her than she planned. Odette may conclude that keeping silent really is a form of deceiving Swann in certain circumstances. And a court may well decide that excluding women from the legal profession denies them the equal protection of the laws.

Such interpretations do not violate any earlier commitment made by the prohibition or undertaking that the interpreter is trying to follow. On the contrary, they represent the interpreter's effort to do justice to the commitment at issue. To be sure, they contradict an original intention concerning the commitment's limits. But to the extent that an interpreter means to honor a commitment, originalism is not on. Commitmentarian interpretation is free to contradict original intentions; it is not free to dishonor commitments.

The next, equally critical point is that Application Understandings are different. They can and often do imply commitments. But before turning to this point, I want to consider an objection, which will require me to say something more general about the kind of argument I have made here.

Interpretive Assurances

The objection is this: a constitutional enactment is not like an individual commitment. When more than one person make a joint commitment, they may make statements to one another concerning the interpretation of their commitment. In the case of a constitution, these statements may come to represent widely shared, publicly settled understandings of the meaning of the text. Such understandings, it might be said, backed up by express public statements, cannot properly be ignored by judges who are supposedly interested in honoring commitments.

But if such understandings are only understandings, not commitments, then no matter how strongly or publicly or clearly stated, they *can* be ignored by judges concerned with honoring commitments. Say that Jane and George commit themselves to becoming a great figure skating twosome. At the time, they both understand and declare to one another that their commitment will not require them to take dance lessons, because figure skating (they believe) has nothing to do with dancing. Their clear statements to one another of this No-Application Understanding make no difference. If they want to honor their commitment, they may discover that they have to take dance lessons.

Had Jane and George made a supplemental commitment, "But in no event shall we take dance lessons," they would then be in a different situation. We might say they had made conflicting commitments or that their second commitment commits them to a certain restricted interpretation of the first commitment. Either way, they no longer have a mere understanding about whether they must take dance lessons. They have committed themselves not to take them. Nothing changes here in the shift from a single person making a commitment individually to a group of individuals doing so collectively.

"But you have misunderstood my point," the objector may say. "The proponents of the Fourteenth Amendment gave public *assurances* that the amendment would not have certain consequences. They made these statements to induce others to consent to the amendment, and very probably others relied on their statements in supporting the amendment. Why don't these interpretive assurances change the commitmentarian analysis? Why don't they count as commitments that later courts must honor?"

I am tempted to say here that no one can complain if courts later ignore such assurances, because everyone in the American legal world is on notice that courts will not necessarily defer to extralegal statements declaring the supposed meaning of a law. This is not anachronistic. In the nineteenth century, courts were considerably more opposed than they are today to the use of legislative history as evidence of the meaning of legal texts. Even into the first decades of the twentieth century, judges characteristically took the position that what the legislators "meant" was irrelevant; it was what they "said"—that is, what they wrote into the law—that counted. Most of the framers and ratifiers of the Fourteenth Amendment would have known quite well that lawmakers' interpretive assurances did not bind judges, and no one could have reasonably relied on the notion that they did.

But there is just enough circularity in this reply that I will not rest on it alone. If, on a commitmentarian view of the Constitution, judges *ought* to count interpretive assurances as binding, then the arguments I have made so far seem incomplete. If lawmakers' interpretive assurances counted as commitments, then in a commitmentarian system, judges *would* defer to such assurances, and people would learn that they could rely on them. Therefore it is worth explaining why judges need not regard interpretive assurances as commitments.

The answer requires us to consider more carefully what kind of rule-making practice we take people to be engaged in when then enacting a constitution.

Rules We Follow When We Follow Rules

At bottom, all I have tried to do, throughout the preceding arguments, is to identify a certain normative practice. There are different rules by which we can be guided when we want to be guided by rules. In other words, there are different practices available to us when we make and follow rules. Making commitments is one such practice. It is a practice with which most of us have some familiarity, even if we do not always clearly recognize it or differentiate it from other, similar normative practices in which we also engage.

But we do not always make commitments when we make rules for ourselves, and if the particular practice of rule-making in which we have engaged is not commitment-based, then the fact that No-Application Understandings are not commitments can be totally irrelevant. In some rule-making practices, *all* original intentions, including No-Application Intentions, could be equally significant for interpretive purposes. Hence when interpreting a given rule, a great deal turns on the kind of normative practice in which the relevant agents are engaged. Consider the practices of contract.

Say that A and B contractually agree never to "deceive" one another. Assume that A and B own companies, or perhaps that A and B *are* companies. Their no-deception agreement pertains to a joint venture the two companies are about to start. Because they do business in different jurisdictions, there is uncertainty about what, if any, fraud laws will apply to their venture. So they have included, in their contract, this no-deception clause.

At the time they execute the contract, A and B understand clearly and specifically that "deception" does not include the mere failure by one party to disclose information to the other about its own financial condition. In this, they are similar to Odette in the earlier example, who understood that "deception" did not refer to omissions. We can imagine that A and B (or their agents) discussed the matter thoroughly before they signed the contract. Both A and B were well aware that each understood "deception" in this way. Both made assurances to the other that "deception" did not include mere failure to disclose financial information.

A few months later, B makes certain investments relying on the belief that A is financially sound. In fact, A is insolvent. B sues A, claiming a violation of their no-deception agreement.

A's answer is that no one affirmatively misrepresented A's finances. There was only, at most, a failure by A to disclose information about its own financial condition. Thus, says A, under the parties' clear understanding of their contract, the no-deception agreement cannot have been violated.

B agrees that there were no material misrepresentations. B replies, however, that omissions concerning a party's financial condition can still amount to "deception." He does not deny the original understanding. Yes, at the time of execution of the contract, A and B both intended (and told each other they intended) that their contract would *not* apply to such omissions. But, B says, A and B made a commitment to each other. B can now see better what is required of agents who have committed themselves not to deceive one another. Such a commitment implies not only refraining from affirmative misrepresentations, but also disclosing material facts when necessary to avoid one party's misleading the other.

There is no difficulty imagining a court categorically throwing B and his commitmentarian whining out of court. If the case were decided in an American jurisdiction, this result would probably be expected. Contracts, the court would be expected to hold, are to be interpreted in accordance with the parties' clearly understood intentions at the time of execution. A's and B's express, shared intention was that failure to disclose financial information would not count as deception. Case closed.

In this story, B's argument about what it means to be "committed" is inapposite. B has tried to ingraft a commitmentarian interpretive stance onto a normative practice to which (at least according to the law of contracts, at least in this case) it does not apply. Neither A nor B made a *commitment* in the sense in which I have been using that term. Rather, they made a *contract*, which American law understands to be governed in special ways by the contracting parties' original expressed intentions.

On this view of A's and B's case, there is no powerful interpretive distinction between Application and No-Application Understandings. The parties' intentions govern. The fact that one is dealing here with a No-Application intention makes no difference.[4]

Now imagine, instead of a commercial contract, an international treaty. A and B are now nations, and they enter into a treaty in which A and B agree not to deny the equal protection of the laws to any person in their respective borders. The main objective of this treaty is, let's say, to ensure that A does not discriminate against B's citizens when the latter have traveled to A, and vice versa. In the negotiations leading up to the treaty, A and B made clear to one another that their agreement would in no way prohibit them from racially segregating any or all public facilities, institutions, or buildings.

A few months later, B sues A under the treaty because A maintains racially segregated public schools. Here too, one of the first decisions an interpreter of this treaty must make is whether to treat A and B as having acted within an intention-based normative practice, in which the full set of original (communicated) intentions plays a privileged role in governing the scope of their obligations, or whether instead they engaged in a commitment-based practice, in which their original No-Application intentions command no overriding interpretive significance (because No-Application intentions are not commitments).

Of course, even on the latter view, the interpreter would not be bound to hold that the equal protection guarantee in this treaty demands an end to racial segregation. The point is only that the interpreter must first decide whether to give special interpretive weight to all of the parties' original intentions, or only to the parties' commitments. The interpreter must, in other words, decide what kind of normative practice the parties have engaged in.

Interpretation should hold a rule-making practice to be intention-based when the normative basis for the undertaking—the basis of its binding force—makes it appropriate to hold an agent to all his intentions at a particular moment in the past. When parties enter into a contract, for example, there is no difficulty conceiving their undertaking in intention-based terms, so long as the normative framework for contract is bargained-for exchange.

In a bargained-for exchange, the parties should in principle get what they bargained for. That is why it is appropriate to honor the parties' express understandings of a contract at the time of execution. Under this principle, there is no place for a distinction between Application and No-Application intentions. If A and B, on entering a contract, share an express, definite understanding that A's promises do *not* oblige A to *x*, and if we are trying to give A and B what they bargained for, this understanding ought to govern future interpretation. B cannot later claim that a court should discount this No-Application Understanding as a "mere intention," rather than a commitment, because B would be trying to get more than he bargained for.

For constitutional law, therefore, interpretation's first question is whether to understand constitutionalism as a practice like contract-making, where original intentions ought to govern interpretation, or a practice of commitment-making, in which mere intentions do not govern. If constitutional law is not viewed in commitment-based terms, then of course commitmentarian interpretation has no particular significance for it.

The last chapter explained why constitutionalism ought to be viewed in commitment-based terms. I will not repeat the arguments, but the conclusion is easily summarized. Understanding American constitutionalism, both descriptively and normatively, requires us to embrace a temporally extended picture of self-government. This idea of self-government over time in turn implies a central place for commitments. Rejecting the presentist conception of self-government means that democracy does not consist ideally of governance by present democratic will, but also, in fundamental part, of adhering to the nation's fundamental, self-given commitments over time. Only this commitment-based account of constitutional democracy explains the Constitution's continuing authority today. That is why commitmentarianism is the right lens through which to read the Constitution.

We are now in a position to answer the objection raised earlier. The objection asked why a commitmentarian judge interpreting the Fourteenth Amendment should not defer to the original No-Application Understandings if the amendment's proponents, in order to induce others to support it, made public statements expressly declaring (their understanding) that the Fourteenth Amendment would not prohibit segregation. The answer is that a judge who took this view would have inappropriately treated the Constitution as a contract, rather than as a collective effort to achieve self-government over time.

We can imagine a kind of hypothetical constitutional conversation in which group A says to group B in 1867, "All we are asking for is your promise to guarantee blacks the equal protection of the law. We understand and openly declare that this promise will not oblige you to stop segregating the races, if you wish to segregate. Moreover, we are willing to offer you valuable consideration if only you will make this promise." If the Fourteenth Amendment were understood to have authority today because it was a bargained-for promise of this sort, then sticking to the original intentions of the parties might well be the right interpretive course.

Most or all of the Constitution's provisions clearly reflect bargain and compromise. As a result, it is possible to view the Constitution as a bargain among individuated actors (whether persons, states, or "interest groups") trying to maximize satisfaction of their own preferences. Any act of legislation can be understood in these terms, as "public choice" theory tells us. But if the Constitution is viewed in these terms, it loses its status and authority as an act of collective self-government by the American people, which alone can adequately explain its claims to continuing authority today.

Constitutionalism is certainly not the only arena in which the question arises whether to view the parties to an agreement as contractors or as co-participants in a union of a different nature. Marriage is another. This is why the "marital contract" has always fit so awkwardly within the framework of contract law. Marriage can be conceptualized along the lines of pure bargained-for exchange. If it is, then its terms should in principle be defined in advance, by the express will of the parties, preferably in a written agreement hammered out through careful negotiation beforehand. The more we conceive of a wedding as the execution of a contract in this sense, the more appropriate it would be for the parties' premarital bargained-for declarations of intention to govern their obligations in future. But if we take marriage to be an attempt to form a relationship not defined by contractual bargaining, the more the language of commitment becomes pertinent.

If we viewed the Fourteenth Amendment as a contract among those who voted for it, then the interpretive assurances made by some voters to others might be conclusive for later interpretation. But constitutions cannot be viewed that way. For if the bindingness of the Fourteenth Amendment depended on a contractual model of this kind, the Fourteenth Amendment would not bind anyone who did not consent to it—a group which would presumably include those who were against it at the time, as well as everyone alive today.

To be sure, viewing the Constitution as a "contract among the states," might alleviate this problem to some extent. But whatever merit that view of the Constitution might once have had, the Civil War sealed its fate. Indeed, given the circumstances of its enactment, the Fourteenth Amendment is particularly ill-suited to the "contract among states" rhetoric. That amendment was rammed down the throats of a recalcitrant South by the victorious forces of the Union. If the Fourteenth Amendment has continuing authority today, it has this authority because it was an act of self-government by the United States, not a contract voluntarily entered into by (among others) the vanquished Southern states. A state cannot as it were protest, "But we only promised to guarantee equal protection of the laws because we were expressly assured that we could keep segregating." The states did not make a "promise" when they ratified the

Fourteenth Amendment; or, to be more precise, the Fourteenth Amendment's binding authority does not flow from any such act of promising by the separate states. Its authority flows from its status as a commitment made by the Union as a whole.

Yes, it is victors' history to say that the Reconstruction Amendments were commitments "made by the nation as a whole," given that they were forced upon the vanquished South. But the victors' perspective—the Union's perspective—is the right one for constitutional interpretation to adopt. When Georgia ratified the Fourteenth Amendment, it was not "promising," but rather participating in, or yielding to, an act of constitution-making by the Union. (Another way to put the same point: the scope of Georgia's obligations under the Fourteenth Amendment would be the same if it had never ratified.) Obviously these are not statements simply of historical fact; they are statements about the right way for constitutional interpretation to understand, from a normative point of view, acts of constitution-making. States are bound by the Fourteenth Amendment not because they "promised" to abide by it in some kind of state-to-state compact, but because that amendment represents a collective, national commitment. As a result, the states' obligations thereunder are not limited by their No-Application Understandings, even if the supporters of the Fourteenth Amendment shared the same No-Application Understandings and made public declarations to that effect.

In contractual matters, the parties ought to get exactly what they bargained for. At least that is the principle. Parties to a contract have a right to complain if they end up with more obligations than they bargained for. With commitments, it is different. Commitments characteristically turn out to require more than the parties who made them bargained for.

Application Understandings

Return now to the main argument. Why should the foundational Application Understandings be regarded as commitments, if No-Application Understandings are not?

For any legal prohibition, No-Application Understandings simply are not candidates for answers to the question, "What commitments have been made here?" By itself, a No-Application Understanding represents, precisely, a *noncommittal* position: an understanding that the prohibition at issue does *not* commit the agent one way or the other with respect to some particular course of conduct. To the extent, therefore, that interpretation is bound by commitments, but not by mere intentions, it is not bound by No-Application Understandings.

By contrast, an Application Understanding can imply a commitment. An Application Understanding is, in this respect as in most others, the opposite of a No-Application Understanding. It declares that the agent *is* committed, one way or another, with respect to some particular course of conduct. Every possible Application Understanding of a commitment is a potential answer to the question, "What commitments have been made here?"

This purely analytic difference between Application and No-Application Understandings is what opens up a logical space between them, making it possible for Application Understandings to be commitments while No-Application Understandings cannot be. But this is only a logical possibility. More is required to make an Application Understanding into a paradigm case.

I am now going to describe a special case of commitment-making. Again, the aim is merely to describe a possible normative activity in which agents can engage. Not every agent need make commitments of the kind I am about to describe. The claim is only that agents can make commitments of this kind, and if they do, commitment-based interpretation will have good reason to treat the foundational Application Understandings as paradigm cases.

Begin again with an illustration. Consider once more Odette, who commits herself against deceiving Swann. We already know that Odette, to the extent that she adopts a commitmentarian stance toward her resolution, need not—should not—regard her original No-Application Understandings as dispositive. But what of her original Application Understandings?

Suppose, this time, that Odette and Swann are married. And suppose that a particular episode induced Odette to make her commitment. To make things as hokey as humanly possible, say that Odette had secretly slept with the handsome Duke, who, it will be recalled, is Swann's best friend. Later, Odette had an uncharacteristic bout of self-loathing over this. It was then that she committed herself never to deceive Swann again.

In this story, Odette never affirmatively lied to Swann. On the other hand, she never told Swann about her liaison with Duke. So in this story (unlike the last one), at the time Odette makes her commitment, she does not believe that it has No Application to omissions. Assume instead that she has not yet thought carefully about this question one way or the other.

But she does think about it when, a few weeks later, away on a business trip, she finds herself once again alone with the handsome Duke, who invites her to his hotel room for a nightcap. Suppose Odette means to honor her commitment. But she also wants to sleep with Duke. An appealing way out of this dilemma occurs to her.

She might, she realizes, interpret her commitment as follows: "deception" refers only to affirmative misrepresentations. On this interpretation, if Odette does not affirmatively lie to Swann, she has not deceived him. She can sleep with Duke and never say anything about it to Swann, without having "deceived" him.

Odette adopts this interpretation. She therefore concludes that she is free to sleep with Duke so long as she does not affirmatively lie to Swann about it. And that's what she does.

But this "interpretation" is a kind of fraud, and Odette knows it. Sleeping with Duke, without telling Swann about it, is exactly what she did before. It is exactly what she committed herself not to do again.

As a matter of logic and English, one can reasonably interpret "deception" to apply only to affirmative misrepresentations. But this interpretation is unavailable to Odette, if she means to keep her commitment. To adopt this "interpretation" is not really an act of interpreting her commitment at all. It is a violation of the commitment, under the guise of interpreting it.

We might say of Odette's commitment: if it means anything, it means not doing *this*. Resisting her desire to sleep with Duke was, for Odette, her commitment's definitive requirement. It was the core commitment itself. Her commitment not to deceive Swann *was*, at a minimum, a commitment not to sleep with Duke again.

Thus Odette's commitment is both specific and general at the same time. She made a commitment concerning a particular course of action (sleeping with Duke again) by committing herself to a more general proposition or principle (not to deceive Swann) of which the particular course of action was, for her, a definitive instance. She made the specific commitment *through* the more general one.

Why would an agent do this? Why didn't Odette simply commit herself not to sleep with Duke again? Perhaps because this narrower proposition would have sounded strange and incomplete to her, as if she were deliberately leaving herself free to cheat on Swann with Marcel or Albertine, so long as she didn't cheat on him with Duke. Therefore she made the commitment more general. And why did she choose to commit herself against *deceiving* Swann? Presumably because, in her experience of the episode that led her to make the commitment, she had a particular understanding of what was wrong with what she had done. It was the gross and harmful deception practiced on Swann that made sleeping with Duke such a dreadful thing to do.

But the crucial point is this: as she committed herself not to deceive Swann any more, Odette was committing herself never again to sleep with Duke. That remained the central, definitive thing she did when she engaged in her act of commitment-making. She meant to impose, and did impose, an obligation on herself not to sleep with Duke again behind Swann's back. How did she do this? She made the more specific commitment *through* the more general prohibition.

So we deal here with a particular kind of commitment, double in nature. The agent makes a specific commitment by making a more general commitment. In these special circumstances it is not the case that the agent has made *only* a commitment to the general proposition—unanchored by any commitment more specific than that—so that commitmentarian interpretation would be concerned only with giving content to the general proposition. On the contrary, in these circumstances, the agent has also made a more specific commitment at the same time, which commitmentarian interpretation is obliged to respect as well.

All this is entirely a matter of contingent fact; in particular, a great deal turns on the agent's intentions. Odette intended to be imposing on herself an obligation never again to sleep with Duke when she committed herself not to deceive Swann. This was an Application Understanding or an Application Intention, but it was not *only* an understanding, and it was not *only* an intention. Odette did not merely *intend* to refrain from sleeping with Duke; nor did she merely *intend* to commit herself to this course of action. She *did* commit herself never again to sleep with Duke. She made this commitment by committing herself not to deceive Swann. Where a foundational Application Understanding plays this decisive role in the agent's actions—where the agent centrally intends to be imposing on himself an obligation not to engage in some specific course of action by committing himself to a more general prohibition (of which the specific course of action is the definitive, paradigmatic instance)—the Application Understanding is itself a commitment.

As such, it binds. Whatever else may be left open for interpretation in Odette's commitment, one thing is certain: she is obliged not to sleep with Duke again. Her resolution "not to deceive" Swann was Odette's way of expressing this very commitment—whatever else might go along with it. To be sure, things can always change in a way that deprives Odette's commitment of its force. Swann might die. Odette and Swann might separate. Or Odette might, for other reasons, repudiate her commitment. Then she would be clear of her commitment and would presumably be free to sleep with Duke at will. But so long as she means to honor her commitment, Odette knows that resolving not to deceive Swann was a commitment, at a minimum, not to do *that* again—not to repeat what she had done already with Duke.

In other words, Odette's commitment had a foundational paradigm case. In these circumstances, commitmentarian interpretation calls for the paradigm-case method: interpretation of the more general commitment must be anchored by the more specific commitment. Because of the distinction it draws between Odette's Application and No-Application Understandings, the paradigm-case approach to the meaning of her commitment differs sharply from an originalist approach, which would take all of Odette's original intentions as equally conclusive. At the same time, the paradigm-case interpretive method differs just as sharply from a moral-philosophical approach.

The paradigm case is given, for Odette, not by philosophy, nor by morality as such, but by her particular history with Swann and Duke. Consider Odette's acquaintance Q, whom we have not met until this sentence. He also happens to have made a commitment against deception; as a matter of fact, Q also committed himself never again to deceive the hapless Swann. But Q's commitment has a very different paradigm case: it involved lying to Swann about the quality of his taste in women. For Q, sleeping with someone without Swann's knowledge—someone other than Odette, presumably—would not be an instance of deceiving Swann at all; it would be a course of conduct wholly irrelevant to his commitment. But for Odette, sexual goings-on behind Swann's back are core instances of deceiving Swann; at an absolute minimum, secretly sleeping with the handsome Duke is right out.

A person who makes a commitment need not have specific, core Application Understandings at the time. A commitment need not have any specific, foundational applications. The point is simply that Application Understandings *can* play this role in our commitments. Agents can and sometimes do make commitments regarding specific courses of action by committing themselves to more general propositions.

Commitments require a performative act. They require an agent to give his word. When the word the agent gives is centrally intended to have specific applications, but is nonetheless more general, the agent has made a double commitment of the kind described.

But can't the agent's original Application Understandings of a commitment be mistaken? Of course. Ken, committing himself to vegetarianism, originally believes that the McSausage Breakfast Sandwich is off-limits. It turns out, however, that the McSausage is made entirely of soybeans. Upon learning the facts, Ken will correctly reject his original Application Understanding as mistaken. But even though Application Understandings can always be mistaken in this way, there is another sense in which foundational Application Understandings can never be mistaken. How can this be? The answer will be given in the next chapter.

Core Constitutional Applications as Commitments

No a priori necessity dictates the existence of any specific, core, actuating applications for the various rights and powers included in the American Constitution. There needn't have been any. But as we have seen, it just so happens that there were, for just about every one of the Constitution's most important rights and powers. And where there were such core, actuating applications, the paradigm-case method comes into play. The original Application Understandings remain binding on interpreters for the same reasons explored previously. These understandings are not merely understandings; they represent commitments in their own right.

The intention to abolish the institutions through which blacks were owned as chattel property was obviously central in bringing the Thirteenth Amendment about. The intention to abolish the black codes played a similar role in bringing about the Fourteenth Amendment. These intentions were not merely intentions. Those who supported the Reconstruction Amendments were centrally committed to abolishing certain specific laws and practices. The First Amendment too was a double commitment of this kind, committing the nation not only to large principles but to certain more specific prohibitions as well: against seditious libel law, against prior restraint, against the creation of a national church, and so on.

Thus we reach the end of the argument. Where the Constitution's commitments have core paradigm cases, they require precisely the interpretive asymmetry observed throughout constitutional doctrine. The foundational Application Understandings bind because they are themselves commitments, even while the No-Application Understandings can be cast aside.

Subsequent Paradigm Cases

What of Application Understandings that emerge after enactment? How are they to be regarded?

Return one last time to Odette, still away on her business trip, who now receives a different proposition from the handsome Duke: he invites her out dancing. Odette considers. Her commitment doesn't call on her to refuse a night out dancing, does it? True, she will not be able to tell Swann about it later; it would make him very upset. But after all, she can't possibly tell Swann every single thing that happens to her. No one does that. So doing some things without telling Swann must be all right. And why shouldn't one of those things be dancing with Duke? As she reflects, Odette comes to be increasingly certain: now that she thinks it over, she realizes that this was her original understanding. All she meant by "not deceiving" Swann was not sleeping with other people behind his back.

So Odette's commitment, according to the understanding at which she has now arrived, does not apply to anything she might do with Duke short of sleeping with him. Even if this was Odette's original understanding, however, it was still a No-Application Understanding. As such it ought, from a commitmentarian perspective, to have no particular interpretive weight.

But say that Odette sticks to this view, which, of course, she is entitled to do. The fact that she is *free* to reject a No-Application Understanding does not mean she *has* to reject it. In any event, out she goes. As it happens, she also goes out dancing with Duke the next night, and the next week too, when they are on another trip together.

Back home, she does not lie to Swann, but neither does she tell him about her nights out with Duke. On these nights, Odette always stops short of sleeping with Duke, but, as you might imagine, not too far short. Now say that Duke, being Swann's best friend, joins Odette and Swann on a few social occasions. Duke also declines to enlighten Swann about his nights out with Odette. At first Odette is relieved that Duke is not giving them away, but after a while she begins to feel a little appalled.

She sees Swann smiling happily, fixing a drink for Duke, exchanging witticisms about men having affairs with their best friends' wives. She sees Swann made ridiculous by the secret she shares with Duke. In short, she sees that Swann is badly deceived.

In this story, Odette has the experience of learning something about her commitment. The lesson (as she sees it) is this: if she really means not to deceive Swann, she can't keep carrying on with Duke as she has been. Her secret nightlife with Duke may or may not be as gross an act of deception as secretly sleeping with him would have been, but it is still deceptive. So she says no the next time Duke asks her out. And she holds to this new interpretation of deception for the rest of her years with Swann. (Which is not to say that she never again cheats on Swann; I said that she holds to this interpretation of her commitment, not that she always honors it.) What is more, the realization that secretly "going out" with other men, even short of sleeping with them, is still an act of deception becomes, for her, an established piece of her commitment's meaning. She accepts this meaning, and her subsequent interpretations of her commitment are built around it. Thus a new paradigmatic Application Understanding comes into place for Odette.

Expressing a mere intention, her original No-Application Understanding was not entitled to any particular interpretive weight. But her new Application Understanding, expressing a commitment, carries considerable weight. So long as she remains serious about not deceiving Swann, her future interpretation of deception is shaped by this new specific commitment that, she now understands, it entails.

From a commitment-based point of view, a No-Application Understanding never obliges. But an Application Understanding of a commitment always carries at least some interpretive force. This force can vary. At a minimum, to break from an Application Understanding is to repudiate what one has previously recognized to be a commitment. This is not an action the agent will take lightly. An agent who adopts the commitmentarian stance is bound to consider carefully whether, in deciding to repudiate what he took himself to be committed to, he is not simply giving in to desire or expediency. In this sense, departing from any Application Understanding demands greater or clearer justification than is required for departures from a No-Application Understanding.

When the Supreme Court holds that a constitutional right prohibits some given governmental action, the Court recognizes and thereby establishes a commitment on behalf of the nation: this particular governmental action will not be allowed. That is why a decision by the Supreme Court that a constitutional right prohibits x carries more interpretive weight than a decision that the right does not prohibit x. It was much easier for the Court to overrule *Gobitis* (which found that compulsory flag salutes in public schools did not violate the First Amendment) one year later in *Barnette* (which found that compulsory flag salutes in public schools did violate the First Amendment) than it would have been for the Court to move in the reverse direction. Throughout the history of American law, the total number of cases in which the Court overruled an earlier recognition of an individual constitutional right can perhaps be counted on one hand (provided that we count the repudiation of the *Lochner* era's rights as a whopping single digit), while cases shifting the law in the other direction—recognizing a constitutional right not recognized before—are legion. There are many reasons for this, but one is that decisions recognizing a constitutional right make a commitment, whereas decisions declining to recognize a constitutional right do not.

In some instances, however, the force of later-developing Application Understandings can be even stronger. They can acquire a greater interpretive status, similar to that of a foundational application. The most obvious constitutional illustration is *Brown*. When and how does this happen?

An Application Understanding is a paradigm case when the agent understands that he can do justice to his commitment only in light of— only within the terms established by—the Application Understanding. In other words, to the extent that a new Application Understanding becomes a "fixed star" or reference point by which future interpretations are measured, interpretation is dealing with a new paradigm case.

A characteristic way for a new Application Understanding to take on this status is through the chain of events described in the last story of Odette and Swann: (1) the new Application Understanding emerges out of a powerful subsequent experience giving the agent the conviction that a lesson has been learned, a lesson about what counts as a violation of the commitment; (2) this new Application Understanding holds up over a substantial period of time, confirming that it does not reflect a mere flip-flop of opinion; and (3) the agent incorporates the new Application Understanding into future conduct and future interpretations of his commitment, so that it comes to work its way ever more significantly into the agent's life. The new Application Understanding (although by the time it has worked its way into the agent's life it will hardly be "new" anymore) need never possess the same inviolable status as a foundational Application Understanding, but if these three criteria are satisfied, it will have become deeply embedded within the overall commitment.

Brown v. Board of Education displays all three of these criteria. It emerged out of a long experience with apartheid in this country; it represented, or came to represent, a profound experience of lessons learned about the real meaning of separate-but-equal and the real meaning of equal protection. As the years and decades passed, *Brown* stood the test of time; indeed, it gained in strength. Finally, *Brown* worked its way ever more deeply into the nation's life, as the Court applied its desegregation principle to more and more public institutions, changing the face of the nation and sparking the antidiscrimination movement that would reshape American law beginning in the 1960s.

Observe that these same three criteria also obtain in the case of the emergence of the Sedition Act of 1798 as a First Amendment paradigm case and then, once again, in the twentieth-century reemergence of sedition laws as paradigmatic First Amendment violations. Both in the late 1790s and again in the first half of the twentieth century, the nation had a profound confrontation with sedition laws, leading eventually to a conviction that core constitutional rights were being violated. This conviction has now stood up over time; the contemporary understanding that sedition statutes (statutes penalizing the criticism of government) are categorically unconstitutional has been bedrock First Amendment law for at least fifty years, if not much longer. And it has plainly worked its way deeply into American culture and social practices.

Similar observation could be made about the famous *Miranda* decision; the protection of art under the First Amendment; the protection of pornography under the First Amendment; the protection of women against governmental sex discrimination under the Fourteenth Amendment; and the Court's holding, in the wake of the Depression, that the federal government had the power, under the commerce clause, to regulate farming (even when the particular farm at issue was located solely within a single state and even when the particular farming activity regulated was not itself an act of interstate commerce). All these subsequently developed Application Understandings today have a status close to that of a foundational paradigm case. None of them is beyond the Court's power to undo, but the Court would be under an obligation to demonstrate compelling justifications for doing so.

I have not tried to say here how courts go about the business of extrapolating rules or principles from paradigm cases. I have tried only to show that in the interpretation of commitments, Application and No-Application Understandings are differently situated. Original No-Application

Understandings never represent commitments, and therefore courts may ignore them, whereas the original, core Application Understandings are commitments, and the courts are bound by them. If this is right, then a commitment-based understanding of constitutional law generates a powerful account of the doctrinal structure that, as shown in Part I, obtains pervasively throughout American constitutional law.

6

Two Objections

I have argued that we can make sense of constitutional law's asymmetric treatment of Application and No-Application Understandings if we view constitutionalism as a matter of honoring commitments. This chapter addresses two important objections to this argument, each of which was mentioned but deferred earlier.

The first objection asserts that even from a commitment-based point of view, Application Understandings are just as open to error as are No-Application Understandings, so that the "commitmentarian" perspective previously described does not successfully motivate the desired distinction between Application and No-Application Understandings. The second objection points out that the Constitution's framers are dead and argues, on this ground, that their commitments can have no binding force on Americans alive today.

Mistaken Application Understandings

Say I have committed myself to eating no more unhealthy food. At the time I made this commitment, there was one particular dish I meant to put definitively off the table: chicken-fried steak. In other words, I had an original Application Understanding that chicken-fried steak was unhealthy and that my new commitment required me to abstain from it. My commitment had precisely the double nature described earlier. I made a specific commitment against eating chicken-fried steak through the more general prohibition against eating unhealthy food. In short, my commitment had a foundational paradigm case.

But science proves me wrong. Chicken-fried steak, it turns out, helps build strong bodies twelve ways. Surely the correct conclusion for me to draw now is that my commitment does not prohibit me from eating chicken-fried steak. Doesn't this simple example prove that Application Understandings can be as erroneous as No-Application Understandings? Doesn't it prove that Application Understandings, even if once regarded as paradigm cases, are entitled to no special interpretive privilege?[1]

I said earlier that No-Application Understandings are never themselves commitments, while Application Understandings can be and often are. In this difference, I said, lies the root of the interpretive structure observed throughout constitutional law. The health-food objection denies this distinction. It suggests that Application Understandings of a commitment are no more commitments, in and of themselves, than are No-Application Understandings. The objection, in essence, says that my claims about Application Understandings misconceived the correct "level of generality" at which to fix the commitment.

Spelling out the level-of-generality argument, someone might put the objection as follows: "When you committed yourself against eating unhealthy food, you did not commit yourself against eating chicken-fried steak, whatever you may have thought. Your commitment was more general: it was to stop eating unhealthy food—nothing more or less. Treating Application Understandings as somehow inviolable makes the mistake of failing to locate the commitment at its proper, higher level of generality."

Translated to the domain of constitutional law, the higher-level-of-generality objection would fit comfortably with at least two familiar approaches to constitutional interpretation. A wing of originalism holds that constitutional interpretation should be governed by the general purposes the founders sought to achieve, even if that means disregarding the founders' more specific intentions. As we saw earlier, Robert Bork invokes such general-purpose interpretation to defend *Brown,* arguing that segregation was inconsistent with the framers' "purpose" of achieving equality, "although the framers did not realize that."[2] Similarly, Lawrence Lessig argues for general-purpose interpretation as a more faithful form of originalism than one gets from standard, specific-intention accounts of originalism.[3]

Another interpretive approach consistent with this way of thinking is the "moral reading" of the Constitution. Here is how a moralist might object to my argument: "I am happy to use the term 'commitment' to describe a constitutional guarantee like the equal protection clause. But the constitutional commitment is, precisely, to the equal protection of the laws, rather than anything more specific. Suppose the equal protection guarantee was originally intended to prohibit what we today call affirmative action. This would clearly be, in your terms, an 'Application Understanding,' but I fail to see why this understanding should be binding today if permitting affirmative action makes the equal protection clause the best it can be. A judge is certainly bound by the concepts the framers used—and hence by their semantic intentions—but not by their more specific conceptions."[4]

Perhaps the simplest answer to both the general-purposivist and the moralist is that they cannot make sense of the fact that American constitutional law has, in fact, systematically and ubiquitously, treated historical Application and No-Application Understandings differently—categorically adhering to the former, while routinely disregarding the latter. But this observation, while important, is not a sufficient answer at this stage of the argument.

The goal in this part is to offer reasons that might explain why constitutional law treats Application and No-Application Understandings so differently. I have said that the idea of commitment explains this differential treatment. The higher-level-of-generality objection denies this. Through hypotheticals like the health-food story told a moment ago, the higher-level-of-generality objections seeks to show that Application Understandings can be just as mistaken as No-Application Understandings, regardless of whether the Constitution's terms are viewed as commitments.

But notwithstanding the health-food story, there remains a sense in which original core Application Understandings of a commitment cannot be mistaken. To see how this is so, it is necessary to consider in greater detail the different ways in which a person's original Application Understandings of his commitments can be mistaken.

Mistakes of Fact

Assume that I originally thought that chicken-fried steak increased the risk of heart attack, promoted obesity, shortened life span, and so on. That's why I thought it was unhealthy. But nutritionists have authoritatively concluded that chicken-fried steak does none of these things. In fact, it is the key to a healthy diet. Having committed myself not to eat unhealthy food, doesn't it follow that I may now abandon my original Application Understanding?

There is no doubt that I can start eating chicken-fried steak again. In that straightforward sense, my original Application Understanding was obviously mistaken. But this is a mistake of a certain kind, and when this particular kind of mistake is more clearly identified, we will see that it does not imply a rejection either of the original Application Understanding or of its paradigmatic status.

The mistake I made was a mistake of fact. I erroneously believed that eating chicken-fried steak, as a factual matter, causes certain adverse health consequences. Hence when I learn that it does not produce these consequences, I naturally conclude that my commitment no longer applies to chicken-fried steak.

Now, a paradigmatic Application Understanding is always an understanding of how a commitment applies to a posited set of facts. In the case of my chicken-fried steak understanding, the set of facts that I assumed to be the case turned out not to be the case. But the facts posited by an Application Understanding do not need to be actual; the posited facts need not be the case. The facts posited by an Application Understanding could be entirely hypothetical. Or they could be true, but mistakenly believed to be hypothetical. Or they could be false, but mistakenly believed to be true. It makes no difference to the Application Understanding itself, nor to its interpretive status.

Assume that the seditious libel prosecution of John Peter Zenger in 1735 was an undisputed foundational paradigm case for the First Amendment. Assume that every framer and ratifier of the Bill of Rights understood that the freedom of speech, if it meant anything, guaranteed that the United States could not prosecute or jail a person for doing what Zenger had done. But say that historians have just now uncovered the original indictment in the Zenger case, and this original document reveals a little mistake in the framers' understanding.

Zenger was not, it turns out, prosecuted for "casting an Aspersion on the Governor General," as was believed by all the framers and ratifiers in 1789. He was actually prosecuted for "casting a Nasturtium at Gouverneur Morris." This is doubly surprising: not only was everyone misinformed about the charge against Zenger, but everyone has always believed that Gouverneur Morris had not yet been born in 1735.

So the factual premises behind the original Application Understanding were a little off. From the point of view of the paradigm-case method, how should judges respond to this new discovery about the true facts of the Zenger trial? Should they hold, perhaps, that throwing flowerpots at Gouverneurs is the true benchmark of protected First Amendment activity?

The new discovery should have no impact on First Amendment law or on the status of the paradigmatic application. Judges should not suddenly take the view that throwing a nasturtium at a Gouverneur is a First Amendment paradigm case. Nor, however, should they hold that the original Application Understanding concerning Zenger is no longer important to First Amendment law. Rather, judges can and should continue enforcing the foundational Application Understanding, taking the facts of the Zenger case as they were (mistakenly) taken at the time. Despite the error, the original core commitment behind the First Amendment would remain a commitment against prosecuting someone for casting aspersions on a governor. In other words, despite the factual error, the original Application Understanding—viewed as an understanding of how the First Amendment applies to a certain posited set of facts—would remain as decisive and as definitive as before.

For this reason, the possibility of factual error underlying an Application Understanding poses no threat to the status of Application Understandings or to the distinction between them and No-Application Understandings. Application Understandings, whether based on real or hypothetical facts, can still represent commitments. The First Amendment would still embody a core commitment to abolish seditious libel prosecutions, paradigmatically exemplified by facts widely supposed to have been the facts of the Zenger trial of 1735, even if it turned out that those facts had nothing to do with the actual Zenger trial of 1735.

The whole business of interpreting a commitment boils down to the problem of deciding how the commitment applies to given sets of facts. A paradigm case offers one fixed answer to this problem. A paradigm case is precisely a posited set of facts or fact patterns with respect to which the commitment is definitively held to apply.

When, therefore, we discover that an original Application Understanding assumed facts that were not really the case, and we wonder whether the commitment would apply to the facts as they really were, we are *not* asking whether to preserve or reject the original Application Understanding. We are asking how the commitment would apply to different facts.

In this important sense, paradigmatic Application Understandings cannot be mistaken. They are not affected by the discovery that the factual premises on which they were based are erroneous. When I learn that chicken-fried steak does not lead to heart attack and so on, I revise my conclusion about whether I can eat chicken-fried steak, but I do not call into question my original understanding on the facts as I then supposed them. Learning the actual facts about chicken-fried steak does not call into question my original understanding that my commitment would have stopped me from eating chicken-fried stead *if* eating chicken-fried steak caused heart attack, obesity, early death, and so on. This is a decisive point, because it explains how a foundational Application Understanding can still retain its paradigmatic force even though based on mistaken facts.

Thus the chicken-fried steak objection does not have the effect claimed for it. It demonstrates that (of course) original Application Understandings can be based on factual error, but it does not undercut the idea that original, core Application Understandings can be regarded as binding commitments, notwithstanding the possibility that they may have rested on a mistake of fact. The core commitment remains defined by the original Application Understanding, even if the facts assumed in that Application Understanding turn out to be hypothetical, rather than actual. If a seditious libel case arises with just the fact pattern mistakenly imputed to the Zenger case, then First Amendment law ought to adhere to the original Application Understanding, even though that understanding did not actually describe the Zenger case itself.

Mistakes of Interpretation

Now consider, however, a different kind of mistake imputed to a paradigmatic Application Understanding. Assume once again that chicken-fried steak was a core original target of my no-unhealthy-food commitment. Stipulate that eating chicken-fried steak will, just as I always thought, lead to obesity, heart attack, and early death. But now imagine that someone says that my original Application Understanding was still mistaken.

His argument runs as follows. "Health is not like weight; it is not something that can be measured irrespective of an organism's functions or purposes. In the case of humans, proper functioning is utilitarian. Each individual should act to maximize overall social utility. Whatever state of a person's body is best suited to achieve this result is 'healthy.' Yes, obesity, heart attack, and early death can sometimes be bad results from a utilitarian point of view. But in your case, it happens that you are and have always been a social net welfare loss. Your utility has always been less than your costs. Hence the quicker the death, the better. So if you will maximize your own happiness by eating nothing but chicken-fried steak, and if at the same time you will hasten your death without a protracted hospital stay, you should eat up."

In this argument, the original Application Understanding is said to be erroneous not because of a mistake in my grasp of the facts, but because of a mistake in my understanding of "unhealthy." As a result, this argument, unlike the mistake-of-fact argument, *does* call for a surrender of the foundational Application Understanding. It holds that the commitment should be interpreted not to apply to the exact set of facts to which they were originally and paradigmatically understood to apply.

In other words, the facts underlying my original Application Understanding are no longer at issue. Rather, it is the meaning of "unhealthy" that has been put in question. The objection says that my original Application Understanding rested on an erroneous idea of the meaning of health.

How does the paradigm-case method reply to this kind of argument? Consider how the same argument would go with respect to constitutional commitments.

Return to the black codes of 1867. Again assuming no factual error, suppose someone insists that the Fourteenth Amendment, properly interpreted, does not make black codes unconstitutional. The black codes of the 1860s were not unconstitutional (this person says), and a reenactment of those codes today would not be unconstitutional either. He argues as follows.

The correct level of generality in interpreting the equal protection clause is established either by the framers' general purposes or by the words of the clause itself. The framers' general purpose (he says) was to achieve "racial justice," and the words used were "the equal protection of the laws." Either way, the commitment was not to anything more specific. And either way, the proper interpretation of the equal protection clause is utilitarian, although the framers did not realize it. The demands of racial justice as well as equal protection are satisfied whenever a law increases overall social utility, so long as each person's utility is counted equally, regardless of race. And black codes do increase social utility, counting each individual's utility equally.

This is not a mistake-of-fact argument. The claim here is not that the framers miscalculated (as a factual matter) the felicific consequences of black codes. The claim, rather, is that the framers held a mistaken view of racial justice or of equal protection. The framers' asserted mistake lay in failing to adopt a purely utilitarian conception of justice or equal protection, and it was this error that produced their mistaken belief that the black codes were unconstitutional.

If commitment-based interpreters were free to attribute this kind of error to an original Application Understanding, then the distinction between Application and No-Application Understandings would indeed collapse. Application Understandings, no matter how central to the enactment of a constitutional provision, would no longer deserve any special interpretive role.

What kind of putative error is said to be in play here? The claim is that an original Application Understanding was erroneous because it rested on what we might call a *mistake of law,* rather than on a mistake of fact. Or better still, we might call this a claim of *interpretive error,* rather than factual error.

The paradigm-case method flatly rejects such claims, insofar as they cut anchor with the foundational paradigm cases. Mistake-of-fact arguments are no problem for the paradigm-case method; a judge pursuing commitment-based interpretation is fully open to all the facts and to all interpretive revisions that might be required as a result of new facts. But the foundational Application Understandings cannot be challenged on grounds of interpretive error.

The foundational paradigm cases are preinterpretive. They precede interpretation; they define its limits and its objects. Hence there can be no claim that they represented misinterpretations. Mistake-of-fact arguments leave the original Application Understandings intact (because those understandings are properly seen as understandings that the commitment reaches a given set of facts, whether or not that set of facts really obtained). But mistake-of-law arguments call for a reinterpretation of the commitment, cutting anchor with the original Application Understandings. The paradigm-case method is therefore open to the former, but closed to the latter.

"But these are assertions, not reasons," a moralist or a general-purposivist will ask. "You are begging the question. The question is, at what level of generality should a constitutional commitment be identified? I say it should be identified at a fairly high level of generality, so that the original Application Understandings are not binding commitments. Your answer is that the constitutional commitment cannot be identified at the higher level of generality because doing so would fail to treat the original Application Understandings as binding commitments. That's not an argument; it's a restatement of your conclusion."

True. The only argument I have made is that paradigm-case reasoning, with its core distinction between Application and No-Application Understandings, is perfectly open to the possibility that an original Application Understanding was based on a mistake of fact. I made this argument in response to the chicken-fried steak objection, which was alleged to prove that original Application Understandings could be obviously erroneous and hence could not plausibly demand interpretive deference. The health-food hypothetical was supposed to undermine the special interpretive weight that I have said belongs to original, core Application Understandings (but not to No-Application Understandings), because it presented a case in which all would have to agree that an original Application Understanding would have to be abandoned as erroneous. But the health-food story involved only a mistake of fact, and hence it raised no serious difficulties.

By contrast, claims that a paradigmatic Application Understanding is infected with *interpretive* error, rather than factual error, *would* challenge the privileged position of Application Understandings. This is just the kind of claim that paradigm-case reasoning rejects.

Why? For all the reasons discussed in Chapters 4 and 5. When Odette commits herself never again to deceive Swann, she knows that one thing counts, beyond cavil, as "deceiving" him: sleeping with Duke. As she reflects on her commitment in future, she knows that any interpretation of "deception" that lets her out of that commitment is fraudulent—a betrayal and a dishonoring of the obligation she imposed on herself.

How does she know that? Why can't she regard this particular Application Understanding as having been an erroneous interpretation of a commitment properly identified at a higher level of generality? Why can't she adopt, in good faith, whatever interpretation of "deception" she thinks best, including an interpretation that frees her to sleep with Duke after all?

She cannot do so, in good faith, because she knows that she wasn't committing herself "at a higher level of generality" unanchored to this particular Application Understanding. She knows that, by committing herself not to deceive Swann anymore, she was, precisely, committing herself at an absolute minimum not to sleep with Duke again. Making that specific commitment through the more general commitment was part of the very structure of the normative practice in which she was engaged.

To repeat: it is of course possible to make a general commitment unanchored by any more specific commitments. But that is not what Odette did. She made her more general commitment and her more specific commitment at the same time. She made the specific commitment *through* the general commitment.

In the same sense, the Fourteenth Amendment is not merely a general commitment to the equal protection of the laws, the privileges and immunities of citizens, and so on. The Fourteenth Amendment committed the nation, at a minimum, not to tolerate black codes of the kind passed by numerous Southern states in the wake of the Civil War. Interpretation of the Fourteenth Amendment begins with this fact about its meaning. Any posited interpretation of the Fourteenth Amendment that knocks out that foundational paradigm case is to be rejected for that reason alone.

When a constitutional provision is enacted, there is always a commitment to a principle or proposition of some sort—the principle or proposition set forth in the text. But when there existed a core application, a foundational paradigm case, for this principle or proposition, there is a double commitment: both to the proposition or principle, and to the specific application. The nation commits itself never again to tolerate x by committing itself to a principle the core meaning of which is that it prohibits x.

The higher-level-of-generality view would free judges to ignore every constitutional provision's foundational paradigm cases. Judges who believed they could jettison specific commitments in favor of higher-level-of-generality commitments could easily adopt the utilitarian reading of the Fourteenth Amendment described earlier, thereby permitting reenactment of the black codes today. According to a "moral reader" of the Constitution, such judges might be making a gigantic mistake, but if so, their mistake would lie in their having chosen utilitarianism as their overarching morality. The "moral reader" would fail to comprehend why the judges' decision would and should be categorically condemned just because it surrendered the foundational paradigm case (judged wrong, that is, without needing to discuss whether utilitarianism is good or bad morality).

American constitutional law begins with specific commitments, sometimes written in blood. This is not a matter of a priori or conceptual necessity; it is a matter of history. The fixed quality of these historical commitments is lost the moment interpreters set themselves up at a "higher level of generality." Only the paradigm-case method can explain the fact that, in American constitutional practice, foundational Application Understandings are systematically regarded as inviolable, structuring the doctrine, while No-Application Understandings are routinely dismissed.

The Framers' Death

Turn now to the claim that the framers, being dead, cannot have committed *us* to anything.

Behind this objection usually lies the ideal of present-oriented self-government: that law, in order to be democratically legitimate, ought to be an effectuation of present democratic will. On this presentist view, the Constitution's authority depends on whether Americans today "consent" to it. From this viewpoint, it is almost laughable to think that the Constitution's ratification two hundred years ago could make it an act of legitimate self-government today.

The response to this has already been given: the present-oriented conception of democracy cannot deliver an acceptable account of American constitutional self-government. It removes from self-government the dimension of time—of temporal extension—and accepts instead the view that self-government consists of governance by the present will of the people, a view the American Constitution rejects. If the temporally extended conception of self-government discussed earlier is not the only intelligible and acceptable conception, it is the one embraced by American constitutionalism. Hence to the extent that this objection relies on a conception of self-government already rejected, the observation that the framers are dead states no objection to the argument here.

But this response is not entirely sufficient. Someone making the objection from the framers' death might disclaim the present-oriented conception of self-government. "You are missing the point," he might say. "I accept the basic idea of self-government over time. I accept that people can bind themselves through their own commitments. But the people who made our Constitution are gone. I'm prepared to accept that people can bind *themselves* through their *own* commitments. What I deny is that some people can bind *others* through their commitments."

But all democratic government (on anyone's account) presupposes that some people can bind others. With respect to any law, including the Constitution, the question of self-government that a democratic citizen is entitled to ask is never, "Did I give myself this law?" It is whether the nation or the appropriate democratic body gave itself the law. On the temporally extended conception of self-government, one way a nation gives itself law is by making constitutional commitments in the past and holding itself to them over time.

"But that is exactly why I reject your attempt to conceptualize democratic self-government on the model of individual self-government," the objector may say. "Democracy cannot be thought of as making and following 'national commitments' without presupposing some mystical idea of a collective, national subject into which the actual, living individuals are somehow subsumed. That is magical thinking. I grant that a majority's decision today can bind a minority today, but that is very different from saying a majority's decision in 1789 can bind the entire country today, on the ground that commitments 'the nation gave itself' two centuries ago remain 'our self-given commitments' today. There is no such 'we.' There is no 'nation.' There are only individuals."

There are no nations?

"Well, all right, there are nations, but there is no such thing as 'national self-government.' Nations are not *selves*. They cannot engage in self-government. They are not agents. Only individuals are agents."

Many people rebel at the idea of collective agency, and especially at the idea of a generation-spanning "we" considered as a self-governing entity. On the other hand, the idea of politics as a collective enterprise in which a people or nation acts as some kind of subject, engaging in self-government over time, runs very deep in Western thought. I will say nothing further about the possibility of "collective subjects" here. There is a simpler way to put things. The question is not whether there is such a thing as a collective *agent*. The question is whether there is such a thing as collective, self-governing *agency*, engaged in by many persons participating in joint, cooperative, deliberative activity over time.

To speak of collective self-government implies no single, mysterious mind behind the nation's constitutional commitments. It does imply the possibility of collective agency, but collective agency can take place without presupposing a collective mind. Collective agency takes place through the individuals who participate in it. The conceptual mechanics of this process are of growing interest to analytic and legal philosophers,[5] but there is nothing mysterious about the phenomenon itself. For present purposes, all that is required is a very simple concept and practice of collective commitment-making, examples of which are easy to find.

Take a law journal. Its members, let's say, consist of second- and third-year students at a particular law school. Suppose this journal is self-governing; its member students attempt to run the journal democratically. After lengthy deliberation, the students enact a new bylaw, which passes by the requisite two-thirds majority, providing that the law journal henceforth will publish only articles "of absolutely no practical relevance." There is a mechanism by which this bylaw can be amended or repealed, but while it stands, it creates—or is supposed to create—a collective commitment, binding on all the individual members, including those who voted against it. Associations are governed by such self-given commitments all the time.

Of course, this "no practical relevance" criterion may prove difficult to interpret and to apply. Say that the law journal has an articles committee that chooses articles for publication. The word "committee"—literally, "committed"—is not fortuitous. A committee is a body to whom a task has been committed, and the individual members of the committee are supposed to be committed to discharging this task on the larger group's behalf.

Now, if all the members of the articles committee were to say, "There is no such thing as a collective commitment; let's take whatever articles we want," their view would be self-fulfilling. The commitment would fail. But no logical compulsion requires them to take this view. The collective commitment, made through individuals' actions, is perfectly sustainable, provided that a sufficient number of the committee's members choose to sustain it and to try to apply it in good faith. This is the task that has been committed to them, and it is supposed to bind them regardless of whether they individually supported the bylaw.

In this perfectly straightforward sense, we can speak of institutional actors making collective commitments without invoking notions of a collective mind, myths of a perfect unity of will at the founding "moment," or any of the other conceptual trappings that might be thought to render the idea of collective commitments mysterious. A commitment-based theory of constitutional law requires nothing fancier from the idea of collective commitments. Constitutional commitments would be launched through a democratic process of enacting a constitutional text, and courts would be among the "committees" to whom these commitments are entrusted.

Now, let's say that two years have passed since the enactment of the no-practical-relevance bylaw. As a result, not one current member of the law journal was a member two years ago, when the vote was taken. All of the individuals who participated in that legislative process have graduated and been replaced by fresh faces. Nevertheless, the bylaw has not been amended or repealed.

Say that the new articles committee is reviewing a particular article for publication. The committee's members like the article; their preference would be to publish it. But all agree that this article has considerable practical relevance. Accordingly, they are about to reject it. But one member of the committee—call him Live-in-the-Moment—opposes the no-practical-relevance standard. Live-in-the-Moment points out that the article in question has absolutely no theoretical relevance, and he says that articles of no theoretical relevance are equally deserving of a place in the journal's pages.

Other committee members respond that articles of no practical relevance are often equally devoid of theoretical relevance, so there is no need to change the rules. But in any event, they add, the law review has already made a decision on this subject, so the case is closed. The committee's job is to honor the law review's collective commitment unless or until it is changed.

Live-in-the-Moment replies, "But *we* never agreed to this no-practical-relevance bylaw. Why are we bound by it? It has nothing to do with us."

This argument can be interpreted in more than one way. An uncharitable interpretation would run as follows. Live-in-the-Moment is saying that the members of the committee did not personally approve the no-practical-relevance bylaw and therefore do not have any obligation to enforce it. This interpretation is uncharitable because it views Live-in-the-Moment as arguing that the members of the articles committee should feel free to subvert the journal's collective commitments whenever they personally did not agree with those commitments.

Another uncharitable interpretation of Live-in-the-Moment's objection would say that he is making a conceptual or ontological argument. The law review has no collective existence as an agent. Individuals are the only real agents; collective agents are figments of the imagination. There is no such subject as the "law review" that could "still have" a rule from two years ago. At any given time, the students on the law review can make rules for themselves, if they like, but they can't make rules for subsequent members. The notion that the two-year-old bylaw is still in force today, after every single member who voted for it is gone, is simply unintelligible. It is "mysticism." It is "cant."

This interpretation of Live-in-the-Moment's argument is uncharitable because it makes his position nonsense. Institutions make rules all the time, and these rules can of course stay in force well after the particular individuals who made the rules have left the institution. There is no conceptual or ontological problem here. If there were, all corporations would be in serious trouble. The argument proves far too much. It undoes not only the law review's no-practical-relevance rule but also the articles committee itself, which was presumably formed under preexisting rules and procedures. It similarly undoes the United States Congress, formed under rules laid down two centuries ago, together with all laws more than a couple of decades old.

Live-in-the-Moment might, however, be making a different point, a normative point. He might be saying that, while the bylaw remains in force, the committee *ought* to ignore it because the present membership of the law review did not and does not approve it. Perhaps he will say: "I didn't mean that we should ignore the will of everyone else on the law review. On the contrary. I took a poll of every member of the law review just this morning, and a majority want this article published. So democracy itself," he concludes, "demands that the committee ignore the bylaw."

Now Live-in-the-Moment has rested his case explicitly on the present-oriented conception of self-government. This returns the argument to its point of departure, so there is little more to be said. Yes, from the point of view of present-oriented self-government, past-made law retains authority only if it accords with the current will of the governed. If one accepts the present-tense ideal of democracy, then a law made a generation or more in the past plainly commands very little legitimate authority today—none at all, it seems, if present democratic will runs against it.

But if we reject this presentism, then Live-in-the-Moment has stated no argument. If we accept the idea of self-government over time under self-given commitments, there is no conceptual difficulty saying that commitments democratically adopted by the law review in the past remain binding on its members today, even if the current members did not themselves make those commitments, and even if they run contrary to present majority preference. The present membership of the journal is free to repudiate the review's commitment, but until they do, self-government dictates adherence to the bylaw, not rejection of it on the grounds that it runs against present majority will in the case at hand.

"But you are still begging the question," Live-in-the-Moment may say. "There is no such thing as 'the journal' above and beyond the real human beings who are currently its members. You can talk about people living under 'self-given commitments' until you're blue in the face. The fact is that the members on the law review today have no reason to see a commitment made two years ago, by other people, as their own."

On the contrary, if the present members of the journal have accepted, implicitly or explicitly, the idea of self-government over time, then they will see a very strong reason to treat the commitment made two years ago as continuing to bind them today. They are trying to run the law review under principles of democratic self-government, and they understand that self-government has a temporally extended dimension. They understand, therefore, that their achievement of self-government depends on their adhering to the journal's collectively made commitments unless those commitments are repudiated and new ones enacted in their place. Not because the journal exists "above and beyond its members," but because this is the way that members of a body or institution attain self-government.

"But if your argument depends on their accepting your ideas about 'self-government over time,'" Live-in-the-Moment may ask, "then doesn't your own argument rest ultimately on what the present members want in the here and now? Aren't you conceding that self-government boils down to what the agents of the present moment want today?"

No. The idea of self-government over time does not depend on people here and now agreeing with it. If a present majority of Americans wanted to get whatever they want here and now—regardless of any past-made constitutional commitments—then the country would clearly face a conflict between the claims of present-oriented self-government and the claims of self-government over time. But this dispute could not be adjudicated in favor of present-tense self-government simply by referring to the present will of the majority. That would beg the question. A present, motivated majority of Americans, insisting on the right of the living to govern themselves, might have the political power to get their lawmakers to violate the Constitution, but their belief that they had thus achieved democratic self-government would not make it so.

At the end of the day, nothing compels the present membership of our law journal to maintain that journal's past commitments, and nothing compels Americans today to maintain the Constitution's commitments. To be sure, these commitments will fail if enough people do not believe in their continuing authority, but it is not present will that allows these past-made commitments to claim authority today. It is the fact that our self-government today is ineluctably part of a larger enterprise, going back into the past and projecting far into the future. If we are to seize the reins of this larger enterprise of self-government, rather than merely trying to maximize satisfaction of our present preferences, we will embrace the possibility of commitment-based self-government over time. We will try to build or to participate in institutions that allow self-given commitments to govern us.

Yes, the framers are dead, and we Americans today find ourselves thrown into the political-legal world that they in part bequeathed to us. The question is not whether we the living *today* committed ourselves to the Constitution's rights and powers. The question is how a democratic nation governs itself. If our answer to that question is (as I have suggested) that a democratic nation governs itself over time, by making and living up to enduring self-given political commitments, then the framers' death does not kill the law they made. The Constitution's commitments remain fundamental parts of the collective project of self-government in which we find ourselves. They can be rejected, of course, but they are not to be viewed as "rejected" just because a majority today prefers to violate them. The whole point of a commitment is to bind in the face of contrary present preferences.

Even if we today were to throw off the "yoke" of the Constitution, we would not have achieved freedom through that simple act of rejection. To achieve freedom, we would have to replace the rejected constitutional commitments with other, enduring commitments, which would in turn exert authority over the next generation of Americans, after we had died, unless and until they rejected them.

Anyone is free, of course, to argue that governance by present popular will is better or more legitimate than governance under enduring, self-given commitments. But those who argue for government by present popular will have stepped outside the enterprise of self-government embraced by American constitutionalism for the last two hundred years. They have also turned away from the human capacity most central to autonomy: the capacity to give ourselves law.

The concept of agents giving themselves law cannot be made intelligible in terms of governance by those agents' present will. Law extends over time. This feature of law is irreducible. It is part of the very concept of law. Law is a regularity, of one sort or another, over time. Governance under law always presupposes the regulation of the future by the past.

Treating democracy as government by present popular will severs the dimension of time from the enterprise of self-government. It offers little or no conceptual space for the authority of past acts of lawmaking. On the contrary, it casts into doubt the authority of all past-made law; it sees no reason why agents should be governed by law made in the past.

Rejecting this presentism, and instead embracing a commitment-based picture of self-government, we gain a conception of democracy that restores to law the central role it deserves, that provides a lasting account of the Constitution's authority, and that explains the distinctive interpretive structure—differentiating between Application and No-Application Understandings—that has shaped constitutional law for two centuries.

III

Constitutional Law Today

7

Has Constitutional Law Stopped Making Sense?

In constitutional law these days, a certain feeling has been hard to avoid over the last several years: there is something going on here, but we don't know what it is.

Beginning in the 1990s, the United States Supreme Court began deciding cases that broke, sometimes profoundly, with preexisting constitutional doctrine. Frequently, these groundbreaking opinions were decided five to four, with the same justices—Rehnquist, Scalia, Thomas, O'Connor, and Kennedy—forming the majority. A list of the most important doctrinal changes would certainly include the following:

Affirmative Action. In a case called *Adarand,* the Court held that all governmental, race-based "affirmative action" measures had to satisfy the nearly always fatal "strict scrutiny" standard of review.[1] In the wake of *Adarand,* lower courts invalidated a number of affirmative action measures, and the Court itself struck down majority-minority redistricting measures,[2] as well as an ethnic preference in a federal law that set monies aside for native Hawaiians.[3]

Commerce Clause. In *United States v. Lopez,* a decision that stunned many constitutional scholars, the Court invalidated the federal Gun-Free School Zones Act on the ground that the law exceeded the limits of Congress's commerce power.[4] This was said to be "the first time in nearly sixty years" that the Court "invalidated . . . a congressional reliance on [the] commerce power."[5] Applying its new commerce clause doctrine, the Court in 2000 struck down important provisions of the Violence Against Women Act, a federal statute prohibiting "gender-based violence."[6]

Eleventh Amendment. This gets a little technical, but, in a reversal of existing doctrine, the Court held that the Eleventh Amendment, which bars federal courts from hearing certain lawsuits brought by individuals

145

against states, applied to most suits arising under federal law. On the basis of this holding, the Court handed down a series of decisions immunizing states from suit even when it was conceded that the state had violated federal statutes protecting individuals from discrimination or other forms of injury.[7]

Religious Exemptions. Overturning prior doctrine, the Court held that individuals had no right to religious exemptions from laws of "general applicability."[8] Preexisting doctrine held that whenever a law imposed a substantial burden on an individual's religious practices, the state must prove a "compelling" justification for denying religious exemptions. Today, under the *Smith* case, the taking of wine at communion could be criminalized under a state statute banning the consumption of alcohol.

Expressive Association. In 2000, the Court ruled that New Jersey could not prohibit the Boy Scouts from expelling a homosexual scoutmaster.[9] The Court held that New Jersey's attempt to ban discrimination on the basis of sexual orientation violated the Boy Scouts' "First Amendment right of expressive association." According to *Boy Scouts,* New Jersey's antidiscrimination law would have forced the Boy Scouts to express a message—tolerance for homosexuality—with which the Scouts did not agree.

There is widespread uncertainty about what these cases mean. One reason for the uncertainty is that it is still much too early to know their full reach. If extended, some of these decisions would have quite radical implications. Under the Court's new commerce clause cases, it is now possible to question the constitutionality of the Endangered Species Act and other important federal statutes that once seemed settled features of the American legal landscape. Under *Boy Scouts,* it is possible to question the constitutionality of nearly all antidiscrimination laws, because all such laws force individuals and organizations to express associational messages with which they might not agree. How far do the new cases go? The answer is not yet known.

On top of this, in 2001, the same five justices responsible for most of the case law just described handed down *Bush v. Gore.* According to most of the American constitutional law academy, including many who supported the result in *Bush v. Gore,* the five-justice opinion in that case rested on patently indefensible legal reasoning.[10] As a result, *Bush v. Gore* raised serious concerns about the willingness of the dominant five justices to use constitutional law as a vehicle to achieve desired results.

Conceivably in response to these concerns, the Court in 2003 once again surprised many, but this time by retreating from some of its most visibly "right-wing" decisions. The Court upheld an affirmative action policy in the University of Michigan Law School's admissions procedures—while also striking down that university's undergraduate affirmative action program.[11] In the same month, the Court in *Lawrence* overruled *Bowers v. Hardwick* and struck down a law criminalizing homosexual sodomy.[12] Although *Lawrence* did not overrule the *Boy Scouts* case (*Boy Scouts* involved the right of associations to exclude individuals on the basis of homosexuality; *Lawrence* involves the right of individuals to engage in homosexual sex), those who saw in *Boy Scouts* a Court irredeemably hostile to homosexuality were quite taken aback by *Lawrence*—either pleasantly or rudely, as the case may be.

Most recently, again eschewing an extreme "right-wing" position, the Court issued important rulings limiting the President's unilateral power to detain prisoners deemed "enemy combatants" in the wars in which the country became engaged after September 11, 2001.[13] These rulings rebuked the White House's assertion of an unfettered authority to deem even American citizens "enemy combatants" and to imprison persons without criminal charges and without judicial review.

What are we to make of all this? I will not discuss every one of these cases in the chapters that follow, nor try to reveal an "inner unity" holding all of them together. The goal will be more modest. Several of the cases just summarized are better viewed as responses to extraordinary events (*Bush v. Gore;* the "enemy combatant" decisions) rather than as doctrinal turning points that might be part of a wide and radical change in constitutional law. Of these cases, I will have little to say. On the other hand, as noted previously, a number of the Court's decisions do mark important reversals in preexisting constitutional doctrine. These are the cases on which I will focus, analyzing them in the light of the arguments made in the first two parts of this book.

Together, Parts I and II offered a new way to make sense of constitutional reinterpretation. Constitutional law has a commitment-based, paradigm-case structure. American judges are free to determine, and often have determined, that the Constitution's commitments require considerably more than was originally contemplated—but not less. For this reason, constitutional law has adhered to historical Application Understandings even as judges have repeatedly overruled No-Application Understandings, unquestionable as those No-Application Understandings may have seemed before.

Through this process, judges can introduce paradigm shifts into the law, creating radically new constitutional doctrine.

But radical reinterpretation is subject to a limiting principle. The new doctrines—the new paradigms—have to answer to the foundational paradigm cases. In the following chapters, I will sketch out—and it will be no more than a sketch—how the current Court's pathbreaking decisions could be examined in light of these considerations.

Road Map

There are two different ways to ask whether the Court's recent case law is justifiable in light of the Constitution's paradigmatic Application Understandings. The first is broad-gauged, casting a wide view over the case law, looking at several different constitutional doctrines all at once. The second bores closely into each doctrinal field, one at a time.

The broad-gauged approach can downplay or disregard entirely the Court's efforts to assign the new decisions to this or that doctrinal compartment, as if the transformative new cases represented standard exercises of ordinary doctrinal logic. In other words, the broad-gauged approach need not take seriously the doctrinal terms in which the new case law presents itself. Rather, it asks whether, below the doctrinal surface of these decisions, a fairly coherent, far-reaching paradigm shift is occurring, cutting across several doctrines simultaneously. If such a paradigm shift is indeed occurring, the task then becomes one of explaining and evaluating it. What underlies the new paradigm shift? What are its core applications or paradigm cases? Most important, what, if any, relationship is there between the new paradigm and the Constitution's historical Application Understandings? This way of doing constitutional analysis is not traditional, but it may be necessary. In some circumstances, it does not make sense to do constitutional analysis the traditional way, because constitutional law will have stopped making sense from a traditional analytic perspective.

The rest of this chapter and the next one follow this line of inquiry. The rest of this chapter shows how constitutional doctrine has during at least one period in American legal history stopped making sense in a particular way. That period in constitutional law is called the *Lochner* era. I am not interested in rehashing the *Lochner* era as an instance of "judicial activism." American constitutional law is ineluctably and properly open to radical reinterpretation. The *Lochner* era has a much more distinctive interest. In a quite particular fashion, to be described below, the *Lochner* cases offer a model of a constitutional paradigm shift that emerged not from paradigm-case reasoning, but from the pursuit of an identifiable agenda—a kind of anti-anti-capitalist agenda—which caused constitutional law to stop making sense in the way we are used to.

Chapter 8 will examine the extent to which this may be happening once again in constitutional law today. It turns out that the *Lochner* era sheds considerable light on the current Court's groundbreaking case law. A large number (but not all) of these cases seem to reveal the pursuit of a new agenda—a kind of anti-anti-discrimination agenda—in constitutional law today, which once again may be causing constitutional law to stop making sense in the way legal scholars expect it to make sense.

Chapter 9 puts aside this possibility and returns to the more close-grained analysis. It looks at three particular areas of constitutional doctrine in which the current Court has issued groundbreaking decisions and asks whether these decisions can be justified in light of the paradigm cases pertinent to those doctrines. Specifically, I will address the Court's recent cases dealing with sexuality, the commerce clause, and racial preferences.

Has Constitutional Law Stopped Making Sense?

Consider federalism, one of the major concerns of the current Court. In some quarters, the Court's new "federalism" decisions, which reintroduce limits on what Congress has the power to do, have provoked a reaction close to outrage, as if unlimited federal legislative jurisdiction were an unwritten constitutional right. I have never quite understood this view. For myself, the thought that the commerce clause might actually mean something does not seem exactly shocking.

Nevertheless, to take the present majority's "federalism" cases seriously, to defend or criticize them in the doctrinal terms in which they present themselves, demands that we see them a certain way—namely, as federalism cases. Sometimes, however, a decision can sound like a federalism case, it can be seen and debated as a federalism case, without actually being a federalism case.

The best examples can be found in the *Lochner* era. Famously, the *Lochner* era Court issued several decisions striking down federal statutes, including laws imposing collective-bargaining, minimum-wage, or maximum-hour requirements, on the ground that Congress had improperly delegated its legislative power or unconstitutionally usurped state legislative authority.[14] This reasoning was on its face perfectly intelligible.

The Constitution limits Congress to its enumerated powers, and Congress's enumerated powers nowhere expressly refer to collective bargaining, wages, or hours of employment. To be sure, Congress has power to regulate "commerce" "among the states," but that power—said the *Lochner* Court—does not authorize a national labor law, because if it did, the implication would be that Congress had control over purely in-state labor relations:

> The apparent implication is that the federal authority under the commerce clause should be deemed to extend to the establishment of rules to govern wages and hours in intrastate trade and industry generally throughout the country, thus overriding the authority of the states to deal with domestic problems arising from labor conditions in their internal commerce.[15]

In other words, federal labor laws do not regulate *interstate* commerce; they attempt to regulate "*intrastate* trade and industry." Moreover, the *Lochner* Court would add in other "federalism" cases, federal labor laws did not regulate *commerce* at all:

> The word "commerce" is the equivalent of the phrase "intercourse for the purposes of trade." The employment of men, the fixing of their wages, hours of labor and working conditions, the bargaining in respect of these things . . . all constitute intercourse for the purposes of production, not trade. . . . Every journey to a forbidden end begins with the first step; and the danger of such a step by the federal government in the direction of taking over the powers of the states is that the end of the journey may find the states so despoiled of their powers . . . as to reduce them to little more than geographical subdivisions of the national domain.[16]

In both these lines of reasoning—that the conditions of labor were not matters of *interstate* trade and that they were not matters of *commerce* at all—the *Lochner* Court's "federalism" reasoning presented itself as a simple act of judicial fidelity to the Constitution's text and to its textually commanded principles of state legislative power.

The embarrassment was that when the *Lochner* Court dealt with *state* labor statutes of the very same kind, the Court would strike down these measures too.[17] The implication of the *Lochner* Court's "federalism" cases was that the regulation of bargaining, of wages, or of the hours of employment was constitutionally confided to exclusive state legislative control. Yet when the states attempted to exercise this control, the *Lochner* Court did not let them.

Which provision of the Constitution was breached this time? The answer was—well, there was no precise answer. No specific constitutional guarantee had been transgressed. So the Court found instead that these state economic regulations violated an unwritten "liberty of contract," which the Court "located" in the due process clause of the Fourteenth Amendment—creating, famously, the oxymoronic doctrine of "substantive due process."

We have been laughing at this constitutional joke for a long time. To be sure, the *Lochner* Court's "liberty of contract" doctrine did not, strictly speaking, contradict its commerce clause doctrine. But the strange and happy coincidence—that is, the felicitous congruence of results, with unwritten constitutional law popping up and preventing states from doing exactly what the Constitution allegedly prevented Congress from doing on strictly "textualist," "federalist" grounds—told the story. The *Lochner* era's "federalism" had little or nothing to do with federalism. The *Lochner* Court's "federalism" cases spoke the language of textualism and federalism, but their true purpose was to keep Congress from passing laws to which the Court was manifestly opposed on other grounds.

The joke, however, could easily have been missed at the time. Lawyers are trained to analyze and assimilate cases by separating them into distinct lines of doctrine. This doctrinal sorting is indispensable; its virtues are obvious. Without it, the legal system could not possibly digest its tens of thousands of cases, nor could individuals develop expertise in particular fields of law. But this practice inhibits vision too, as do the blinders on a horse. While directing and focusing attention, it also tends to suppress appreciation of how differing lines of case law relate to one another. By failing to see these interdoctrinal relationships, we can be misled into taking cases seriously long after they have stopped making sense.

Considered on their own, the *Lochner* "federalism" cases could be debated and defended just as if they really offered a serious effort to grapple with the problems of allocating power between the federal and state governments under the specific textual grants and reservations of power laid out in the Constitution. Unfortunately, those who tried to understand the *Lochner*-era case law this way were in a sense duped. They turned out to be engaged in a bootless, credulous enterprise.

The constitutional case law of the *Lochner* era could not, in reality, be understood in the doctrinal terms in which it presented itself. Those who tried to make sense of it in doctrinal pieces were victims of, or participants in, a charade. The *Lochner* case law made sense only as a whole—and made sense only in the sense that, taken as a whole, the cases revealed an agenda that was driving them, quite apart from any specific considerations of constitutional language, history, doctrine, or principle.

What was this agenda? It was not, as is sometimes supposed, libertarianism. Classical libertarianism holds that government may not legislate morality, but the *Lochner* Court had no trouble with state morals legislation. The Court never, for example, came close to invalidating state sexuality or bigamy laws, which obviously violate libertarian principles. Nor did the Court invalidate Sunday laws or even prohibition laws; indeed, it upheld a criminal conviction under a statute prohibiting schools from "mixing" white and black students, a statute that libertarians would have decried.[18] A *Lochner*-era decision striking down prostitution laws on "liberty of contract" grounds would have been unthinkable—even though perfectly logical.

Even in cases dealing solely with economic issues, the *Lochner*-era case law is not well captured by the idea of a "liberty of contract." As Justice Holmes liked to point out, there were numerous blatant restraints on purely economic exercises of the "liberty of contract," such as usury statutes, that the *Lochner* Court never called into question.

A better way to understand the *Lochner* decisions would be as follows. The *Lochner* justices perceived in the legal and social developments of their era what they took to be a grave threat to the American constitutional order. But this threat did not translate comfortably into any available precepts of constitutional text, history, or principle. What was this threat? The *Lochner* justices were keenly aware of a growing pro-worker, anticapitalist movement in America and the rest of the world. Labor unions, increasing employee rights, condemnations of unequal wealth, vilification of capitalist greed and oppression, growing calls for wage and price regulations—all were important pieces of this movement. Socialism was, of course, no mere academic topic in this period. Nor was it only a serious movement in faraway lands like Russia. By 1918, the leader of the American Socialist Party would be jailed for his inflammatory speeches; two years later, still in prison, Eugene Debs would receive almost a million votes in the presidential election.

Socialism was probably perceived by many in the American legal and political establishment as the most urgent and serious then-existing threat to the nation, its liberties, its values—all that the Constitution stood for.

It may be unfair to say that the *Lochner* justices were "anti-labor." A more accurate characterization is probably *anti-anti-capitalist.* They were determined to oppose measures they must have regarded as threats to the basic capitalist premises of American liberty and prosperity.

The trouble was that the Constitution did not quite address these threats. The Constitution's solicitude for private property and contract is clear; hence the *Lochner* justices could well have understood their concerns as quintessentially constitutional. But the Constitution was not enacted against a background of threatening socialism.

To be sure, anxiety over democracy's conflict with unequal wealth was well known to the framers, and the Constitution reflects this anxiety. But the Constitution does not prohibit government from confiscating private property, so long as the taking is compensated. It says absolutely nothing against minimum-wage or maximum-hours laws, so long, at least, as the obligation of existing contracts is not impaired. To be sure, the Fourteenth Amendment contained language capacious enough to support any result, but it was enacted to deal foremost with slavery and discrimination of the kind exemplified by the black codes. Indeed, in earlier cases, the Supreme Court itself had already come close to holding that the Fourteenth Amendment had no application to matters other than racial discrimination. The "war" between labor and capital, which some in the early 1900s perceived or feared, was a product of an industrial revolution not unthinkable in 1789 or 1867, but certainly not salient then in anything like the form it would later assume.

In other words, the threat of labor unions and quasi-socialist laws in America was a new species of threat, which the Constitution's text and history did not specifically meet. But for the justices of the *Lochner* Court, that did not make the danger any less real or urgent. The *Lochner* cases are full of references to an ominous danger of just this kind. "[I]nterference on the part of the legislatures of the several States with the ordinary trades and occupations of the people seems to be on the increase," the Court noted in *Lochner* itself. "It is impossible for us to shut our eyes to the fact that many of the laws of this character, while passed under what is claimed to be the police power for the purpose of protecting the public health or welfare, are, in reality, passed from other motives."[19]

What hidden, illicit motives was the Court referring to? The answer was strangely anticlimactic. "It seems to us that the real object and purpose," the Court wrote, "were simply to regulate the hours of labor between the master and his employes."[20]

This declaration of the "real" legislative purpose, as if merely stating it were enough to condemn it, puzzles the contemporary reader. What exactly is wrong with regulating the hours of labor? But from an anti-anti-capitalist perspective, the Court's declaration makes good sense; little more needed to be said. If interfering with the free market in labor is viewed as a threat to fundamental American values and liberties, not to mention prosperity, then "simply to regulate the hours of labor" would indeed be an improper legislative object.

Within an anti-anti-capitalist paradigm, pro-labor legislation is an attack on the entire system of free enterprise and hence on the very institution of private property. A private property system inevitably generates inequalities of wealth. To say that a state can pass laws "simply to regulate the [terms] of labor" is to say that state power can be used to try to eliminate these inequalities, which is neither possible nor legitimate in any system that prizes the liberty and prosperity generated by the institution of private property. Or so it seemed to the *Lochner* majority:

> No doubt, wherever the right of private property exists, there must and will be inequalities of fortune; and thus . . . it is . . . impossible to uphold freedom of contract and the right of private property without at the same time recognizing as legitimate those inequalities of fortune that are the necessary result of the exercise of those rights. . . . And since a State may not strike [those rights] down directly it is clear that it may not do so indirectly, as by declaring in effect that the public good requires the removal of those inequalities that are but the normal and inevitable result of their exercise. . . . The police power is broad, . . . but it cannot be given the wide scope that is here asserted for it, without in effect nullifying the constitutional guaranty.[21]

There was just one little problem: the *Lochner* Court was never able to specify what "constitutional guaranty" it was referring to. The passage just quoted comes from one of the *Lochner* Court's "yellow-dog" cases, striking down a law that forbade employers to fire their workers for joining a union. Which constitutional right, exactly, would "in effect" be "nullified" by such a law? Nothing in the Constitution expressly prohibited pro-labor legislation. Nothing prohibited unions. Nothing prohibited laws intended to facilitate unionization or to give workers a right to unionize. Justice Holmes made all these points in his *Lochner*-era dissents. Certainly no constitutional text or principle prohibited *all* laws derogating from a pure laissez-faire capitalism. It would have been impossible to ban all such laws.

As a result, the *Lochner* Court's suspicions about a creeping redistributive or pro-labor bias in state or federal legislation could not be easily translated into operative constitutional terms. The Court perceived a grave threat to the American constitutional order—the threat of an attack on capitalism itself—but was unable to identify any clear constitutional text or language in which to articulate this threat. Thus the Court was obliged to achieve its results through a variety of different doctrinal devices, generating decisions with a distinctly adventitious, and even surreptitious, character.

If a federal statute authorized the President or other actors to establish minimum wages or maximum hours, these laws would be attacked on nondelegation grounds. But if Congress did the regulating itself, its laws would be struck down as exceeding the reach of the commerce clause. In these cases, the Court could rest, quite intelligibly, on the judiciary's traditional and clear duty to adhere to the letter of the Constitution and to the Constitution's allocation of powers. But when *state* governments passed the offending laws, the Court suddenly had to become much more creative. Because no specific constitutional text served the purpose, the Court would have to announce an unwritten constitutional right—the "liberty of contract"—to do the job.

But even this "liberty of contract" was a mask. This is a critical point. It was not as if the *Lochner* Court "came clean" in the liberty of contract cases, acknowledging the true principle that it was inscribing into constitutional law. The *Lochner* majority, not genuinely libertarian, was unprepared to invalidate a host of laws equally infringing the "liberty of contract": prostitution laws, usury laws, Sunday laws, restrictions on common carriers. Somehow the "liberty of contract" did not apply in these cases. Somehow it applied only to the new anticapitalist laws, such as minimum-wage and maximum-hour legislation, price regulations, and "yellow-dog" statutes.

In other words, the *Lochner* Court never quite acknowledged the true agenda that underlay the results it sought to achieve. It masked this agenda behind talk of "federalism" and a "liberty of contract." It continually issued decisions, across several different doctrines, that achieved the desired results, but that could not really be understood in the doctrinal terms in which they presented themselves.

The most remarkable single illustration of the illusory nature of the *Lochner* Court's doctrinal manipulations was probably *Coronado Coal Co. v. United Mine Workers.*[22] In *Coronado,* a mining company sued a mine-workers union, claiming that their threat to strike violated the Sherman Act, a federal antitrust statute. As a matter of doctrinal logic, the case should have been easy to dismiss.

To begin with, under the Court's then-existing commerce clause precedents, federal law clearly did not reach mining or labor relations (matters of "production," not "commerce"). If that were not enough, the liberty-of-contract doctrine ought to have protected striking workers from governmental prohibitions. Most workers labored under "at-will" terms of employment—meaning that they were hired, legally speaking, on a day-to-day basis, dischargeable any time. This at-will status guaranteed the employer a right to fire workers for any reason or no reason, but it also meant that workers had the right to withdraw from work at any time. Workers who entered into a contract with one another to exercise this right to leave work (that is, to strike) were therefore taking advantage of their "liberty of contract." Nevertheless, contrary to everything the Court was then saying with respect to both the commerce clause and the "liberty of contract," the Court held that the Sherman Act did prohibit the workers from striking.

The sharpness of *Coronado*'s conflict with the Court's other cases is quite remarkable. In earlier commerce clause cases, the Court had expressly held that the Sherman Act could not constitutionally be applied to a monopoly in the *ownership* of the factories that produced a certain good, on the ground that production was not itself commerce, despite the fact that a monopoly over production would significantly affect interstate commerce. Yet *Coronado* held that the Sherman Act could constitutionally apply to a strike agreement among *workers* in the production of a certain good, on the ground that the strike would significantly affect interstate commerce. Similarly, the yellow-dog cases held that when the "liberty of contract" was exercised in a manner designed to *block* union activity, government could *not* interfere, but *Coronado* held that when the "liberty of contract" was exercised to *pursue* union activity, government *could* interfere. *Coronado* made little or no sense in terms of the *Lochner* Court's official doctrine, but it made excellent sense within the Court's anti-anti-capitalist agenda.

In other words, the *Lochner* cases made sense, but not the kind of sense traditionally expected of constitutional law. Taken one at a time, each *Lochner*-era case or line of cases could have been (and was) taken perfectly seriously in interpretive terms, to be analyzed and debated in all the conventional ways that constitutional lawyers and academics know so well. But those who took the *Lochner* case law seriously in this way were engaged in a fool's errand. The truth was that the constitutional interpretation of the *Lochner* era did not deserve to be taken seriously *as* constitutional interpretation. The law had stopped making sense that way. It still made sense, but in a very different way.

The question is whether this might be true again today. The next chapter explores this possibility.

8

The Anti-Anti-Discrimination Agenda

There is considerable disagreement in constitutional law circles about how to understand what is going on in constitutional law today. A number of scholars, some friendly to the Court, some unfriendly, have taken the view that the new case law displays certain unifying features that give it coherence. The most superficial critical analyses charge the Court with a new "judicial activism."[1] Sympathizers, by contrast, see a new "textualism" at work.[2]

These characterizations are polar opposites. The reason one sees both claims is that the current Court (like the *Lochner* Court) has displayed *both* textualism *and* activism. The Court has, for example, insisted on heeding the plain meaning of the word "enforce" in Section 5 of the Fourteenth Amendment and on the significance of the word "commerce" in the commerce clause. But at the same time, the Court has leapt entirely outside the text (as I will discuss further below) in its freedom-of-association cases and in its Eleventh Amendment jurisprudence. For this reason, the "textualist" and "activist" tags are manifestly insufficient.

Another set of polar opposite views runs as follows. According to critics, the Rehnquist Court is seized with the idea of "judicial sovereignty," or more specifically the sovereignty of the Supreme Court. According to the friendlier view, the Rehnquist Court is determined to decentralize power: to push the levers of power down from federal government to the states, and from the states to associations and individuals.

This chapter begins by considering—and rejecting—these two accounts. Then I advance an alternative hypothesis, suggesting that the Court's recent constitutional case law may be unified in a quite different way. The hypothesis will be that today's Court (like the *Lochner* Court) is using whatever doctrinal devices it can find to effectuate a substantive agenda—which I will call an anti-anti-discrimination agenda.

Judicial Sovereignty and the Tocquevillian Court

According to the critical view, the Rehnquist Court is, essentially, seeking to usurp the political branches. The Court is after nothing less than "judicial sovereignty,"[3] no longer accepting that the other "branches have equal standing to interpret" the Constitution.[4] The majority of the justices harbor a "disrespect [for Congress] bordering on contempt"[5] and are not sympathetic to state legislators either. On the contrary, these justices are determined to show that the Court has "a monopoly on constitutional interpretation,"[6] that its word on constitutional meaning is final, exclusive, and supreme.

The trouble with this "judicial sovereignty" account is that it lacks any explanatory power.

Any case that finds anything unconstitutional can be attacked as an exercise of "judicial sovereignty." Virtually every time the Court strikes down a statute, the justices assert the supremacy of their own constitutional judgment, with the implicit corollary that the other "branches do not have equal standing to interpret the text." Imputing to the majority a disdain for the political branches is certainly consistent with every case in which the Court has struck anything down, but it would be consistent with the Court's decisions no matter what the Court was striking down. As a result, this view tells us nothing about why the Justices have struck down the particular laws they have—the number of which remains infinitesimal compared to the total amount of legislation and regulation in force. Explaining everything, the "judicial sovereignty" view explains nothing.

In every period of American constitutional history, opponents of the Court's constitutional invalidations cry out against "judicial activism" and "government by judiciary." This was the repeated complaint of "conservatives" who opposed *Brown, Miranda,* and *Roe,* while "liberals" in those days championed expansive judicial review. Today, the shoe is on the other foot. Little separates yesterday's claims of "government by judiciary" from today's claims of "judicial sovereignty," except the political views of those who make the claims. Of course, if it is embarrassing for constitutional "liberals" suddenly to discover the vices of "activism" at just the moment when conservative justices took control of the Court, it is equally embarrassing for constitutional "conservatives" suddenly to forget those vices at the very same moment.

The friendly account of the Rehnquist Court is almost the diametric opposite. On this view, far from nursing ambitions of concentrating power in its own hands, the reigning paradigm of the Rehnquist Court is "decentralization": the Court is determined to shift power out and down at all levels. Although "not fully articulate," the driving force behind the Rehnquist Court's new case law is a "Tocquevillian" recognition that the true "vibrancy, innovation, and beneficence of American society did not come from its rulers but bubbled up from below."[7]

But this "Tocquevillian" account of the Rehnquist Court has the same problem as the "judicial sovereignty" account. It too applies to almost any possible decision invalidating any law or governmental action. Whenever the Supreme Court strikes down an act of Congress, the Court has either empowered states or empowered individuals—and hence has necessarily "decentralized" power. And in almost every case in which the Court strikes down *state* action on constitutional grounds, the freedom of individuals or associations is again increased—"decentralizing" power. Hence it is hardly surprising that most of the Supreme Court's surprising new decisions fit comfortably into the "Tocquevillian" picture.

But there is one kind of case in which the Supreme Court can invalidate state laws without spreading power down to more local levels. When the Court strikes down state regulations on the ground that they are "preempted" by federal regulations, the Court *recentralizes* power. So preemption doctrine is a test case for the "Tocquevillian" view. On that view, we would expect the current Court to resist claims of preemption; we certainly would not expect the Court to expand preemption doctrine, striking down state laws that would have been upheld under preexisting preemption law.

But this is in fact what has happened. Over the last decade, the Court has been markedly sympathetic to preemption claims and has indeed pressed preemption doctrine further than prior cases demanded.[8] In these cases, the Court has invalidated state laws on the ground that federal law occupies the field, thus recentralizing power rather than decentralizing it. These cases make little sense on the "Tocquevillian" account. In addition, the Court's religious exemptions doctrine (under which the Court *upholds* more laws than it used to) contradicts the decentralization account. A decentralizing Court would presumably be highly solicitous of religious exemption claims, which would empower diverse religious individuals or communities at the expense of centralized, governmental power. But *Smith* does just the opposite.

The fundamental problem, however, with both the "judicial sovereignty" and "decentralization" accounts is that nearly every case in which the Supreme Court strikes something down on constitutional grounds will *both* further judicial sovereignty and decentralize power. Thus the hostile and friendly accounts of the Rehnquist Court are not really opposites; they are mirror images, explaining very little. Out of all the laws of the land, the current Court has struck down an infinitesimal number. The critical task, therefore, is not to propound a theory that would be consistent with the Court striking down almost anything—which would leave us wondering why the Court has not struck down thousands more laws than it has. The task is to understand better why the Court has invalidated the few, particular laws it has.

In the remainder of this chapter, I consider the possibility that a very different agenda lies behind the Court's recent constitutional case law. This account of the Court's decisions will not have the all-inclusiveness of the "judicial sovereignty" or "decentralization" stories, but it may have more explanatory power. It may not capture all the Court's recent case law, but it may do better at explaining the cases it does capture.

Note on Method

I am going to be arguing that the constitutional texts and principles on which the Court relies in its transformative case law—such as federalism, the Eleventh Amendment, and the freedom of speech—are actually stalking horses for a substantive agenda. I will try to show, for example, that most of the Court's federalism cases are not really federalism cases at all— that they cannot be intelligently explained or debated in the doctrinal terms in which they present themselves. This is a difficult showing to make, but an important one, if the idea of an unacknowledged anti-antidiscrimination agenda is to have its strongest purchase.

How could this showing be made? One way to suggest that certain members of the Supreme Court are deeply but perhaps covertly hostile to antidiscrimination laws would be to rely on biographical or personal information about them, such as stories alleging that the Chief Justice participated as a young political operative in efforts to stop blacks from voting, or certain crude psychoanalyses of Justice Thomas. I disclaim this kind of argument, which, whatever its merits for other purposes, is unreliable and unproductive for the law.

Another reason that might persuade some people not to take the current Court's constitutional reasoning seriously can be summarized in a single case name: *Bush v. Gore*. The majority's opinion in that case was so extraordinarily indefensible in legal terms that it predisposes many to skepticism about the five justices who decided it. But in the argument that follows, I will not rely on *Bush v. Gore,* which was after all so singular a case in so many ways that generalizations based on it are perilous.

Instead, I will pursue the same method used previously to reveal the agenda underlying the *Lochner* Court's case law. This method might be called juxtaposition across doctrines, by which I simply mean examining how decisions from one doctrinal category relate to those from others. Thus the place to begin is with the Court's "federalism" decisions, which turn out to betray the same embarrassments as did the "federalism" decisions of the *Lochner* era. Consider first the Court's new Eleventh Amendment case law.

The Eleventh Amendment

The facts of *University of Alabama v. Garrett*[9] were relatively simple. Patricia Garrett worked as Director of Nursing for a state university. After undergoing surgery for breast cancer, she was demoted to a lower-paying job as a nurse manager. She sued the university under the Americans with Disabilities Act (ADA), which prohibits employers, both governmental and private, from discriminating against disabled people. Garrett sought money damages, alleging that the University of Alabama demoted her not because of a genuine inability to perform her job, but because of her breast cancer and the cancer treatment she had received.[10]

The Supreme Court rendered a 5–4 decision. The split among the Justices followed a familiar pattern, with Chief Justice Rehnquist joined in the majority by Justices O'Connor, Scalia, Kennedy, and Thomas. These five Justices dismissed the case under the Eleventh Amendment. *Garrett* thereby joined a string of recent decisions giving the Eleventh Amendment new constitutional bite.[11]

A little legal background: as noted previously, the Eleventh Amendment bars federal court jurisdiction over certain suits brought against a state.[12] Before 1996, the Eleventh Amendment was generally understood not to apply when an individual brought suit against a state under a valid federal statute. Under pre-1996 law, the Eleventh Amendment would have been no bar to Garrett's suit (which arose under the ADA, a federal statute). In 1996, however, the Court held that the Eleventh Amendment *did* apply to most suits arising under federal law.

But not all such suits. The Court did not go so far, for example, as to rule that individuals could no longer enforce the equal protection clause against states in federal court. Such a holding would have been virtually unthinkable, gutting the Fourteenth Amendment to an extent inconceivable today. Rather, the Court reaffirmed that Congress could constitutionally override the Eleventh Amendment when it passed legislation pursuant to the Fourteenth Amendment, Section 5 of which authorizes Congress to pass "appropriate legislation" to "enforce" the equal protection clause and the Fourteenth Amendment's other provisions.[13] Thus if a federal statute falls within Section 5 of the Fourteenth Amendment, then the statute is not restricted by the Eleventh Amendment, and individuals can sue states under it.

As a result, the ultimate question in *Garrett* was whether the ADA fell within Congress's Section 5 powers. The Court's answer was no: the ADA did not "enforce" the equal protection clause. The word "enforce," according to the Court's reasoning, which on this point is solidly textualist, does not mean "interpret" or "alter." Thus under Section 5, Congress has the power only to enforce the equal protection clause, not to change its meaning. But the equal protection clause, as the Court interprets it, does not bar discrimination against disabled people in the way that it bars discrimination against blacks or women. The equal protection clause (as the Court interprets it) generally permits states to deny disabled people rights or privileges granted to others, provided only that the state action can pass a lenient "mere rationality" test.[14] The ADA goes much further and hence could not be said merely to "enforce" the equal protection clause. Accordingly, the Eleventh Amendment remained controlling, and it barred Garrett's suit.

Taken seriously as Eleventh Amendment doctrine, *Garrett* raises deep and potentially disturbing questions of constitutional principle. With *Garrett* and its predecessor cases, the present Court has created a constitutional doctrine that is, in a way, very odd. The *Garrett* majority did not hold the ADA unconstitutional, not even as applied to state employers. Although the majority found that the ADA was not a valid piece of Section 5 legislation, the ADA remains under *Garrett* a perfectly valid piece of commerce clause legislation.[15] In other words, the ADA remains completely binding (under the commerce clause) on all employers, whether private or governmental, and the Court assumed, for purposes of the decision, that Alabama had violated Garrett's statutorily mandated legal rights.[16] The five Justices' holding was "merely" that Garrett was barred from enforcing these rights, because of the state's immunity from suit under the Eleventh Amendment.

It is important to get a firm grip on what this means. Suppose that, just because she lost a breast to cancer, Alabama decided to cut Garrett's salary by half, even though she did all her work and did it as competently as every other employee in her position. Alabama would have broken the law. There would be no dispute about Garrett's legal rights. Under the ADA, Garrett would be legally entitled to the money she ought to have been paid. Under *Garrett*, however, she could not collect it.

Garrett would have a legal right to the wrongly withheld pay, but the courts would be barred to her. (State courts would be barred to her under state law.[17]) She would have a legal right, but she would have no legal right.

So the first thing to observe about the Court's new Eleventh Amendment case law is that it creates a quite odd legal regime, in which some individuals whose rights have been indisputably violated do not have a right to enforce their rights in court. This is an unusual result in American law.

Most people know the case that principally inaugurated constitutional law in America. It was *Marbury v. Madison*.[18] In that case, Chief Justice Marshall's opinion for the Court did not merely hold that the judiciary could rule a federal statute unconstitutional. His opinion also held that every individual, having established the violation of his legal rights, had a right to go to court to have those rights vindicated, even if the perpetrators of the legal injury were the very highest officers of government.

Marshall wrote: "[W]here a specific duty is assigned by law, and individual rights depend upon the performance of that duty, . . . the individual who considers himself injured, has a right to resort to the laws of his country for a remedy."[19] This was no mere technicality: "The government of the United States has been emphatically termed a government of laws, and not of men. It will certainly cease to deserve this high appellation, if the laws furnish no remedy for the violation of a vested legal right."[20] And again: "The very essence of civil liberty certainly consists in the right of every individual to claim the protection of the laws, whenever he receives an injury."[21]

So *Garrett* puts a dent—some might say a gouge—in a deep, longstanding principle of American law. *Marbury* announced the fundamental individual right that underlies all other legal rights: the right to go to a court for protection and redress when one has been treated unlawfully, especially by the government. Individuals in Garrett's situation no longer have this right.

To be sure, *Garrett* did not leave Garrett wholly without remedy. As the majority pointed out in a helpful footnote, the United States government always has the constitutional power to sue states.[22] Why? The majority does not say, but presumably the reason is that the federal government is not covered by the Eleventh Amendment, which bars suits against states only by "Citizens of another State" and by "Citizens or Subjects of any Foreign State."[23] Thus it was always possible that the United States might sue Alabama on Garrett's behalf and then remit the damages to Garrett.

But the United States is not obliged to do that. The United States *may* choose to sue a state on an individual's behalf, but it has no *duty* to do so. It is as if under *Garrett,* disabled people who suffer monetary damage because of discrimination by a state employer are living in a classical international law regime, where individuals have no legal standing in their own person, and a seeming violation of their legal rights is not a violation of *their* legal rights after all, but at best a violation of the rights of their national government, which may or may not, depending on political factors and resource constraints, choose to bring a claim on their behalf before an international tribunal (formerly known as federal court).

Now, everything I have said to this point remains firmly within the conventional debate about whether *Garrett* is right or wrong as a matter of Eleventh Amendment doctrine. And nothing I have said demonstrates that *Garrett* is a legally indefensible Eleventh Amendment result. As readers might imagine, *Garrett* and its predecessor cases have prompted a plentiful debate in the academic journals retelling the history of the Eleventh Amendment, theorizing about the constitutional status of state "sovereign immunity," and analyzing the Eleventh Amendment's interplay with Section 5 of the Fourteenth Amendment.[24]

But the point here is not to pursue that debate. On the contrary, the question is whether it makes sense to have this sort of debate—the kind that takes the Court's new constitutional doctrine seriously. To begin to see why it might not make sense, readers need to know a little more about the oddness of the Court's new Eleventh Amendment case law.

The Sameness of the Other

As noted, the Eleventh Amendment bars federal court jurisdiction over suits against any state brought by "Citizens of another State." Readers unfamiliar with the facts of *Garrett* might therefore infer that Garrett was a citizen of some state other than Alabama. Not at all. Garrett was an Alabama resident.[25] She was a citizen of the same state she was suing.

In other words, to reach the desired result, the five Justices in *Garrett* had to do more than dent a constitutional principle established in *Marbury v. Madison*. They had to read "another" to mean "the same." In case anyone has not noticed, these two terms are antonyms.

Once upon a time, judicial conservatives criticized those who saw in the Constitution words that were not there, like "privacy." *Garrett* goes one better. *Garrett* reads a word that *is* in the Constitution to mean its opposite.

It is virtually impossible to think of a law (or indeed any sentence in English) in which "the same" and "another" could be intelligibly interpreted as interchangeable terms. A useful comparative exercise might be to imagine the Court holding, in a double jeopardy case, that "the same offense" also included "another offense," so that nobody convicted of one crime could ever be prosecuted again.[26] Another useful exercise would be to imagine that same holding again (by "another" in this sentence, I meant "the same").

Or how about a case holding that the Eleventh Amendment's ban on *federal* court jurisdiction meant a ban on *state* court jurisdiction too? Surely if the Court began to play that kind of trick with the Eleventh Amendment, people would have to acknowledge that we were no longer dealing, in any serious way, with an "Eleventh Amendment doctrine" at all. A note for the noncognoscenti: the Court already *has* "extended" the Eleventh Amendment to cover state court jurisdiction.[27]

There is a single sentence in the *Garrett* majority opinion devoted to the same/other problem: "Although by its terms the [Eleventh] Amendment applies only to suits against a State by citizens of another State, our cases have extended the Amendment's applicability to suits by citizens against their own States."[28] (This sentence strangely echoes Justice Brandeis's famous statement seventy-five years ago that although the due process clause by its terms applies only to matters of procedure, case law had established the existence of substantive due process as well.[29] The difference is that the *Garrett* majority intended no irony.) The string of precedents offered by the five Justices to support this proposition—with the exception of a one-hundred-year-old case dubious in its logic and authority—consists entirely of recent decisions.[30]

The Court's new Eleventh Amendment decisions represent, at best, pure unwritten constitutional law. It is impossible to take seriously, as an act of interpretation, a construction of the word "same" to mean "another," or a construction of "federal" jurisdiction to refer to "state" jurisdiction. On occasion, the Court has conceded as much.[31]

The suspicion that arises here is not of bad faith. It is rather a conviction that the Court's "Eleventh Amendment" doctrine cannot be profitably understood as Eleventh Amendment doctrine at all. The Court is advancing an unwritten principle of state sovereign immunity, and occasionally it purports to do so under the rubric of interpreting the Eleventh Amendment. Once this conclusion is acknowledged, the real question is whether the Court's other "federalism" holdings can be taken any more seriously, as an interpretive matter, than the "Eleventh Amendment" doctrine that seemingly furthers this "federalism." On this question, it is critical to examine the new case law restricting state power.

For example, in *Boy Scouts*, the Supreme Court—or rather five members of the Supreme Court, the same five listed previously—concluded that New Jersey could not constitutionally bar the Scouts from expelling a scoutmaster on the basis of his homosexuality.[32] What constitutional provision did New Jersey violate when it tried to stop the Boy Scouts from discriminating on the basis of sexual orientation? The Court's answer: the First Amendment. The majority ruled that New Jersey's statute impermissibly intruded upon the Scouts' "First Amendment freedom of expressive association."[33]

Predictably, *Boy Scouts* has generated considerable debate of the conventional doctrinal sort, taking the case seriously as a First Amendment case and arguing over its First Amendment implications. This debate is natural; I have contributed to it myself.[34] Here, however, the goal is to step back from this debate, in order to ask whether it makes sense to take *Boy Scouts* seriously as a First Amendment case at all. Could the "freedom of expressive association" be the present Court's "liberty of contract"— that is, the unwritten constitutional right that felicitously pops up to prevent states from doing exactly what the Court has been supposedly telling us, in its "federalism" cases, that Congress cannot do without usurping state authority?

Thinking through this possibility requires that we first identify more carefully the elements of the simple but suspect doctrinal configuration that obtained during the *Lochner* era.

Pseudo-Federalism

Described most starkly, the *Lochner* embarrassments were caused by the Court's simultaneous embrace of two very different lines of cases.

Start with a set of self-professedly textualist federalism cases. The opinions in these cases, involving federal statutes, must display a strict respect for constitutional text, as if protecting the letter of the Constitution were the Court's hard but unavoidable duty. At the same time, they must also display a serious concern for state legislative sovereignty and autonomy. Questions of mere policy—of balancing interests, of deciding how useful or needful a challenged statute might be—must be rigorously put aside, typically with remarks to the effect that such questions are not properly judicial in nature and must never divert the Court from its duty to respect the Constitution's text. (As in: "It is not the province of the Court to consider the economic advantages or disadvantages of [federal wage and hours laws]. It is sufficient to say that the Federal Constitution does not provide for it."[35]) On this basis, the Court must strike down federal statutes, holding that Congress has intruded into the states' legislative territory.

Now add a very different kind of holding, this time involving *state* statutes. Here, the Court must suddenly become textually cavalier. All thought of strict adherence to the constitutional text must disappear without a trace. Instead, the Court must discover an unwritten right demanding rigorous judicial scrutiny. In enforcing this unwritten right, moreover, the Court's hard but unavoidable duty will be to evaluate how useful or needful the challenged statute really is, and to this end the Court will purport to balance all the pertinent individual and state interests to determine if the statute was sufficiently justified or necessary. Above all, this unwritten right must fortuitously stop states from passing the very same kind of measures that, if passed by Congress, would be unconstitutional because under the Court's textualist federalism cases, the pertinent legislative authority lies with the states.

The present Court's "federalism" cases have all the characteristics of the first line of cases just described. Here, the Court has admirably and ostentatiously insisted that its decisions be guided by the Constitution's text. This is so not only in the Court's recent commerce clause holdings but in its reasoning on Section 5 of the Fourteenth Amendment as well. A good illustration of both can be found in the Court's invalidation of the civil remedy provision of the Violence Against Women Act (VAWA), decided once again by the same five Justices.[36]

Violence against women, according to the *Morrison* majority, is not "economic in nature" and is therefore outside the reach of Congress's commerce power.[37] It is also (the Court held) outside the reach of

Congress's Section 5 power, which empowers Congress only to "enforce" the provisions of the Fourteenth Amendment.[38] Here the Court returns a "commercial" element to the commerce power and strictly construes the word "enforce" in Section 5, thereby respecting the Constitution's allocation of powers between the federal and state governments. Indeed, as noted previously, the Court in construing Section 5 of the Fourteenth Amendment has emphasized its duty to respect the constitutional text: a congressional power to "enforce," the Court has repeatedly said, must plainly be distinguished from a power to "define" or "interpret."[39] Thus Section 5 allows Congress only to pass laws calculated to redress conduct that would violate the Fourteenth Amendment as construed by the judiciary.[40]

In other words, Congress has no general power to create new civil rights or to prohibit discrimination beyond what would count as unconstitutional discrimination under the Fourteenth Amendment itself (as determined judicially). This was why the Court in *Morrison* found that Congress had exceeded its powers when passing the Violence Against Women Act. Because the Fourteenth Amendment's provisions (as interpreted by the judiciary) apply only to state action, Congress has little or no power under Section 5 to reach private conduct.[41]

The *Morrison* majority made clear that it was not deciding whether VAWA was good or bad policy. Although supporters of the law marshaled copious evidence that state laws had not successfully curbed violence against women and that such violence not only was bad for women but also had substantial adverse economic effects on the nation, the Court essentially held that such evidence was not germane to the constitutional issue.[42] VAWA dealt with gender-based conduct and therefore arguably with a form of sex discrimination, but this was private, "noneconomic" discriminatory conduct, which under the Constitution was not a "truly national" concern, but rather a "local" matter.[43] In other words, the Court rejected the idea that the constitutionality of VAWA depended on the law's usefulness or necessity; VAWA had to be struck down out of respect for the categorical distinctions drawn in the constitutional text (the distinction between commerce and noneconomic activity, as well as the distinction between enforcing the Fourteenth Amendment and reinterpreting it).

Without doubt, *Morrison* and its predecessor cases are legally defensible. Their textualism gives them purchase, and their textual interpretations are not unreasonable. To be sure, even on their own terms, they are debatable. For example, the Court's pronouncements on the meaning of "enforce" in Section 5 of the Fourteenth Amendment seem to ignore the Court's own case law construing the very same word as it appears in the almost identical Section 2 of the Thirteenth Amendment.[44] In Thirteenth Amendment cases, the Court has found that the enforcement power allows Congress to define "badges of servitude" well beyond the judicial construction of these terms.[45] Without confronting its Thirteenth Amendment case law, the *Morrison* Court relied instead on the *Civil Rights Cases*,[46] an 1883 decision reflecting the same constitutional premises, and the same hostile or niggardly attitude toward the Fourteenth Amendment, that produced such revered precedents as *Plessy v. Ferguson*,[47] *Bradwell v. Illinois*,[48] and the *Slaughter-House Cases*.[49]

Nevertheless, *Morrison* and the other decisions in this line of cases are well within the ambit of defensible legal decisionmaking. These cases can easily be read and debated as if they offered a serious effort to grapple with the proper allocation of powers between the federal and state governments under the specific grants of power found in the Constitution. Once again, I am not trying to join this debate. I am trying to ask whether we ought to be having it—whether, in other words, we can take seriously the Court's commerce clause and Section 5 cases as "federalism" cases. And this question comes into focus when we juxtapose these cases with the Court's "freedom of expressive association" holding in *Boy Scouts v. Dale*.

The Freedom of Expressive Association

Does the freedom-of-association doctrine announced in *Boy Scouts* create the same suspect doctrinal configuration that the liberty-of-contract doctrine produced during the *Lochner* era? *Boy Scouts* is but a single case, and it is far too soon to know what the eventual shape of the Court's freedom-of-association doctrine will be. Nevertheless, *Boy Scouts* does reveal the critical elements.

First, there can be no doubt that *Boy Scouts* displays, textually speaking, a most generous and expansive approach to constitutional meaning. The First Amendment does not make any reference to a "freedom of association," nor is that right referred to anywhere else in the Constitution. Yet there is no suggestion in the opinion that this absence of textual grounding makes any difference to the Justices in the majority (the same majority that decided the Court's federalism cases).

While the "federalism" cases ostentatiously insist on a strict and narrow respect for the actual language of the Constitution, refusing to add so much as a jot to what the Constitution textually provides, there is not a hint in *Boy Scouts* that the particular terms of the First Amendment should in any way dictate or even guide the Court's conclusion. On the contrary, *Boy Scouts* is as refreshingly unhampered by narrow textual considerations as were the Warren Court cases that first recognized a constitutional "freedom of association."[50]

Second, the *Boy Scouts* majority understands the "freedom of expressive association," as the *Lochner* Court understood the "liberty of contract," to demand a judicial balancing of interests in order to evaluate the needfulness of a challenged law, in pointed contrast to the Court's "federalism" cases. According to *Boy Scouts,* once plaintiffs show that a law burdens their "freedom of expressive association," a court must place these burdens on the "scales," balancing them against the state interests served by the law.[51] Because New Jersey had not shown that allowing organizations like the Boy Scouts to discriminate against homosexuals would threaten compelling harms to individuals or to society, the Court held in favor of the Scouts.

The parallel to *Lochner* here is unmistakable. According to *Lochner,* once plaintiffs showed that a law burdened their "liberty of contract," a court had to engage in the very same kind of interest balancing, scrutinizing the needfulness of the law at issue.[52] In *Lochner,* the Court found that New York had not shown that allowing bakers to work more than ten hours a day threatened substantial harms, either to bakers or to society more generally. It was precisely this superlegislative quality of the *Lochner* regime—in which the Court expressly arrogated to itself the power to review legislators' judgment of how needful a particular law was—to which most objections to *Lochner* were directed.[53]

Finally, and most important, *Boy Scouts* just happens to prevent states from passing the kind of measure that, according to the Court's "federalism" cases, ought to have been a core prerogative of state legislative authority. As noted previously, a central implication of the Court's federalism cases is that Congress has no general power to define and prohibit discrimination as it sees fit. This has been the Court's repeated refrain throughout its major "federalism" decisions. The Violence Against Women Act sought to define and remedy "gender-based" assaults as a form of sex discrimination, but because this discrimination was neither "economic in nature" nor prohibited by the Fourteenth Amendment, the statute exceeded Congress's powers. *Garrett*'s Section 5 holding turned on the fact that the Constitution prohibits only "irrational" treatment of the disabled, whereas the Americans with Disabilities Act requires employers to hire and accommodate disabled people even when a "rational" employer might not do so.[54] The Religious Freedom Restoration Act of 1990 essentially sought to create a disparate impact antidiscrimination regime for religious observers; again the Court found that Congress had exceeded its powers, because the act's prohibitions extended beyond the kinds of religious discrimination recognized as unconstitutional by the Supreme Court.[55]

If these decisions were true federalism cases, the implication would be that the power to define what conduct counts as illegal discrimination—beyond what is directly barred by the Constitution itself—is a power peculiarly within the prerogatives of state and local lawmakers. The implication ought to be, therefore, that when state or local lawmakers exercised this power, the judiciary would respond with, at a minimum, considerable deference. The implication ought *not* to be that when local lawmakers pass antidiscrimination laws, the Supreme Court will suddenly leap into a textually cavalier, superlegislative mode, finding that such laws burden an unwritten constitutional right. Yet just as the *Lochner* Court performed this self-contradicting two-step through the device of the "liberty of contract," so too, *Boy Scouts* achieves this result through the "freedom of expressive association."

The "freedom of expressive association" recognized in *Boy Scouts* is, when all is said and done, a constitutional right to discriminate. Of course, judges will not describe it this way. They will refer to it as a right "not to associate," or to engage in "expressive association," or to exercise "associational freedom." But the fact remains that *Boy Scouts* is the first case in the modern period, and perhaps the first case in American history, to rule in favor of a party asserting on free-speech grounds a constitutional right to discriminate.

To be sure, the five Justices' *Boy Scouts* opinion concedes that the right to discriminate on expressive grounds is "not absolute."[56] Instead, when a law burdens this right, it merely triggers strict scrutiny—which, as everyone knows, is almost always fatal. But how far does this right extend? In what situations does it apply? The answer given in the *Boy Scouts* opinion is astonishingly broad.

According to the five Justices, "freedom of expressive association" claims are not limited to associations formed to advocate or to express a particular viewpoint. "The First Amendment's protection of expressive association is not reserved for advocacy groups. But to come within its ambit, a group must engage in some form of expression, whether it be public or private."[57] The Court repeats the same point later in its opinion: "[A]ssociations do not have to associate for the 'purpose' of disseminating a certain message in order to be entitled to the protections of the First Amendment. An association must merely engage in expressive activity that could be impaired in order to be entitled to protection."[58] So long as a law "significantly affect[s]" an association's "expression," the law cannot be applied to that association unless it is the "least restrictive means" of "serv[ing] compelling state interests."[59]

The *Boy Scouts* majority not only announced a broad view of the kinds of associations that can assert expressive-association claims, but also adopted the most expansive possible position on the kind of review applicable to an association's claim that a challenged law "significantly affect[s]" its expression. According to the *Boy Scouts* majority, in deciding whether a law really has a "significant" impact on an association's expression, the courts must take the association's word for it. "As we give deference to an association's assertions regarding the nature of its expression, we must also give deference to an association's view of what would impair its expression."[60]

Imagine, then, an all-white homeowners' association. The homeowners seek an exemption from laws prohibiting racial discrimination. They claim that their rejection of black residents is an attempt to communicate—to one another, to their children, and to the world—the undesirability of racial mixing. As a result, antidiscrimination laws significantly impair their expression. Why aren't these homeowners entitled to the same strict scrutiny that the Boy Scouts received? The answer is: they probably are.

And why stop with nonprofit associations? Assume hypothetically that Coors, the beer manufacturer, expressly declared that it seeks to communicate traditional views about the natural roles that men and women are meant to play, that these views are central to the firm's creed (or to its marketing strategy), and that being forced to hire women "significantly affect[s]" its ability to express these views. Nothing in the *Boy Scouts* opinion suggests that a sex discrimination law would not have to pass strict scrutiny before it could apply to Coors in these circumstances.

The truth is that virtually every antidiscrimination law could be found to violate the "freedom of expressive association," just as the "liberty of contract" could be found to be transgressed by virtually every commercial and labor law. This is because antidiscrimination laws are nothing other than laws regulating association, and virtually every association "engage[s] in some form of expression, whether it be public or private." I do not suggest, and I do not believe, that the five Justices who decided *Boy Scouts* will go on to strike down core applications of Title VII any time soon. Instead, the *Boy Scouts* holding can be expected to be limited in a number of ways.

To begin with, distinctions among kinds of associations are likely to be made. For example, despite the contrary language in *Boy Scouts,* the Court (or the lower courts) may hold that for-profit, commercial associations, participating in the "public" marketplace, cannot make "expressive association" claims.[61] The distinction would be arbitrary, but not unprecedented. It would be comparable to the *Lochner* Court's holding that businesses "affected with a public interest" could not make "liberty of contract" claims.[62]

In addition, the Court can be expected to reaffirm that some or many antidiscrimination laws, in some or many contexts, serve sufficiently compelling interests to pass strict scrutiny. In this way, the Court will be able to sustain the nation's "established" antidiscrimination statutes, while allowing itself plenty of leeway to block newfangled, overly progressive definitions of discrimination. This would be comparable to the *Lochner* Court's willingness to permit long-established interferences with the liberty of contract (Sunday laws, usury prohibitions), while striking down newfangled, too-progressive interferences, such as the minimum wage.

The result would be a loopholed, exception-ridden doctrine essentially enabling five Justices to strike down discrimination laws whenever they find them most intrusive. If this is what *Boy Scouts* portends—and it is hard to see how a result of this kind can now be avoided—the "freedom of expressive association" will be to antidiscrimination law exactly what the "liberty of contract" was to labor law.

The point, once again, is not that these considerations make *Boy Scouts* wrong. That judgment depends on what one is looking for in a Supreme Court decision. The question raised here is solely whether it makes sense to take the Court's "federalism" and "First Amendment freedom of association" cases seriously in the doctrinal terms in which they present themselves.

On this question, the simple facts are as follows. The "federalism" battle waged by five Justices of the Supreme Court has rejected a general congressional power to define and prohibit discrimination on the ground that this power is "local," rather than "national." This battle has, moreover, proclaimed itself in the name of two things: respect for the constitutional text and respect for the prerogatives of state power. Yet in *Boy Scouts,* the Court struck down a *state* antidiscrimination measure *without a hint of textual support in the Constitution.*

The coincidence is sufficient to make reasonable people wonder. We need to start thinking seriously about the possibility that the Court's federalism cases should not be taken seriously as federalism cases (as efforts to allocate power between the federal and state governments) and that, instead, a more substantive agenda unites the Court's cases across a variety of distinct doctrines. What might this agenda be?

The Anti-Anti-Discrimination Agenda

One hypothesis would run as follows. A view commonly associated with "conservatives" or "neoconservatives" today holds that the "liberal" antidiscrimination movement has taken a turn deeply threatening to America's fundamental values and freedoms. This view does not reject the ideal of formal equality under law; nor does it necessarily reject "traditional" antidiscrimination laws like Title VII. But it condemns many of the newer trends in antidiscrimination law and thinking, in which it sees an attack on important American institutions.

The perceived threats include the erosion of meritocracy; the fostering of divisive racial, ethnic, and gender politics; the corrosive idea that if some people fare worse under neutral standards or laws of general applicability, those people have been "discriminated" against; the corrosive idea that being expected to speak English (well or at all) is a form of "discrimination"; the explosion of antidiscrimination norms and lawsuits in the workplace to the point where it is supposed to be almost impossible for American businesses today to fire women or minorities; the unfair rejection of qualified whites from prestigious positions or educational opportunities in favor of undeserving minorities or women; the legitimization of same-sex marriages; and, of course, the general attack on the Western canon by a new emphasis on "marginalized" voices.

These developments—real or imagined—inspire in many people an anxiety that the core premises of their society are threatened by a relativist, antimeritocratic, anti-American antidiscrimination ideology gaining ascendancy in the "liberal media," among "liberal" intellectual elites, and most important, among "liberal" legislators and other governmental decision makers. It is not impossible that five Justices of the Supreme Court are moved by these fears, just as several Justices appear to have been moved earlier in this century by the fear that American society was profoundly threatened by an anticapitalist ideology.

Just as the *Lochner* Court felt that the Constitution must protect against anticapitalist legislation, even if the Constitution nowhere specifically addressed this threat, so these five Justices would feel that the Constitution must protect against the new forms of antidiscrimination legislation. Hence these five Justices would face the same problem the *Lochner* Justices faced, and they would be forced into the same kind of indirection. Their case law, taken as a whole, would reveal a coherence and a thematic unity only fortuitously related to the various doctrinal innovations they announced. Sometimes these Justices would present themselves as sticklers for the constitutional text, yet in other cases they would become (without comment) textually cavalier, invoking utterly unwritten constitutional rights and principles. Sometimes these Justices would be federalist (on textual grounds), but their "federalism" doctrine would just happen to apply principally to antidiscrimination laws, while at other times the same Justices would (invoking unwritten law) strike down state law regulating the same subject matter that the Court had just told us was especially confided to state (rather than federal) authority. In other words, their decisions would reveal, below the surface, an *anti-anti-discrimination* agenda.

The anti-anti-discrimination agenda would be especially hostile to claims that a person has been "discriminated against" when he has merely been asked to abide by the same laws everyone else must; racial or gender preferences; "identity politics"; measures banning discrimination against groups, such as homosexuals, not covered by "traditional" antidiscrimination law or thinking; laws extending the concept of discrimination in new ways, such as a prohibition of "gender-based violence"; laws that say employers are "discriminating" against disabled people if they do not provide them with special accommodations; and any other laws extending the concept of discrimination beyond the confines that the Court itself has laid down.

Needless to say, these concerns match up almost bracingly with a number of the Court's most important recent constitutional innovations. To summarize the leading cases once again:

Expressive Association. The "freedom of expressive association" as defined in *Boy Scouts* is, precisely, a constitutional right to discriminate. To be sure, the Court says this right must be balanced against competing interests, but *Boy Scouts* puts the Court in a position to exercise superlegislative review of almost every application of almost every antidiscrimination law, striking down those (like the prohibition of discrimination against homosexuals in *Boy Scouts*) that five Justices find impolitic.

Eleventh Amendment. Of the handful of laws against which the Court has applied its new "Eleventh Amendment" doctrine, two have been important antidiscrimination laws. The Court has held that individuals cannot sue states under the Americans with Disabilities Act[63] or under the federal Age Discrimination Act.[64]

Commerce Clause. Interestingly, the Court's newly invigorated "commerce clause" doctrine, despite all the attention it has received, has been invoked to strike down exactly two laws. One of them just happened to be an important new antidiscrimination law. This was the Violence Against Women Act, a law that essentially portrayed violence against women, and states' alleged failure to redress it, as a form of "gender-based" discrimination.[65]

Affirmative Action. The *Adarand* decision obviously fits within an anti-anti-discrimination paradigm. The principle of color blindness precisely refuses to accept the "politically correct" antidiscrimination ethos in which "reverse discrimination" is an acceptable tool for fighting discrimination. Consistent with *Adarand* and the anti-anti-discrimination paradigm, the Court has also struck down majority-minority redistricting measures, as well as an ethnic preference employed in connection with the disbursement of monies in Hawaii.[66] On the other hand, the recent *Grutter* case (upholding an affirmative action program at the University of Michigan Law School) marks a significant retreat on this front.

Religious Exemptions. The specific doctrinal change effected by *Smith* was, precisely, to eliminate claims of discrimination by religious people who had been asked merely to abide by the same laws that everyone else must.[67] Under *Smith*, individuals cannot claim that laws of "general applicability" discriminate against their religion just because those laws happen to burden their religious practices. Instead, free-exercise plaintiffs need to show religious discrimination—a deliberate targeting of their religion or religious practices.

Thus the most transformative constitutional decisions by the Supreme Court over the last decade all point toward the operation of a new anti-anti-discrimination paradigm in constitutional law. Moreover, in a number of other areas where the Court has not broken substantially new doctrinal ground, but has applied old doctrinal frameworks in controversial ways, some of the Court's most important decisions also squarely fit within this anti-anti-discrimination paradigm:

Section 5 of the Fourteenth Amendment. As noted previously, the Court's new commerce clause and Eleventh Amendment doctrines have given a new importance to Section 5 of the Fourteenth Amendment. (Under older case law, the Court did not have to reach the Section 5 issues, but because Congress can escape the limits of the Court's new commerce clause and Eleventh Amendment jurisprudence under Section 5, the Court has had to render several important Section 5 holdings.) In its Section 5 cases, the Court has expressly held that Congress has no power to extend the concept of unlawful discrimination beyond the confines of the Court's definition of unlawful discrimination. Thus the Americans with Disabilities Act could not be upheld under Section 5 because the ADA recognizes forms of unlawful discrimination against the disabled that the Court does not. Similarly, the Age Discrimination Act could not be upheld under Section 5 because that measure recognizes forms of unlawful discrimination against older people that the Court does not. And the Religious Freedom and Restoration Act, which in essence would have set up a disparate-impact antidiscrimination regime for religious groups, also had to be struck down as outside Congress's Section 5 powers.[68]

"Disparate Impact" Discrimination. In important nonconstitutional cases, five Justices of the Court have rejected "disparate impact" discrimination claims (that is, claims of discrimination based merely on disproportionate harms to a class of persons, rather than on intentional discrimination against that class of persons). In 1989, the Court cut back sharply on "disparate impact" discrimination claims under Title VII,[69] but Congress quickly overrode the Court's ruling in the Civil Rights Act of 1991.[70] In 2001, five Justices held that Title VI, which prohibits discrimination in certain federally funded programs, does not authorize a private right of action for "disparate impact" discrimination. Interestingly, the case involved an English-only policy; the Court held that plaintiffs could not sue Alabama for discrimination

merely because that state had begun conducting drivers' license examinations only in English.[71]

Sex Discrimination. In 2001, the Court, rejecting a claim of discrimination against men, upheld a law granting birthright citizenship to a child born abroad of unwed parents where the mother was a U.S. citizen, but imposing more stringent requirements for the acquisition of citizenship where the father was a U.S. citizen. In addition to upholding here an instance of "traditional" differential treatment of men and women, the Court in this case also, more significantly, may have endorsed a test for sex classifications considerably more lenient than the one that the Court had embraced in previous cases. Previously, the Court had held that state actors had to show an "exceedingly persuasive justification" supporting any sex-based classification. But in the 2001 decision, the Court seemed to retreat from this test, upholding the challenged statute without demanding "exceedingly persuasive" proof of the necessity of differential treatment.[72]

On all these fronts, under widely varying doctrinal rubrics, invoking sharply conflicting constitutional principles and interpretive methods (for example, lurching from textualism and federalism to unwritten law and intervention into state regulations), the Court's case law over the last decade may have been driven by an anti-anti-discrimination agenda.

It does not follow, however, that the Justices in the majority are therefore to be accused of bad faith. When limiting federal antidiscrimination statutes in favor of state sovereignty, when limiting state rights-granting statutes in favor of federal sovereignty, and when guaranteeing the Boy Scouts' right to expel homosexuals, the five Justices who have rendered most of these decisions probably understand themselves to be vindicating constitutional values of the highest magnitude. They presumably see in the laws they have struck down genuine threats to constitutional principles.

But like the *Lochner* Court, the current Court has responded to this new constitutional threat through doctrinal guises that tend to mask the actual coherence of its new case law. The current majority has introduced an anti-anti-discrimination agenda into constitutional law, but, because this agenda does not fit comfortably with available constitutional text or principles, it has had to operate under cover.

Counterexamples and Countervailing Considerations

That a constitutional agenda is pursued under cover does not necessarily mean that it is unjustifiable. If the new paradigm were acknowledged and its principles articulated, it might be more defensible than the judges pursuing it recognize. If one were convinced that an anti-anti-discrimination agenda was now driving American constitutional law, the question to ask would be how well the Court's case law captures the Constitution's historical paradigm cases.

I doubt very much that paradigm-case reasoning would support an anti-anti-discrimination agenda. Astonishingly, arguments have occasionally been made that the Thirteenth Amendment implies a right to discriminate against racial minorities in some contexts: a right not to "serve" blacks if one doesn't wish to.[73] It is very hard to believe, however, that the core applications of any of the Reconstruction Amendments—race slavery, the black codes, the denial to blacks of the suffrage—could in good faith be interpreted to exemplify a constitutional anti-anti-discrimination principle. On the contrary, these paradigm cases stand plainly for antidiscrimination principles. Thus from the point of view of paradigm-case reasoning, the Reconstruction Amendments offer scant justification for an anti-anti-discrimination agenda. If anything, the paradigm cases of those amendments stand against the introduction of an anti-anti-discrimination paradigm in constitutional law.

What about "the freedom of association"? Doesn't this freedom have deep roots in American constitutionalism, and couldn't the anti-anti-discrimination paradigm be built, as *Boy Scouts* suggests, around the core applications of this freedom?

The "freedom of association" can mean many things. It can refer, for example, to "intimate associations."[74] (A freedom of intimate association might suggest, for example, a right to marry or to have sexual relationships with whomever one pleases.) The "freedom of association" can also refer to the right of individuals to form parties and other groups to pursue political objectives. Such associations are undoubtedly protected by the First Amendment from state efforts to disrupt, persecute, or harass them due to the positions they espouse.[75] But if an anti-anti-discrimination agenda is said to rest in the "freedom of association," then a very different meaning of that freedom is in play. The "freedom of association" would then have to refer to a constitutional right to refuse to associate with others on whatever grounds one wanted—a general right to discriminate.

The "freedom of association" has in fact carried this meaning for many people in American constitutional history. It should not be forgotten that the "freedom of association," understood precisely in this sense—as a right to discriminate, both in the private and public spheres—was a segregationist rallying cry in the mid-twentieth century. *Brown*'s opponents, including state supreme court judges, referred to white people's freedom not to "associate" with blacks as one of the cherished values of the "free world":

> A victorious crusade of the N.A.A.C.P. for the special privilege of Negroes to intrude upon white people in their private affairs can only be won at the expense of the traditional freedom of personal association which has always characterized the free world."[76]

Plessy v. Ferguson was of course premised on the claim that the Fourteenth Amendment "could not have been intended" to "enforce . . . a commingling of the two races upon terms unsatisfactory to either."[77] Similarly, Herbert Wechsler's famous critique of *Brown* maintained that integration could not be accomplished without violating some individuals' "freedom of association."[78]

One might have thought, therefore, that *Brown* itself—a paradigm case of a status nearly equal to that of the foundational Application Understandings—stood for a rejection of the idea that individuals' racial associational preferences had the status of a constitutionally protected interest or right. For if the "freedom of association" in this expansive sense is a constitutional right, then, just as Wechsler argued, it becomes hard to see why racial segregation laws cannot be defended on the ground that the state is merely attempting to protect its citizens' constitutional rights—their freedom not to associate with members of other races. To be sure, a state school system seriously attempting to satisfy its citizens' racial associational preferences would have to offer not only segregated schools but also mixed-race schools for those parents who desired them. If it did so, however, the state could plausibly be said to be doing its best to vindicate the associational preferences of all its citizens, and thus to have a very strong constitutional justification for its actions—*if* those associational preferences really were constitutionally protected interests.

The fact that offering whites-only, blacks-only, and mixed-race schools is not and has never been a constitutional option under *Brown* demonstrates that *Brown* implicitly rejected the notion that individuals have some kind of general constitutional right to the satisfaction of their associational preferences. If there were such a right, segregated public schools would have a much stronger claim to constitutionality than *Brown* recognized. If *Boy Scouts* resurrects the "freedom of association" in this sense it calls into question not only all antidiscrimination laws but also, to some extent, *Brown* itself.

It is important to observe, however, that the Supreme Court's decided case law does not go nearly this far. It is not directed against Title VII or other "traditional" antidiscrimination laws. It is directed against more recent developments in antidiscrimination law and thinking. But for just this reason, the Court has put itself in a logically difficult position. Like the *Lochner* Court's anti-anti-capitalist agenda, the present Court's anti-anti-discrimination agenda lacks a consistent principle. It is organized around perceived *new* threats to American values and institutions—threats to meritocracy from affirmative action, to national identity from "identity politics," to heterosexually defined marriage, to the ability of employers to fire workers without undue fear of a discrimination lawsuit, to the freedom of employers or others to exclude homosexuals—and hence to threats that neither the Constitution's text nor its history specifically meets.

There is little point extending this discussion further. It is premature. The Court's case law over the last decade has not been sufficiently of a piece to justify a conviction that the anti-anti-discrimination agenda is now part of American constitutional law. If there are anti-anti-discrimination principles emerging in the case law, it is not yet clear what these principles will be.

In fact, the Court has decided several cases that stand as important counterweights to the anti-anti-discrimination agenda. In *Romer v. Evans*,[79] the Court struck down a Colorado constitutional amendment forbidding Colorado cities from enacting ordinances prohibiting discrimination on the basis of homosexuality. In *United States v. Virginia*,[80] the Court held that Virginia's exclusion of women from the state's premier, public military academy violated the equal protection clause. In 2003, the Court upheld an affirmative action program,[81] found that individuals could sue states under a "nontraditional" federal antidiscrimination statute,[82] and struck down a state law criminalizing homosexual sodomy.[83]

The simple fact may be that of the five Justices who have decided so many of the current Court's transformative decisions, one or two—perhaps Kennedy or O'Connor—may be less adamant in their commitment to the anti-anti-discrimination agenda. If so, and if their ambivalence produces occasional anomalous results, then in this respect too the anti-anti-discrimination agenda is similar to the *Lochner* era's anti-anti-capitalist agenda, which was also riddled with exceptions. Indeed, anomalies are hardly surprising when the Court pursues an unacknowledged and jurisprudentially under-theorized agenda. In the absence of clear, explicit rules, a new paradigm invites inconsistency. The "softness" of one or two Justices makes such departures almost inevitable.

Nevertheless, the Court's decisions in 2003 make it impossible to know what the future direction of the Court's most important doctrinal innovations will be. The anti-anti-discrimination paradigm has not yet won the day. Instead, therefore, of exploring further a new constitutional paradigm that would unite the Court's decisions across a variety of doctrines but that may not exist, it makes sense to consider the Court's decisions in a more conventional fashion, taking them seriously in their own doctrinal terms, and asking whether these doctrines are supportable by reference to the Constitution's paradigm cases. This is the task taken up in the next (and final) chapter.

9

Sex, Commerce, Preferences

In this chapter, I consider three important constitutional fields in which the Supreme Court has issued transformative decisions, asking in each case whether the Court's decisions are justifiable according to paradigm-case reasoning. The three areas are the right of privacy, Congress's commerce power, and racial preferences for minorities (affirmative action).

The Right of Privacy—*Lawrence*

In June 2003, the Court reversed *Bowers v. Hardwick* and held unconstitutional a Texas statute criminalizing homosexual sodomy.[1] *Lawrence* should be celebrated by all who stand against the endless campaign to vilify and torment "homosexuals." But in the main, the actual opinion produced by the *Lawrence* Court is not satisfying as a matter of constitutional interpretation, and it is not supported by paradigm-case reasoning.

Lawrence should and will probably be regarded as a "right of privacy" decision, although some of its language suggests (for reasons not made clear in the opinion) a shift away from the vocabulary of privacy to that of liberty. Does *Lawrence* indicate a paradigm shift in constitutional law?

The Court's 2000 decision in *Boy Scouts v. Dale* may have led some to believe that a majority of the present Justices were simply antihomosexual. From this point of view, *Lawrence* marks a clear shift, or at least a big swing of the pendulum, returning the Court to the path it charted in *Romer v. Evans,* in which six Justices (the same six who formed the majority in *Lawrence*) struck down a Colorado constitutional amendment repealing local efforts to prohibit antigay discrimination. But a swing of this sort is not a "paradigm shift" in the sense in which I have used that term.

A paradigm is an interpretive framework; it is the normative and conceptual frame of reference within which judges develop doctrine. To say

184

that *Lawrence* has effected a paradigm shift would mean that the Court has created a new interpretive framework for the Fourteenth Amendment or, more specifically, for the right of privacy. Does *Lawrence* indicate such a paradigm shift? Possibly.

Justice Kennedy's opinion for the Court in *Lawrence* says many things, invoking a number of quite different thoughts as possible justifications of the Court's holding. Some of these break no new constitutional ground; others would, if taken seriously, imply radical innovations in constitutional doctrine. It is not yet possible to know which of the strands of *Lawrence*, if any, the Court will pick up in later cases as it develops the doctrine. Only time will tell, then, whether *Lawrence* marked a paradigm shift.

For example, at one point in his opinion for the Court, Justice Kennedy quotes a 1992 case called *Casey* and says:

> "At the heart of liberty is the right to define one's own concept of existence, of meaning, of the universe, and of the mystery of human life. Beliefs about these matters could not define the attributes of personhood were they formed under compulsion of the State." Persons in a homosexual relationship may seek autonomy for these purposes, just as heterosexual persons do.[2]

Here the *Lawrence* Court breaks no new interpretive ground, but rather endorses *Casey*'s abstractions, purporting to apply them to the case at hand. True, the language quoted is so magniloquent that it is virtually contentless—any action could fall within the "right to define one's own concept of existence, of meaning, of the universe"—but *Casey*'s grand vapidity means only that *Casey* itself created no new interpretive framework or paradigm for the right of privacy.

In other parts of the opinion, Justice Kennedy stresses that antisodomy laws "demean the lives of homosexual persons."[3] In these passages, the Court breaks new ground in the sense that it recognizes—as it did not in *Hardwick*—a constitutional offense in the stigmatization effected by laws banning homosexual sex. Equal protection principles, however, have long recognized that stigmatizing laws are constitutionally suspect. Perhaps, in these passages, the Court is simply, finally, applying this equal protection principle to laws criminalizing homosexuality.

Other parts of *Lawrence*, however, are much more suggestive. The opinion begins with a grand declaration that "[l]iberty presumes an autonomy of self," and the language of individual autonomy (rather than equality) is the dominant language of the opinion. There is a strong display of constitutional respect for all "intimate" conduct and relationships, where "intimate" seems to have vaguely sexual connotations. One passage in *Lawrence,* however, goes much further. Toward the end of his opinion, Justice Kennedy says that the Court should have accepted the following proposition in *Hardwick* and does accept it now: "[T]he fact that the governing majority in a State has traditionally viewed a particular practice as immoral is not a sufficient reason for upholding a law prohibiting the practice." This thought, if taken seriously, would have profound implications for American constitutional law.

A venerable line of liberal philosophical thought holds that the state may never "legislate morality." On this view, each individual has a right to "pursue happiness after his own fashion," and law is illegitimate when it imposes some people's moral judgments on others. The famous saving corollary is that the state may prohibit individuals from doing harm. Murder can be prohibited not because it is immoral, but because it inflicts harm on its victims. When, however, in the words of the *Lawrence* Court, adults engage in "consensual" conduct, inflicting no "injury" on others or on "institutions that the state has a legitimate interest in protecting," there is apparently no harm of the relevant kind. In such cases, a state attempting to ban such conduct can invoke only moral condemnation, and mere moral condemnation is constitutionally insufficient. If this way of thinking becomes the constitutional law of the United States, then *Lawrence* will indeed have effected a profound paradigm shift, establishing at long last that the Fourteenth Amendment, although it may not have enacted Spencer's *Social Statics,* did enact a good portion of Mill's *On Liberty.*

The chief problem with this new paradigm, from the point of view of the paradigm-case method, would be the absence of paradigm cases.

The *Lawrence* opinion presents itself as an interpretation of the Fourteenth Amendment, but one searches that opinion in vain for any sign of an interpretive engagement with the text of that amendment or its paradigm cases. Instead, the opinion begins with the Court's past privacy decisions. In principle, this is a perfectly defensible way of proceeding from the point of view of paradigm-case reasoning. The right of privacy, like any other constitutional doctrine, has its own paradigm cases, established by precedent, and hence this characteristic form of constitutional argument—reasoning from settled precedent—is very much a part of the paradigm-case method. But if there is one paradigm case most associated with, and most definitive of, the right of privacy, it is surely *Roe v. Wade,* and the no-legislating-morality principle, along with its corollary harm principle, does not capture *Roe.*

The act of abortion inflicts several harms that would render it prohibitable under a principle that states may prevent harmful conduct. There is, first and most fundamentally, the killing of a living thing. I have never accepted the view that states can deem an embryo a human being (or "person") from the moment of conception, but as Ely pointed out almost thirty years ago, we don't usually suppose that law can prevent harms *only* to human beings. That would be news to anyone who supports laws preventing cruelty to animals, not to mention the Endangered Species Act.

Moreover, a woman's decision to abort can undoubtedly adversely affect human beings, such as the biological father, whose consent to her abortion is specifically *not* required under *Roe.* For the nonconsenting father, the woman's vindication of her "right to decide whether and when to have a child" deprives him of a similar right. Finally, according to many, abortion's availability promotes sexual practices and attitudes that generate a wide variety of social costs.

To recognize that abortion can do harm is not to criticize *Roe.* A good deal of conduct that the Constitution protects is harmful. Religious fundamentalism can be harmful in many ways, but it does not therefore lose its constitutional protection. The point is simply that *Roe* is poorly explained through a principle that requires us to see abortion as a perfectly harmless act.

Of course, from the point of view of the paradigm-case method, the primary question would not be whether *Lawrence*'s no-legislating-morality principle captures *Roe,* but whether *Roe* itself is supportable through paradigm-case reasoning. A satisfying justification of *Roe,* from the commitment-based perspective, would require a showing that the principle for which *Roe* stands is rooted solidly in the Fourteenth Amendment's foundational paradigm cases. Can such a showing be made? Interestingly, the answer is yes.

To make this showing in depth would require a chapter of its own, but the overall argument can be summarized briefly as follows. The Fourteenth Amendment's core applications involved numerous, notorious efforts by Southern states to use law to keep the newly freed blacks in a condition close to that of slavery: forcing them into menial occupations, obliging them to work for white landowners, and so on. Now, a notorious but quite definitive hallmark of female slavery in the American South (as elsewhere) was its sexual and maternal component. Slave women were routinely forced to have sex, to bear children, and to raise children against their will. There is no difficulty seeing in *Roe v. Wade* the proposition that a free woman cannot be forced into motherhood against her will. Indeed, *Roe* stands quite precisely for that very proposition, which in turn could itself be seen as part of a more general principle condemning all state efforts to force particular occupations on individuals, or otherwise to instrumentalize them as masters could do to their slaves. If *Roe* and the right of privacy are understood to stand for a principle of this sort—and they can be[4]—then they find strong support in the paradigm-case method.

The right of privacy can be conceptualized in many ways. But if an explanation of privacy is to have power in terms of paradigm-case reasoning, it ought both to capture *Roe v. Wade* and to draw its principles from the Fourteenth Amendment's core applications. An "anti-instrumentalization" account of privacy might do both those things. Unfortunately, the *Lawrence* opinion, to the extent that it tries to explain the right of privacy under a no-legislating-morality principle, does neither. It fails to capture *Roe* and draws little if any support from the Fourteenth Amendment's distinctive paradigm cases.

But it is unsurprising that an opinion espousing a constitutional principle against legislating morality (even if limited to "intimate" conduct) can claim little support in paradigm-case reasoning. For if there were such a constitutional principle, its paradigmatic applications would be found in laws that, far from being long prohibited in the United States, have been long embraced. Prostitution laws, for example, would seem a paradigmatic instance of legislating morality, as would bigamy and polygamy laws, and possibly incest laws, to the extent they apply to consensual conduct between adults. Yes, someone could try to defend all of these laws on "nonmoral" grounds of health, safety, or lack of "meaningful" consent, but these arguments can hardly be admissible here, because the very same arguments could obviously be made with respect to antihomosexuality laws.

In fact, Justice Kennedy's opinion for the Court in *Lawrence* expressly signals that the Court is not calling prostitution laws into question, perhaps suggesting that a law will not fall under the Court's no-legislating-morality principle if the conduct prohibited is "commercial" in nature. I would like to see the argument explaining why prohibiting commercial sex is *not* legislating morality, whereas prohibiting homosexual sex *is*. I would also be curious to hear whether Justice Kennedy thinks that *all* intimate relationships lose their protection when they have a monetary element, in which case the right to intimate relationships is not going to be very broad after all. Perhaps Justice Kennedy means that prostitution's commercial component makes it regulable under the commerce clause, in which case he should not be accused of contradicting or eviscerating the no-legislating-morality principle, but only of confusing the question of whether a law violates the right of privacy with the totally irrelevant question of whether the same law would be within the ambit of Congress's commerce power.

Obscenity and nudity laws are also worth considering. These laws are currently viewed as constitutional, but are they not legal prohibitions resting on moral disapproval? Perhaps it will be said that "offensiveness" is different from moral disapproval; violations of community standards of offensiveness, someone might say, are harms the law may legitimately address. This kind of logic might save obscenity and nudity laws, but it would equally save antihomosexuality laws.

I am not defending prostitution or obscenity laws. The point is that these laws, as well as a host of others, demonstrate that American constitutional jurisprudence has never embraced the principle that government may not "legislate morality." Hence a fundamental paradigm shift would indeed be in play if *Lawrence* really does constitutionalize that principle. The official American understanding has always been that legislators have the prerogative, or even the duty, to protect the "health, safety *and morals*" of their constituents. Needless to say, legislators may not legislate morality when doing so would violate a constitutional right, but there has never been any general prohibition in American constitutional jurisprudence against laws based on morality. Our entire legal system would probably be unconstitutional if there were. The civil rights revolution of the 1960s, embodied in Title VII and the many other laws prohibiting discrimination, would almost certainly be unconstitutional under a principle that the state may not legislate morality. Discrimination inflicts no force or fraud on anyone. What is illegal discrimination if not conduct deemed unjust and immoral by contemporary American law?

The "harm" that racist property sellers inflict on those to whom they will not sell is not the kind of "direct injury" that Mill or libertarian philosophers characteristically describe as legally cognizable. The discriminating seller does not use force or fraud; he and his customers engage in purely consensual conduct, merely refusing to deal with others. If we say that discrimination is not "fully consensual" because those with whom the discriminator refuses to deal do not consent to this exclusion, then we would have to stop calling "consensual" a good deal of seemingly consensual practices—heterosexuality and homosexuality, for example. But if we defend Title VII as it should be defended, in the language of equality and justice, then we are defending it on the basis of a moral judgment. Antidiscrimination laws represent the considered, hard-fought moral judgment of a majority of this political community that racial discrimination (as well as other comparable forms of invidious discrimination) is, in most contexts, reprehensible and should therefore be prohibited. That is why libertarians like Richard Epstein argue against antidiscrimination laws.[5]

I doubt very much that the *Lawrence* majority would strike down Title VII on the ground that morality "is not a sufficient reason for upholding a law." I doubt they even recognize that the no-legislating-morality principle calls Title VII into question; racial and sex discrimination seem so obviously wrong and prohibitable to the contemporary American mind that we don't tend to notice that discrimination's "harm" is not the kind of harm that the classical harm principle acknowledges. But this shows only that the no-legislating-morality principle represents a way of thinking that is quite foreign to American law. If *Lawrence* embraces this way of thinking, it can claim support in libertarian philosophy, but not in the paradigm-case method, which would demand that a paradigm shift of this magnitude be justified by a showing that the new interpretive framework can compellingly explain why certain paradigmatically unconstitutional laws are unconstitutional. The no-legislating-morality principle has the opposite effect: it would explain why a number of laws central to our legal system are actually unconstitutional. There is nothing inherently wrong with calling into question the constitutionality of long-accepted laws, but if it is to be done, it should be done on the basis of a paradigm shift that can claim powerful support in the distinctive paradigm cases of the constitutional provision that is purportedly being interpreted.

To repeat: I am not arguing that *Lawrence* was wrongly decided. But the opinion given to us by Justice Kennedy, for all its other merits and all its transcendent aspirations, is sadly lacking in terms of constitutional interpretation. The absence of paradigm-case reasoning in that opinion is an essential part of the problem.

Commerce

Beginning with the 1995 *Lopez* decision, the Court introduced a new interpretive framework to commerce clause doctrine. Previously, under rulings handed down in the early 1940s, the Court had held that Congress could apparently regulate any activity, including in-state activity, so long as that activity had, in the aggregate, an "effect" or "substantial effect" on interstate commerce. Because nearly all activity, in the aggregate, has some such effects—sneezing, in the aggregate, affects the interstate market in facial tissue—the reach of the commerce clause seemed virtually limitless. And in fact, the Court did not find that a single federal law overstepped the bounds of that power from the 1940s to the early 1990s.

Lopez changed the doctrine. According to *Lopez*, Congress cannot regulate in-state activity on the basis of adverse effects on interstate commerce unless the activity in question is "commercial" or "economic" "in nature."[6] Using this test, the Court in *Lopez* struck down the federal Gun-Free School Zones Act and, in the *Morrison* case, provisions of the Violence Against Women Act. The Court found that carrying guns near a school was not "economic" activity, nor was gender-based violence, even if these activities had serious, adverse effects on interstate commerce.

As I said earlier, I have a hard time understanding the outrage with which some greeted *Lopez*. The reach of the commerce power ought to be limited. But the Court chose the wrong approach in *Lopez*.

The discussion of the commerce clause in Chapter 3 highlighted a very early and probably foundational application of that clause: Congress's ability to require the removal of a bridge or other obstruction that hindered traffic on a navigable waterway. As was also discussed previously, an in-state bridge is not itself "commerce among the states." The construction of such a bridge clearly did not have to be, in itself, "commercial" or "economic in nature" in order to fall within Congress's commerce power. If the bridge obstructed interstate commerce, nothing turned on the question of whether it had been built for economic purposes or whether, instead, it had been built wholly by unpaid volunteers for a wholly noneconomic purpose—say, to allow parishioners easy access to a church across the water.

In other words, in this paradigm case, Congress's power arises from the effect on interstate commerce, not from the notion that the bridge was itself "economic in nature" (which it may or may not have been).

Thus the *Lopez* rule runs afoul of the paradigm case.[7] Under *Lopez*'s economic-in-nature test, the fact that a bridge interfered with commerce would not give Congress a basis for ordering its removal (unless, fortuitously, in a particular case, the bridge itself happened to be "economic in nature," whatever that might mean).

Was *Lopez* incorrect, then, from the point of view of the paradigm-case method? Should the Court return to the rule that Congress may regulate any activity, so long as that activity, in the aggregate, has some substantial adverse effects on interstate commerce?

Yes and no. What has to be avoided is an unlimited-power reading of the commerce clause. This reading has to be avoided not because it would be merely unwise or un-originalist. It has to be avoided because it fails to satisfy the minimal requirements of paradigm-case interpretation. An interpretation of the commerce clause turning that clause into an unlimited grant of congressional jurisdiction does not do justice to the text in light of its specific paradigm cases. It mocks the text and its paradigmatic applications; in fact, it mocks the entire text of Article I, Section 8, which becomes ridiculous when one of Congress's eighteen enumerated powers is read as a universal grant of legislative authority.

To be sure, an unlimited-power reading of the commerce clause is *consistent* with the paradigmatic applications of the clause, but only factitiously so. It would be consistent with *any* specific applications of the commerce clause. In theory, judges could "interpret" the establishment clause to bar all federal laws in harmony with any particular religion, thus barring *all* congressional legislation. This reading would be consistent with the clause's foundational Application Understandings, but again only coincidentally so. It would be consistent with the paradigm cases no matter what they were. An unlimited-power reading of the commerce clause, like an unlimited-prohibition reading of the establishment clause, fails to capture in any meaningful sense the specific commitments behind the clause it purports to interpret.

How, then, should judges extrapolate from the paradigmatic power that Congress was to have to regulate in-state bridges over navigable waterways, without turning the commerce power into an unlimited grant of federal legislative authority? If the paradigm case suggests that Congress can reach even *noneconomic, in-state* activities with substantial effects on interstate commerce, and if in twenty-first-century America virtually *all* activities have substantial effects on interstate commerce, aren't we obliged to recognize an unlimited commerce power?

The solution to this riddle is not difficult. The bridge case stands for the proposition that Congress clearly acts within its commerce power when it regulates in-state activity to eliminate injuries to interstate or international commerce. (For shorthand, I will henceforth use "commerce" to refer to interstate or international commerce.) This proposition suggests that Congress can indeed potentially reach virtually all activity under the commerce clause, but only so long as that activity threatens adverse effects on commerce *and* only to the extent that Congress is genuinely seeking to redress those effects. What makes the bridge regulation clearly constitutional is that Congress is acting to address an obstruction to commerce. It does not follow that Congress could pass *any* regulation of a bridge obstructing commerce—for example, a regulation providing that no individuals who engage in homosexual marriage can cross the bridge. In other words, the paradigm case suggests a *purpose-based* limitation on Congress's commerce power, when Congress uses that power to reach in-state activity. Congress can regulate in-state activity to address potential threats to commerce, but cannot use the fact that an in-state activity has substantial effects on commerce as a pretext for regulating that activity for noncommercial purposes.

This modest bit of paradigm-case reasoning allows us to see precisely where both pre-*Lopez* and post-*Lopez* commerce doctrine goes wrong. Recall *Wickard*, the 1942 case in which the Supreme Court upheld under the commerce clause a federal law regulating how much wheat a farmer could grow on his own land for his own use. Whatever one might think of the likely economic consequences of allowing Congress to dictate the maximum amount of wheat farmers can grow, it is clear that in doing so, Congress was not acting out of some anti-wheat moral animus. The regulation was an effort (whether foolish or sound) to reverse the deflationary spiral of the Great Depression, and hence it fell within the scope of the commerce clause. As discussed earlier, the paradigm-case method finds no difficulty in the New Deal proposition that "[t]he power to regulate interstate commerce embraces the power to protect that commerce from injury whatever may be the source of the dangers which threaten it, and to adopt any appropriate means to that end."[8]

The mistake in pre-*Lopez* doctrine did not lie in *Wickard*. The mistake came when the New Deal Court added to *Wickard*'s holding a different one, which eliminated the requirement that Congress must be acting "to protect [interstate] commerce from injury." Rejecting this purpose-based constraint, the Court in *U.S. v. Darby* held that the "motive and purpose of a regulation of interstate commerce are matters for the legislative judgment upon the exercise of which the Constitution places no restriction."[9] It was *Darby*, added to *Wickard,* that produced an unlimited commerce power.

True, *Wickard* opened up virtually all in-state activity to Congress's potential commerce clause jurisdiction, because virtually all activity, in the aggregate, has some "substantial effect" on commerce. *Wickard* did not, however, hold that Congress could regulate such activity *for any purpose.* Similarly, even though *Darby* held that Congress's purpose was irrelevant to commerce clause analysis, Darby itself did not imply an unlimited commerce power, because the *Darby* Court made that statement in connection with a federal law directly regulating the interstate sale of goods. But when *Darby*'s holding was added to *Wickard*'s, Congress merely had to show that an activity had some substantial aggregate effect on commerce (which it could nearly always do), and this showing allowed Congress to regulate the activity for any purpose it chose. The result was that Congress could regulate *virtually any activity for any purpose.* Now, the power to regulate any activity for any purpose is the very definition of unlimited legislative authority, which is why, once *Darby* had been added to *Wickard,* the Court never again found that any congressional statute overstepped the bounds of the commerce power.

Thus pre-*Lopez* doctrine went wrong in holding that judges could not scrutinize the ends or purposes behind Congress's regulations once Congress showed that an in-state activity had substantial effects on commerce. It went wrong, in other words, when it removed the requirement that Congress must be acting, in such cases, with the purpose of eliminating or ameliorating harm to commerce. This conclusion would sustain *Wickard* and would exactly capture the paradigmatic bridge case, but would allow the Court to reject a claim of commerce clause jurisdiction when Congress attempted to use the effects-on-commerce rationale as a pretext to justify a law it passed for other reasons, as was arguably the case of both the Gun-Free School Zones Act and the Violence Against Women Act.

The problem with post-*Lopez* doctrine is that it fails to restore this purpose-based inquiry. It asks whether the activity regulated is "economic in nature," when it should ask whether Congress's purpose is "economic in nature."[10] If antiglobalization enthusiasts sabotaged bank accounts on a large scale, damaging commerce, Congress would have the power to penalize such hacking—even though the saboteurs' conduct was not itself "commercial" or "economic in nature." (We could assume, hypothetically, that their actions were politically motivated, that they were not being paid, that they were not trying to advance anybody else's commercial activity, and so on.) When Congress tries to reach conduct that is not in itself interstate or international commerce, it is the commercial nature of Congress's regulatory purpose, not the commercial nature of the activity regulated, that should be dispositive.

Taking this thought further would require a more careful definition of the purposes permissible when Congress acts under the commerce clause. Clearly, a purpose of removing threats to commerce is legitimate. But other commerce-related purposes might be permitted as well.

For example, it may be that Congress ought to have power to redress not only potential harms *to* commerce but also potential harms caused *by* commerce. Interstate commerce is obviously responsible for various harms, such as environmental degradation. State governments have a limited ability to cure such harms, not least because a state that passes strict environmental measures may find that businesses relocate outside its borders, in which case interstate commerce might be responsible not only for the environmental damage but also for the absence of state regulations counteracting that damage. There is no reason why a purpose-based restriction on the commerce power could not take these factors into account, holding that Congress may reach in-state activity both to protect commerce from injury and to redress injuries from commerce.

Affirmative Action

In 2003, in a case called *Grutter*, the Court surprised many by upholding (again by a 5–4 majority, with Justice O'Connor providing the "swing" vote) the University of Michigan Law School's affirmative action admissions program. The Court followed *Adarand*, but found that the law school's program satisfied "strict scrutiny." In a separate decision, the Court struck down the University of Michigan's undergraduate affirmative action program, which, unlike the law school's program, used a formalized point system for admissions and which allotted all "minority" candidates a fixed number of extra points.[11]

Taking the two decisions together, the rule the Court seemed to announce is that affirmative action is constitutional in higher education so long as it is implemented through sufficiently nebulous and covert criteria. This compromise position may or may not prove stable. For now, however,

Grutter stands as a significant backing off from the rule of strict color blindness that *Adarand* seemed to portend.

What does the paradigm-case method say about affirmative action? There is no doubt that the Court's decision in *Grutter* is well supported by paradigm-case reasoning. But this is not saying too much, because a rule of color blindness would also have been supportable to some extent. From the Fourteenth Amendment's paradigm cases, which involved discrimination against blacks, it is possible in theory to derive either an anti-caste principle of the kind that tolerates affirmative action or a color-blindness principle that cuts against it.

Still, the paradigm-case method may have an additional important contribution to make here, because strict color blindness would prove surprisingly difficult to square with the Fourteenth Amendment's foundational commitments if it were adopted in combination with certain other features of existing equal protection law. In other words, a rule of color blindness could be rendered consistent with the Fourteenth Amendment's core applications, but only if significant modifications were made to existing doctrine—modifications that anti-affirmative-action justices would very probably reject.

The paradigm-case argument for *Grutter* is straightforward. The paradigmatic instance of racial discrimination in American constitutional history is of course discrimination against blacks. Slavery, the black codes, and Jim Crow all involved governmental actors deliberately seeking to perpetuate white supremacy. By contrast, laws singling out blacks (and other racial minorities) for special rights or privileges in the allocation of governmental benefits were not originally considered paradigmatic violations of equal protection principles. On the contrary, the very Congress that framed and promulgated the Fourteenth Amendment passed several laws explicitly granting blacks special benefits.[12] There is no difficulty capturing the Fourteenth Amendment's paradigm cases with a principle that does not categorically prohibit efforts to assist blacks or other racial minorities by giving them some measure of preferential treatment in the allocation of government benefits or opportunities.

But if there was an original understanding that laws granting special benefits to "colored persons" did *not* violate the equal protection clause, it was a No-Application Understanding, and today's judges are free to reject it. A rule of strict color blindness could therefore reject this original No-Application Understanding without contravening the paradigm-case method. Strict color blindness would be clearly unsupportable from an originalist viewpoint (segregation was originally considered permissible, and segregation is of course a violation of color blindness), so it is a little embarrassing to see our self-professed "originalist" judges righteously insisting on a color-blind equal protection clause. Nevertheless, color blindness would certainly be consistent with the Fourteenth Amendment's paradigmatic applications.

But there would still be a problem with color blindness, given other features of contemporary doctrine. Fourteenth Amendment law nearly always permits state actors to single out groups in need of assistance—or deemed to be in need of assistance by the legislature—for preferential treatment. Numerous laws grant special privileges or benefits to the very poor, veterans, the disabled, large but putatively struggling corporations, farmers, victims of terrorist attacks, and so on. But under a rule of strict color blindness, blacks and other racial minorities could not be singled out for such advantageous treatment.

It might be replied that this discrepancy is the fair price that racial minorities must pay for their protection against discrimination. In other words, it might be said, it is obtuse to complain that color blindness blocks racial minorities from receiving preferential treatment. Color blindness also safeguards racial minorities from hostile laws. Thus color blindness is perfectly evenhanded, someone might say, and therefore cannot be deemed to treat racial minorities in any sort of unfair or disadvantageous manner.

But contemporary constitutional doctrine creates a problem with this logic. There are many groups, in addition to racial minorities, protected against hostile discrimination by modern equal protection law. Yet these groups *can* be singled out for *favorable* treatment in the allocation of governmental benefits. A state could not specifically prohibit poor persons or veterans from eating at certain restaurants, from pursuing certain occupations, or, probably, from exercising *any* right or privilege enjoyed by others. That would be unconstitutional discrimination. Yet states can and do specifically assist the poor or veterans with specially favorable treatment in the allocation of governmental benefits. But under strict color blindness, blacks and other racial minorities would be denied this privilege.

In other words, color blindness puts racial minorities in a worse position than that of other minorities under existing equal protection law. The mentally ill, to take another example, are protected from invidious discrimination under the equal protection clause,[13] but they can be and are occasionally singled out for preferential treatment, receiving welfare benefits or other benefits denied to others. Color blindness denies this advantageous possibility to blacks.

Now, it may be replied that racial affirmative action programs differ from, say, welfare programs, because affirmative action, however benign in intent, has pernicious consequences for the very groups whom it ostensibly benefits. In other words, affirmative action is in reality (it might be said) deeply harmful to blacks, even if these harmful consequences are unintended, and it ought to be struck down out of solicitude for black interests. Justice Thomas has adopted this argument in his opinions, and the *Adarand* majority explained itself in similar terms. Strict scrutiny of affirmative action programs was necessary, the Court said in *Adarand,* because such programs had the unintended consequence of promoting invidious racial stereotypes.

This unintended-consequences argument may be the best defense of *Adarand* and a strict color-blindness rule, but once again, it runs afoul of other parts of existing equal protection law. The unintended-harm argument maintains that preferences for racial minorities must be struck down (or at the very least subjected to "strict scrutiny") because such preferences promote stereotypes of racial inferiority, thereby producing deeply adverse (though unintended) consequences for affirmative action's supposed beneficiaries. But in every other context in equal protection law, the Court specifically refuses to strike down state action (or even to subject it to "strict scrutiny") solely on the basis of unintended harms to minorities, including the unintended promotion of invidious racial stereotypes.

The use of standardized tests, for example, has notoriously promoted stereotypes of racial inferiority. Under current equal protection doctrine, however, blacks cannot claim discrimination or demand strict scrutiny of such tests on this ground. This is the rule of a famous case called *Washington v. Davis*.[14] Rather, they would have to show that such tests were used *deliberately* to harm them.

Thus in the absence of an overhaul in equal protection law in which the rule of *Washington v. Davis* was abandoned, the unintended-consequences argument cannot be used in defense of *Adarand* without involving the Court in serious difficulties. If *Adarand* or a strict rule of color blindness is explained on the basis of affirmative action's unintended harms to minorities, then, given the rest of existing equal protection law, a strange result is produced. When blacks confront state action that unintentionally disadvantages them, they have no discrimination claim. But when whites confront state action that singles out blacks for benefits, they can claim discrimination *on the ground that the state action unintentionally harms blacks.*

It will be replied that the color-blindness principle applies only to measure that explicitly treat persons differently on the basis of race, whereas the rule of *Washington v. Davis* applies to racially neutral measures. This reply misses the point. *Washington v. Davis,* along with many other, similar cases, holds that unintended harm to minority groups is not by itself a constitutional evil: it is not, as such, a ground for invalidation or for the imposition of strict scrutiny. Now, if laws with explicit racial classifications are said to be constitutionally evil in some fashion that categorically distinguishes them from racially neutral measures, that evil cannot, consistent with *Washington v. Davis,* be said to consist in the asserted fact that racial classifications inflict unintended harms on minorities. For under *Washington v. Davis,* such harm is not a constitutional evil. Thus to the extent that *Adarand* is defended on the basis of the unintended harm that affirmative action inflicts on minorities, there is indeed a conflict with the *Washington v. Davis* principle.[15]

In essence, *Adarand* completed a paradigm shift in equal protection law. The interpretive framework governing discrimination claims under the equal protection clause used to be organized around "suspect *classes.*" Under *Adarand,* the interpretive framework is plainly organized around "suspect *classifications.*" Strict scrutiny is triggered not by the disadvantaging of suspect classes, but by the use of a suspect classification (no matter which group is advantaged or disadvantaged). Organizing equal protection doctrine around the concept of suspect classifications might be defensible in itself; certainly, it can be squared with the Fourteenth Amendment's paradigm cases. But the results are quite strange given existing Fourteenth Amendment case law, and they will remain strange unless significant bodies of current doctrine are changed. If, for example, we ask why the rich cannot claim unconstitutional discrimination when governmental benefits are extended only to the poor, the well-understood answer (under existing case law) is that the wealthy are not a "suspect class" and hence are not entitled to strict scrutiny of the benefits program at issue. In general, under existing case law, no group that does not meet certain well-established criteria—such as relative political powerlessness and a history of discrimination—can claim "suspect class" status, entitling it to the strict-scrutiny standard of review. But under *Adarand,* there is one group entitled to strict scrutiny even though it does not meet these criteria: whites.

To understand the peculiarity of these results, imagine that South Carolina adopted the following amendments to its constitution to govern preferential treatment and claims of discrimination under state law:

I. Preferential Treatment for Needy Groups
   A. On any rational basis, any minority group disadvantaged or in need of assistance may be given preferential treatment in the allocation of state benefits, contracts, employment, or other advantageous opportunities.
   B. Exception: Blacks shall be denied this privilege, and so shall every other racial minority.
II. Purpose Requirement
   A. Invidious purpose is an essential element of any claim of discrimination; mere unintended harm to, or disparate impact on, a group of individuals is insufficient.
   B. Exception: When state action singles out blacks or other racial minorities for *benefits,* no invidious purpose need be shown. Instead, such state action shall be automatically subjected to strict scrutiny due to the harm it inflicts on its beneficiaries, however unintended that harm may be.
III. Suspect Class Requirement
   A. Even when a group of individuals is specifically excluded from or disadvantaged by an allocation of state benefits, a claim of discrimination by that group shall not receive the strict scrutiny standard of review unless the group is a "suspect class" as that term is defined by the precedents of the United States Supreme Court.
   B. Exception: White people may demand strict scrutiny of any allocation of governmental benefits that excludes or disadvantages them regardless of whether they would qualify as a "suspect class" as that term is defined by the precedents of the United States Supreme Court.

Most readers, I venture to say, would be taken aback by Section B in all of these imaginary provisions. Most of us, I think, would be quite troubled to think that a state could explicitly deny racial minorities a legal privilege granted to all other minority groups. Or that it could make unintended harm a basis for a holding of unconstitutionality discrimination only when a law singles out racial minorities for benefits. Or that a state could explicitly exempt whites from the "suspect class" showing that every other group has to make in order to obtain strict scrutiny of a law that disadvantages them. At the very least, these provisions are in deep tension with what we have long understood to be the Fourteenth Amendment's core commitments.

Yet these provisions merely codify the precise legal effects of *Adarand* or of a strict rule of color blindness, given other well-accepted features of equal protection law. Which is to say: while the Court could coherently try to derive color blindness from the paradigmatic unconstitutionality of the black codes, the principle of color blindness surprisingly and perversely becomes itself a kind of black code when it is combined with the rest of current equal protection law. Under *Adarand,* blacks and other racial minorities are virtually alone denied a legal privilege granted to all other groups of comparable size and need (the privilege of receiving preferential treatment without having to pass through the fire of "strict scrutiny"), while whites alone receive the advantages of "suspect class" status without satisfying any of the criteria ever identified as definitive of that status.

It would seem, therefore, from the point of view of paradigm-case reasoning, that the *Grutter* Court was right to back away from a strict implementation of the strict-scrutiny regime announced in *Adarand.* Unless other major sectors of equal protection law are changed, a rule of color blindness that prohibited legislators from singling out racial minorities for preferential treatment would end up singling out racial minorities for unfavorable treatment and would therefore produce results difficult to reconcile with the Fourteenth Amendment's fundamental commitments.

Conclusion

The purpose of constitutional theory is, and always has been, to hold the mirror up to constitutional law. The difficulty is twofold.

First, this mirror cannot quite be true. Theory provides its own light, which a true mirror would not, and in this illumination the reflected object will be given a wholeness it might not otherwise possess. That is the value of constitutional theory, but also its weakness. It has its own commitments, which boil down to the fact that, to one degree or another, it necessarily enters into the aspirations of that which it theorizes. These commitments, unfortunately, may always prove unjustified.

Second, to take constitutional law's full measure would require a glass reflecting not only its past and present, but also its future. The meaning of a constitutional case decided today is never established here and now, but only over time. The "Rehnquist Court," assuming there ever was such a thing, is already a historical object, but every contemporary effort to encapsulate this object is doomed to a radical incompleteness.

The extraordinary events of the last few years—the election contest of 2000, the terrorist attacks of 2001, and the wars that followed—have had significant, utterly unpredictable effects on the "Rehnquist Court," casting a shadow on it (and all of constitutional law), clouding its legacy, mixing its messages, and bringing the composition of the Supreme Court to a potentially decisive turning point, on which the fate of American constitutional law for the next twenty-five years or more may well depend. As a result, there are inherent limitations in the project undertaken by the last part of this book. The aim there was to take the measure of some of the most important constitutional decisions of the last ten years, and to do so in two different ways: taking the cases all together, and taking them in doctrinal units. Neither method avoids the limitations just mentioned. By the day after tomorrow, cases like *Lopez* or *Boy Scouts* or *Adarand* could be the roots of constitutional forests, standing for propositions grand and sweeping, or they may have been plowed under, leaving little trace.

Constitutional theory is therefore obliged to take the long view. That was the aim of this book's first two parts. If I have said anything of lasting importance in this book, it is to be found there—in the commitment-based picture of the Constitution, with its paradigm-case method and its core distinction between Application and No-Application Understandings.

Notes
Index

Notes

1. Introduction: Radical Reinterpretation

1. The term is Bobbitt's. See, e.g., Philip Bobbitt, *Constitutional Fate: Theory of the Constitution* (1982) (identifying six primary "modalities" of constitutional argument—historical, textual, structural, doctrinal, ethical, and prudential). According to Bobbitt, when these various argument-forms point to different results, judges are left to their own individual moral sensibilities. Philip Bobbitt, *Constitutional Interpretation* 163–70 (1991). See also Richard H. Fallon, Jr., "A Constructivist Coherence Theory of Constitutional Interpretation," 100 *Harv. L. Rev.* 1189 (1987).
2. Boy Scouts of America v. Dale, 530 U.S. 640 (2000).
3. Hyman v. City of Louisville, 132 F. Supp. 2d 528, 543 (W.D. Ky. 2001) ("the Supreme Court [has] held that two types of relationships are entitled to protection under the Freedom of Association Clause of the First Amendment"). For other judicial references to this "clause," see Van Wie v. Pataki, 267 F.3d 109, 111 (2nd Cir. 2001); Baird v. California Faculty Ass'n, 2000 U.S. Dist. LEXIS 13594 at 13 (E.D. Cal. 2000).
4. Robert H. Bork, *The Tempting of America: The Political Seduction of the Law* 76 (1990).
5. See, e.g., id. at 75 (conceding that "those who ratified the amendment did not think it outlawed segregated education").
6. See, e.g., Robert Post, "Theories of Constitutional Representation," 30 *Representations* 13, 23–29 (1990).
7. See, e.g., Ronald Dworkin, *Freedom's Law: The Moral Reading of the American Constitution* (1996).
8. See Bruce Ackerman, *We the People: Foundations* ch. 4 (1991).
9. See Chapter 9.
10. For an excellent overview of the degree of openness to doctrinal change implied by various approaches to constitutional interpretation, see Walter F. Murphy, James E. Fleming, and Sotirios A. Barber, *American Constitutional Interpretation* (2d ed. 1995).
11. Lessig was particularly clear about the originalist premises of his interesting and influential elaboration of the changed-circumstances idea. See Lawrence Lessig, "Fidelity in Translation," 71 *Tex. L. Rev.* 1165, 1267–68 (1993).

12. "[N]otions of an 'evolutionary' or 'living Constitution'" were common in "Classical and Progressive" legal thought. Robert W. Gordon, "The Struggle over the Past," 44 *Cleve. St. L. Rev.* 123, 131 (1996). The phrase was already an object of disparagement for the present Chief Justice thirty years ago (see William H. Rehnquist, "The Notion of a Living Constitution," 54 *Tex. L. Rev.* 693 (1976)), but others have continued to give this idea eloquent expression: "The document that the plurality construes today is unfamiliar to me. It is not the living charter that I have taken to be our Constitution; it is instead a stagnant, archaic, hidebound document steeped in the prejudices and superstitions of a time long past." Michael H. v. Gerald D., 491 U.S. 110, 141 (1989) (Brennan, J., dissenting).

13. Richard A. Posner, "Pragmatism Versus Purposivism in First Amendment Analysis," 54 *Stan. L. Rev.* 737, 739 (2002) ("The point is not that the judge has some kind of moral or even political duty to abide by constitutional or statutory text, or by precedent; that would be formalism. It is merely that continuity and restraint in the performance of the judicial function are important social goods, and any judge proposing to innovate must consider not only the benefits of the innovation but also the costs in injury to those goods.").

14. Ackerman, *Foundations,* chs. 2–3.

15. The objection against "selective" use of historical understandings is the nub of every objection to "law-office history." See, e.g., Martin S. Flaherty, "History 'Lite' in Modern American Constitutionalism," 95 *Colum. L. Rev.* 523, 554 (1995); Alfred H. Kelly, "Clio and the Court: An Illicit Love Affair," 1965 *Sup. Ct. Rev.* 119, 122 n.113. For an exception tending to prove the rule, see Michael W. Dorf, "Integrating Normative and Descriptive Constitutional Theory: The Case of Original Meaning," 85 *Geo. L.J.* 1765, 1810 (1997) (arguing for a "heroic originalism" that would reject original meanings "too distasteful to count").

16. Morton J. Horwitz, "Republican Origins of Constitutionalism," in Paul Finkelman and Stephen E. Gottlieb, eds., *Toward a Usable Past: Liberty under State Constitutions* 148 (1991).

17. H. Jefferson Powell, *The Constitution and the Attorneys General* 9 (1999). Powell demonstrates this point at length and in detail in his superb *A Community Built on Words: The Constitution in History and Politics* (2002).

18. On all the propositions in this paragraph, see infra Chapter 2.

19. The term "suspect class" is notoriously under-defined, but this much has always been clear: (1) blacks are the paradigmatic instance of such a class; and (2) laws singling out blacks adversely are the paradigmatic instance of state action requiring "strict scrutiny." See infra Chapter 2.

20. See Frank Michelman, "Law's Republic," 97 *Yale L.J.* 1493, 1522–23 (1988); Laurence Tribe, "The Curvature of Constitutional Space: What Lawyers Can Learn from Modern Physics," 103 *Harv. L. Rev.* 1, 5 (1989). For a claim that constitutional law is undergoing a "paradigm shift" today,

see Seth Waxman, *Defending Congress,* 79 N.C. L. Rev. 1073, 1075–76 (2001). For a thoughtful discussion of this claim, see Christopher H. Schroeder, "Causes of the Recent Turn in Constitutional Interpretation," 51 *Duke L.J.* 307, 312–15 (2001). For a systematic attempt to bring Kuhnian ideas to bear on American constitutional law, see Robert Justin Lipkin, *Constitutional Revolutions: Pragmatism and the Role of Judicial Review in American Constitutionalism* (2000).

21. See, e.g., H. L. A. Hart, *The Concept of Law* ch. 7 (1961). As Hart famously put it, judges interpreting a "no vehicles in the park" rule could be expected to look to "the paradigm, clear cases (the motor-car, the bus, the motorcycle)." Id. at 125.

2. Rights

1. For a discussion of the Supreme Court's treatment of free speech prior to 1917, see Michael Gibson, "The Supreme Court and Freedom of Expression from 1791 to 1917," 55 *Fordham L. Rev.* 263 (1986). For a more general treatment of pre-1917 free-speech jurisprudence, see David Rabban, "The First Amendment in Its Forgotten Years," 90 *Yale L.J.* (1981).

2. See Roth v. United States, 354 U.S. 476, 482 (1957) ("The guaranties of freedom of expression in effect in 10 of the 14 States which by 1792 had ratified the Constitution, gave no absolute protection for every utterance. Thirteen of the 14 States provided for the prosecution of libel, and all of those States made either blasphemy or profanity, or both, statutory crimes. As early as 1712, Massachusetts made it criminal to publish 'any filthy, obscene, or profane song, pamphlet, libel or mock sermon' in imitation or mimicking of religious services. Acts and Laws of the Province of Mass. Bay, c. CV, § 8 (1712), Mass. Bay Colony Charters & Laws 399 (1814).").

3. This would certainly be true on the view that the freedom of speech protected only against prior restraints. See infra note 14.

4. I use "freedom of speech" throughout as a shorthand for the freedoms of speech and of the press.

5. See, e.g., Lovell v. Griffin, 303 U.S. 444 (1938) (striking down ordinance prohibiting distribution of handbooks, advertising, or literature within the city of Griffin, Georgia without obtaining written permission from City Manager); Near v. Minnesota, 283 U.S. 697, 718 (1931) ("The fact that for approximately one hundred and fifty years there has been an almost entire absence of attempts to impose previous restraints upon publication relating to the malfeasance of public officers is significant of the deep-seated conviction that such restraints would violate constitutional rights."). Narrowly tailored licensing schemes for allegedly obscene films and for narrow categories of commercial speech, such as securities registration statements, have been allowed. See, e.g., Freedman v. Maryland, 380 U.S. 51 (1965) (films); cf. Lowe v. SEC, 472 U.S. 181 (1985) (discussing circumstances in which SEC can demand that investment advice be issued only by persons licensed to do so).

6. New York Times Co. v. United States, 403 U.S. 713 (1971).

7. Nebraska Press Ass'n v. Stuart, 427 U.S. 539, 559 (1976); Doe v. Dep't of Pub. Safety *ex rel.* Lee, 271 F.3d 38, 50 (2d Cir. 2001).

8. Carroll v. President & Comm'rs of Princess Anne, 393 U.S. 175, 181 & n.5 (1968).

9. For an attempt at such an explanation, see Thomas Emerson, "The Doctrine of Prior Restraint," 20 *L. & Contemp. Probs.* 648, 656–60 (1955). But see R. Barnett, "The Puzzle of Prior Restraint," 29 *Stan. L. Rev.* 539 (1977); Vincent Blasi, "Toward a Theory of Prior Restraint: The Central Linkage," 66 *Minn. L. Rev.* 11 (1981); Paul Freund, "The Supreme Court and Civil Liberties," 4 *Vand. L. Rev.* 533, 533–39 (1951); William T. Mayton, "Toward a Theory of First Amendment Process: Injunctions of Speech, Subsequent Punishment, and the Costs of the Prior Restraint Doctrine," 67 *Cornell L. Rev.* 245 (1982).

10. Carroll v. President & Comm'rs of Princess Anne, 393 U.S. 175, 181 and n.5 (1968).

11. See, e.g., Cohen v. California, 403 U.S.15 (1971) (reversing conviction of individual arrested for wearing a jacket in a courthouse bearing the words, "Fuck the Draft"). The *Cohen* Court did not mention the fact that "all of [the 14 States which by 1792 had ratified the Constitution] made either blasphemy or profanity, or both, statutory crimes." Roth v. United States, 354 U.S. 476, 482 (1957).

12. J. Stephen, *A History of the Criminal Law of England* 350 (1834).

13. See, e.g., Vincent Blasi, "The Checking Value in First Amendment Theory," 1977 *Am. B. Found. Res. J.* 521; V. Buranelli, ed., *The Trial of Peter Zenger* (1957).

14. See, e.g., L. Levy, *Emergence of a Free Press* xii–xv (1985). As late as 1907, the Supreme Court seemed to endorse this position, see Patterson v. Colorado, 205 U.S. 454, 462 (1907), which can be traced to Blackstone. See 4 W. Blackstone, Commentaries on the Laws of England * 151–52 (1769) ("The liberty of the press [consists] in laying no previous restraints upon publications, and not in freedom from censure for criminal matter when published."). For contrary views, see Zechariah Chafee, Jr., *Free Speech in the United States* 21 (1941) (arguing, in part on the basis of the prominence of the Zenger trial, that the First Amendment was originally intended to "wipe out the common law of sedition and make further prosecutions for criticism of the government . . . forever impossible"); William T. Mayton, "Seditious Libel and the Lost Guarantee of a Freedom of Expression," 84 *Colum. L. Rev.* 91 (1984).

15. The Act prohibited the publication of, inter alia, any "scandalous" or "malicious" "writings against the government of the United States . . . or the President . . . with intent to . . . bring them [into] contempt or disrepute." Act of July 14, 1798, 1 Stat. 596.

16. See, e.g., Levy, *Emergence,* at 282.

17. See, e.g., Lee v. Weisman, 505 U.S. 577, 626 (1992) (Souter, J., concurring) (observing that Sedition Act would be "patently unconstitutional by modern standards").

18. Rossignol v. Voorhaar, 316 F.3d 516, 525 (4th Cir. 2003).

19. Abrams v. United States, 250 U.S. 616, 630–31 (1919) (Holmes, J., dissenting).

20. 376 U.S. 254 (1964).

21. 376 U.S. at 273–74.

22. This was Kalven's point in his well-known article published immediately afterward. See Harry Kalven, Jr., "The New York Times Case: A Note on 'The Central Meaning of the First Amendment,'" 1964 *Sup. Ct. Rev.* 191, 194.

23. *E.g.*, Lovell v. Griffin, 303 U.S. 444 (1938).

24. Id. at 452.

25. West Virginia State Bd. of Educ. v. Barnette, 319 U.S. 624, 642 (1943).

26. Id.

27. See, e.g., State v. Mockus, 120 Me. 84, 113 A. 39 (1921) (upholding conviction for blasphemy); Commonwealth v. Kneeland, 37 Mass. (20 Pick.) 206 (1838) (Shaw, C.J.) (same); People v. Ruggles, 8 Johns. 290 (N.Y. 1811) (Kent, C.J.) (same).

28. In *Ruggles,* the defendant had called Jesus a "bastard" and his mother a "whore." Chief Justice Kent wrote: "Nor are we bound, by any expressions in the constitution, as some have strangely supposed, either not to punish at all, or to punish indiscriminately the like attacks upon the religion of *Mahomet* or of the grand *Lama;* and for this plain reason, that the case assumes that we are a christian people, and the morality of the country is deeply ingrafted upon christianity, and not upon the doctrines or worship of those impostors." 8 Johns. at 295.

29. In *Kneeland,* the defendant was convicted after declaring that he did not believe in God and viewed the story of Christ as a "fable." 37 Mass. (20 Pick.) at 216.

30. See, e.g., State v. West, 263 A.2d 602, 605 (Md. App. 1970).

31. A pivotal Supreme Court decision was Cantwell v. Connecticut, 310 U.S. 296 (1940) (overturning conviction of a man who vituperatively criticized religion in general and Catholicism in particular). For an excellent short discussion of the history of blasphemy law and its changing position in American constitutional thought, see Robert C. Post, "Cultural Heterogeneity and Law: Pornography, Blasphemy, and the First Amendment," 76 *Calif. L. Rev.* 297, 306–24 (1988).

32. Compare, e.g., Everson v. Board of Educ., 330 U.S. 1, 11 (1947) (holding that the First Amendment was intended to strip government of "all power to tax, to support, or otherwise to assist any or all religions"), with Gerard V. Bradley, *Church-State Relationships in America* 19–68 (1987) (arguing that First Amendment, as originally understood, was not intended to prohibit nonpreferential assistance to religion).

33. See, e.g., Robert L. Cord, *Separation of Church and State* 6–7 (1982); Thomas J. Curry, *The First Freedoms: Church and State in America to the Passage of the First Amendment* 194–95, 197–98 (1986).

34. Massachusetts guaranteed the equal "protection of the laws" to "every denomination *of Christians*," and required elected officers to declare themselves Christian. See Mass. Const. of 1780, pt. 1, art. III, cl. 5 (emphasis added); pt. 2, ch. VI, art. I. New Hampshire and Vermont limited elected office to Protestants. See N.H. Const. of 1784, pt. 2; Vt. Const. of 1786, ch. II, §XII. Even in Rhode Island, Jews were denied full citizenship. I. B. Richman, Rhode Island: A Study in Separatism 180–81 (1905). In Connecticut, irregular church attendance cost 3 shillings; in Massachusetts, 10 shillings. Bradley, *Church-State Relationships*, 21. Needless to say, such laws were not limited to New England. For a brief survey, see Morton Borden, *Jews, Turks, and Infidels* 11–20 (1984).

35. See, e.g., Mass. Const. of 1780, Decl. of Rights, art. III, cl. 1; Curry, *First Freedoms*, 166–84.

36. Edward S. Corwin, "The Supreme Court as National School Board," 14 *L. & Contemp. Probs.* 3, 12 (1949); see Akhil Reed Amar, "The Bill of Rights as a Constitution," 100 *Yale. L.J.* 1131, 1157 (1991); Jed Rubenfeld, "Anti-disestablishmentarianism: Why RFRA Really Was Unconstitutional," 95 *Mich. L. Rev.* 2347, 2351–57 (1997).

37. Madison's original draft of the establishment clause, presented to Congress on June 8, 1789, read, "nor shall any national religion be established." 1 *Annals of Congress* 434 (Joseph Gales, ed., 1834). When the New Englanders protested against the later wording of the clause, "no religion shall be established by law," Madison proposed reinserting the word "national." Id. at 731. Fearing that Congress might yet have power to undo, or disestablish, state ecclesiastical arrangements, the New Englanders were still "not satisfied," id., but all agreed that Congress was to be prohibited from establishing a national church.

38. See, e.g., Cord, *Separation of Church and State,* chs. 1–2.

39. Everson v. Board of Educ., 330 U.S. 1, 15–16 (1947).

40. See supra note 36.

41. See, e.g., Torcaso v. Watkins, 367 U.S. 488 (1961) (striking down Maryland law requiring that holders of office declare their belief in God). In fact, the *Everson* Court's rejection of laws that "aid all religions," *Everson*, 330 U.S. at 16, probably was inconsistent with original No-Application Understandings.

42. See, e.g., Steven D. Smith, *Foreordained Failure: The Quest for a Constitutional Principle of Religious Freedom* ch. 1 (1995) (criticizing incorporation); Kurt T. Lash, "The Second Adoption of the Establishment Clause," 27 *Ariz. St. L.J.* 1085 (1995) (defending it); William K. Lietzau, "Rediscovering the Establishment Clause: Federalism and the Rollback of Incorporation," 39 *DePaul L. Rev.* 1191 (1990).

43. See, e.g., Smith, *Foreordained Failure,* 5 (criticizing *Everson* as a "dismal historical performance"); Daniel O. Conkle, "Toward a General Theory of the Establishment Clause," 82 *Nw. U. L. Rev.* 1113, 1142 (1988) ("The language of the fourteenth amendment, coupled with the federalistic motivation for the establishment clause, make it exceedingly difficult to argue that the framers and ratifiers of the fourteenth amendment intended to incorporate the establishment clause for application against the states.").
44. Lietzau, "Rediscovering the Establishment Clause," 1210.
45. The most important works to see on this point include Akhil Reed Amar, *The Constitution and Criminal Procedure* (1997) and Telford Taylor, *Two Studies in Constitutional Interpretation* (1969).
46. In Wilkes v. Wood, 98 Eng. Rep. 489 (C.P. 1763), 19 How. State Trials 981, Lord Camden, then Chief Justice Charles Pratt, ruled illegal the searches and seizures aimed at John Wilkes, a member of the House of Commons and a critic of the government. See Amar, *The Constitution and Criminal Procedure,* 1–45 (discussing centrality of the Wilkes affair to the enactment and historical understanding of the Fourth Amendment).
47. United States v Bridges, 344 F3d 1010, 1014 (9th Cir. 2003) (quoting Payton v. New York, 445 U.S. 573, 583 (1980) (footnote omitted)).
48. Stanford v. Texas, 379 U.S. 476, 480 (1965).
49. See Amar, *The Constitution and Criminal Procedure,* 69–71.
50. Kyllo v. United States, 533 U.S. 27 (2001).
51. Illinois v. Krull, 480 U.S. 340, 354 (1987) ("a person subject to a statute authorizing searches without a warrant or probable cause may bring an action seeking a declaration that the statute is unconstitutional and an injunction barring its implementation").
52. See, e.g., Amar, *The Constitution and Criminal Procedure,* 71 ("The Court has simply misread the original linkage between the Fourth Amendment's two different commands.").
53. Eben Moglen, "Taking the Fifth: Reconsidering the Origins of the Constitutional Privilege Against Self-Incrimination," 92 *Mich. L. Rev.* 1086, 1122 (1994).
54. See, e.g., David Dolinko, "Is There a Rationale for the Privilege against Self-Incrimination?," 33 *U.C.L.A. L. Rev.* 1063, 1064 (1986) (describing privilege as "historical relic"); Henry J. Friendly, "The Fifth Amendment Tomorrow: The Case for Constitutional Change," 37 *U. Cin. L. Rev.* 671 (1968); McCormick, "Some Problems and Developments in the Admissibility of Confessions," 24 *Tex. L. Rev.* 239 (1946).
55. John H. Langbein, "The Historical Origins of the Privilege Against Self-Incrimination at Common Law," 92 *Mich. L. Rev.* 1047, 1074 (1994).
56. See Leonard W. Levy, *Origins of the Fifth Amendment: The Right against Self-Incrimination* 131–35 (1968); 8 John H. Wigmore, *Evidence in Trials at Common Law* at 267–89 (John T. McNaughton ed., rev. 1961).

57. See, e.g., Pennsylvania v. Muniz, 496 U.S. 582, 596 (1990) (internal citations omitted); Michigan v. Tucker, 417 U.S. 433, 440 (1974); Murphy v. Waterfront Comm'n, 378 U.S. 52, 55 (1964).

58. See *Tucker,* 417 U.S. at 440; Escobedo v. Illinois, 378 U.S. 478, 485 (1964); Miranda v. Arizona, 384 U.S. 436, 461 (1966).

59. Long after the Star Chamber was abolished, defendants were expected to speak, and in a variety of ways systematically compelled to speak, at their own trials, a practice present in America up to, during, and after the revolutionary period, without any sense that the privilege was violated thereby. See John H. Langbein, "Historical Origins," 1048–73; Moglen, "Taking the Fifth," 1090–1110, 1123–28.

60. See, e.g., Langbein, "Historical Origins," at 1080 n.142; Moglen, "Taking the Fifth," at 1100 ("the solution was not to examine them under oath").

61. See *Escobedo,* 378 U.S. at 485; *Miranda,* 384 U.S. at 461.

62. 260 U.S. 393 (1922) (Holmes, J.).

63. See Mugler v. Kansas, 123 U.S. 623 (1887). But cf., e.g., Wynehammer v. People, 13 N.Y. 378 (1856) (striking down liquor prohibition statute) (when "a law annihilates the value of property, [the] owner is deprived of it [within] the spirit of a constitutional provision intended expressly to shield private rights from the exercise of arbitrary power").

64. See, e.g., Andrus v. Allard, 444 U.S. 51 (1979) (upholding prohibition of the sale of bald and golden eagle feathers). Any new statute prohibiting the use or sale of a new narcotic has the same effect.

65. Miller v. Schoene, 276 U.S. 272 (1928).

66. The case was complicated by the fact that the owners of the overlying property (but not necessarily the tenants) had bought the land from the mining company, and had agreed in their deeds to waive any claims they might otherwise have had for damage resulting from the mining below. But even given this provision in the deeds, or indeed perhaps because of it, the state statute could still clearly have been deemed necessary to prevent serious harms—for example, injury to children inhabiting dwellings that might have collapsed due to mining below.

67. Lucas v. South Carolina Coastal Council, 505 U.S. 1003 (1992).

68. Loretto v. Teleprompter Manhattan CATV Corp., 458 U.S. 419 (1982).

69. Kaiser Aetna v. United States, 444 U.S. 164 (1979).

70. Compare *Loretto* with Penn Central Transp. Co. v. New York City, 438 U.S. 104 (1978).

71. See Euclid v. Ambler Realty Co., 272 U.S. 365 (1926) (upholding zoning ordinance despite owner's claim that his property decreased in value from $10,000 per acre to $2,500).

72. Compare United States v. Pewee Coal Co., 341 U.S. 114 (1951) (mine taken over during wartime; compensation due) with United States v. Central Eureka Mining Co., 357 U.S. 155 (1958) (mine shut during wartime; no compensation due).

73. See, e.g., Gardner v. Trustees of the Village of Newburgh, 2 Johns. Ch. 162, 166–67 (N.Y. Ch. 1816) (Kent, Ch.); Fred Bosselman et al., *The Taking Issue* 106–21 (1973); William Michael Treanor, Note, "The Origins and Original Significance of the Just Compensation Clause of the Fifth Amendment," 94 *Yale L.J.* 694, 695–97 (1985). On military impressments, see 1 Henry St. George Tucker, Blackstone's Commentaries app. at 305–06 (Philadelphia, Birch & Small 1803) (stating that the compensation clause "was probably intended to restrain the arbitrary and oppressive mode of obtaining supplies for the army and other public uses, by impressment, as was too frequently practiced during the revolutionary war, without any compensation whatever").

74. See 1 Julius L. Sackman, *Nichols' The Law of Eminent Domain* §§1.1–1.44 (rev. 3d ed. 2003).

75. Theodore Sedgwick, *A Treatise on the Rules Which Govern the Interpretation and Application of Statutory and Constitutional Law* 501, 524 (New York, Voorhies 1857); Stephen A. Siegel, "Understanding the Nineteenth Century Contract Clause: The Role of the Property-Privilege Distinction and 'Takings' Clause Jurisprudence," 60 *S. Cal. L. Rev.* 1, 76–81 (1986).

76. John F. Hart, "Land Use Law in the Early Republic and the Original Meaning of the Takings Clause," 94 *N.W.U. L. Rev.* 1099, 1148 (2000).

77. See id. at 1156 (criticizing *Pennsylvania Coal*).

78. "By each power [taxation and eminent domain] a forced contribution is exacted for the public good, but taxation exacts the money which is supposed to represent the contributor's share of the public expense, while the eminent domain exacts specific property for specific uses." Carman F. Randolph, *The Law of Eminent Domain in the United States* 22–23 (1894). Another treatise distinguished the police power from eminent domain in similar terms: "Under the one, the public welfare is promoted by regulating and restricting the use and enjoyment of property by the owner; under the other, the public welfare is promoted by taking the property from the owner and appropriating it to some particular use." John Lewis, *A Treatise on Eminent Domain* §6, at 15–16 (1st ed. 1888).

79. See, e.g., Penn Central Transp. Co. v. New York City, 438 U.S. 104, 127 (1978); Park Ave. Tower Assocs. v. City of New York, 746 F.2d 135, 138 n.1 (2d Cir. 1984).

80. For further discussion of the concept of a using, the history of the compensation clause, and the case law, see Jed Rubenfeld, "Usings," 102 *Yale L.J.* 1077 (1993).

81. The very first such case was probably Pumpelly v. Green Bay Co., 80 U.S. (13 Wall.) 166 (1871), finding a taking when plaintiff's land was flooded in connection with a state canal project. As Justice Harlan later pointed out, Pumpelly's "property was, in effect, *required to be devoted to the use of the public,* and, consequently, he was entitled to compensation." Mugler v. Kansas, 123 U.S. 623, 668 (1887) (emphasis added). See also, e.g., Portsmouth Harbor

Land & Hotel Co. v. United States, 231 U.S. 530 (1922) (plaintiff's land used as firing range by army); U.S. v. Causby, 328 U.S. 256, 262 & n.7, 264 (1946) (airplanes landing at neighboring airport descending directly over plaintiff's land; Court found that state was "*using* a part of [plaintiff's property] for the flight of its planes"; "as much of an appropriation of the *use* of the land as a more conventional entry upon it") (emphasis added); U.S. v. Pewee Coal Co., 341 U.S 114 (1951) (plaintiff's mines temporarily run for benefit of U.S. army); Kaiser Aetna v. United States, 444 U.S. 164, 180 (1979) (plaintiff's marina opened up for public access; "if the Government wishes to make [plaintiff's property] into a public aquatic park," it must "pay[] just compensation"); Lucas v. South Carolina Coastal Council, 505 U.S. 1003 (1992) (development of plaintiff's beachfront property enjoined so that property could serve as a storm-protection barrier and wildlife habitat; Court noted that when land must by law be left in natural, undeveloped condition, there is a "heightened risk that private property is being *pressed into some form of public service*") (emphasis added).

82. In addition to the cases just cited, see also, for example, Justice Brennan's highly influential opinion in San Diego Gas & Electric Co. v. City of San Diego, 450 U.S. 621, 652 n.18 (1981) (Brennan, J., dissenting) (purpose of city ordinance "was 'to have the property remain . . . in its natural state so open space and scenic vistas may be preserved. In this sense the property *is being used by the public.*'") (emphasis added); Hoeck v. City of Portland, 57 F.3d 781, 788 (9th Cir. 1995) (demolition of abandoned building did not require compensation) ("to state a cause of action for inverse condemnation, Hoeck must show that his property was taken *for a public use*") (emphasis added); Finks v. United States, 395 F.2d 999, 1004 (Ct. Cl.) (seven-judge panel) ("The vehicles were impounded and plaintiffs were deprived of their possession. . . . There was no . . . *use* of the vehicles" however, and hence no compensation was required) (emphasis added); Customer Co. v. City of Sacramento, 10 Cal. 4th 368, 399 (1995) (Kennard, J., concurring) (denying compensation for damage caused to store by police after fugitive sought to hide inside store) ("Because in this case Sacramento *did not put the property it destroyed to any affirmative, productive use,* Customer Co. has no right to compensation under the just compensation clause.") (emphasis added).

83. United States v. Caltex (Philippines), Inc., 344 U.S. 149, 153, 155 (1952).

84. See Rubenfeld, "Usings,"1151–58.

85. Robert Bork, *The Tempting of America: The Political Seduction of the Law,* 75 (1990). Despite occasional efforts to rebut this proposition, see, e.g., Michael W. McConnell, "Originalism and the Desegregation Decisions," 81 *Va. L. Rev.* 947 (1995), the evidence for it is fairly overwhelming. For good, brief discussions, see Herbert Hovenkamp, "The Cultural Crises of the Fuller Court," 104 *Yale L.J.* 2309, 2337–43 (1995) (reviewing Owen M. Fiss, *Troubled Beginnings of the Modern State, 1888–1910* (1993)); Michael J.

Klarman, "*Brown,* Originalism, and Constitutional Theory: A Response to Professor McConnell," 81 *Va. L. Rev.* 1881 (1995).

86. See, e.g., Eric Foner, *Reconstruction: America's Unfinished Revolution, 1863–1877,* at 198–201 (1988); 1 Walter L. Fleming, ed., *Documentary History of Reconstruction* 279–81 (1906).

87. See, e.g., Foner, *Reconstruction,* 198–205, 257; Akhil Reed Amar, "The Supreme Court, 1999 Term—Foreword: The Document and the Doctrine," 114 *Harv. L. Rev.* 26, 64–65 (2000); Michael Kent Curtis, "Resurrecting the Privileges or Immunities Clause and Revising the Slaughter-House Cases without Exhuming Lochner: Individual Rights and the Fourteenth Amendment," 38 *B.C. L. Rev.* 1, 30–34 (1996).

88. 83 U.S. (16 Wall.) 36 (1873).

89. See id. at 70 (reasoning that the privileges or immunities clause of the Fourteenth Amendment made no substantial change in preexisting law). "Unique among constitutional provisions, the privileges and immunities clause of the Fourteenth Amendment enjoys the distinction of having been rendered a 'practical nullity' by a single decision of the Supreme Court." Edward S. Corwin, *The Constitution of the United States of America* 965 (1953).

90. *Slaughter-House,* 83 U.S. (16 Wall.) at 70.

91. 100 U.S. 303 (1879).

92. See Ex parte Virginia, 100 U.S. 339, 364, 367 (1879) (Field, J., dissenting). Justice Field's dissent in *Ex parte Virginia* served also as the dissenting opinion in *Strauder.*

93. Id. at 308.

94. Id. at 307–08.

95. Id.

96. Brown v. Board of Educ., 347 U.S. 483, 494 (1954).

97. See, e.g., Michael J. Klarman, "An Interpretive History of Modern Equal Protection," 90 *Mich. L. Rev.* 213, 232–33 (1991).

98. See, e.g., Gayle v. Browder, 352 U.S. 903 (1956) (buses); Holmes v. City of Atlanta, 350 U.S. 879 (1955) (public golf courses); Mayor of Baltimore v. Dawson, 350 U.S. 877 (1955) (public beaches and bathhouses); Loving v. Virginia, 388 U.S. 1 (1967) (miscegenation).

99. 163 U.S. 537, 559 (1896) (Harlan, J., dissenting).

100. Id. at 560 (Harlan, J., dissenting).

101. And this is, essentially, what Black said about *Brown* fifty years ago. See Charles L. Black, Jr., "The Lawfulness of the Segregation Decisions," 69 *Yale L.J.* 421, 427 (1960).

102. *Plessy,* 163 U.S. at 544–45 (emphasis added).

103. Id.

3. Powers

1. U.S. Const. Art I, § 8, cl. 1.

2. See, e.g., Alexander Hamilton, "Report on Manufactures" (1791), reprinted in 2 Philip B. Kurland & Ralph Lerner, eds., *The Founders' Constitution* 446–47 (1987).

3. Charles Warren, *The Making of the Constitution* 475 (1928).

4. Thomas Jefferson, *Writings* 529 (State of the Union Address of 1806) (Merrill D. Peterson, ed., 1984). Twenty years later, Jefferson still took the same view. See id. at 1509–12 (letter to William Branch Giles, Dec. 26, 1825).

5. 30 Annals of Cong., Senate, 14th Cong., 2nd Sess. 211, 212 (1817).

6. U.S. Const. Art I, § 8, cl. 17.

7. 3 Annals of Cong., House of Representatives, 2nd Cong., 2nd Sess. 386–87 (1792). Madison continued: "In fact, the meaning of the general terms in question must either be sought in the subsequent enumeration which limits and details them, or they convert the Government from one limited, as hitherto supposed, to the enumerated powers, into a Government without any limits at all." Id.

8. See McCulloch v. Maryland, 17 U.S. (4 Wheat.) 316 (1819). A much later case supporting the narrow view of the spending power is Kansas v. Colorado, 206 U.S. 46, 91–92 (1907). Contemporary originalists occasionally still endorse this view. See, e.g., Raoul Berger, *Federalism: The Founders' Design* 100–19 (1987). There is, however, some early evidence of congressional spending outside the national regulatory power, as then understood. See, e.g., 1 *Corwin on the Constitution* 253–70 (R. Loss, ed., 1981); David Currie, "The Constitution in the Supreme Court: The New Deal, 1931–1940," 54 *U. Chi. L. Rev.* 504, 535–36 n.148 (1987).

9. U.S. v. Gerlach Live Stock Co., 339 U.S. 725, 738 (1950). The Court noted: "It was not until 1936 that this Court . . . declared for the first time . . . that, in conferring power upon Congress to tax 'to pay the Debts and provide for the common Defence and general Welfare of the United States,' the Constitution delegates a power separate and distinct from those later enumerated, . . . and that Congress has a substantive power to tax and appropriate for the general welfare, limited only by the requirement that it shall be exercised for the common benefit as distinguished from some mere local purpose." Id. See also, e.g., Ivanhoe Irrigation Dist. v. McCracken, 357 U.S. 275 (1958).

10. Helvering v. Davis, 301 U.S. 619, 640–41 (1937). See South Dakota v. Dole, 483 U.S. 203, 208 n.2 (1987) (observing that the "level of deference to the congressional decision is such that the Court has . . . questioned whether 'general welfare' is a judicially enforceable [concept]").

11. The leading case is *Dole,* which upheld a federal law conditioning 5 percent of federal highway monies on states' adopting a specified drinking age. For commentary critical of *Dole,* see, for example, Lynn A. Baker, "Conditional Federal Spending after *Lopez,*" 95 *Colum. L. Rev.* 1911 (1995); Mitchell N. Berman, "Coercion Without Baselines: Unconstitutional Conditions in Three Dimensions," 90 *Geo. L.J.* 1, 30–42 (2001).

12. *Dole,* 483 U.S. at 211–12 ("in some circumstances the financial inducement offered by Congress might be so coercive as to pass the point at which 'pressure turns into compulsion'") (quoting Steward Machine Co. v. Davis, 301 U.S. 548, 590 [1937]).
13. Nevada v. Skinner, 884 F.2d 445, 449–50 (9th Cir. 1989).
14. Id. at 450.
15. See, e.g., Bork, *Tempting of America,* 56–57; Albert S. Abel, "The Commerce Clause in the Constitutional Convention and in Contemporary Comment," 25 *Minn. L. Rev.* 432, 442–64 (1941); Raoul Berger, "Judicial Manipulation of the Commerce Clause," 74 *Tex. L. Rev.* 695 (1996); Richard A. Epstein, "The Proper Scope of the Commerce Power," 73 *Va. L. Rev.* 1387, 1451 (1987); see also, e.g., United States v. Lopez, 514 U.S. 549, 584–602 (1995) (Thomas, J., concurring). But cf. Grant S. Nelson & Robert J. Pushaw, Jr., "Rethinking the Commerce Clause: Applying First Principles to Uphold Federal Commercial Regulations but Preserve State Control Over Social Issues," 85 *Iowa L. Rev.* 1, 40–41 (1999) (arguing the contrary).
16. The expansive effect-in-the-aggregate test was most clearly stated in Wickard v. Fillburn, 317 U.S. 111 (1942) (upholding federal regulation limiting amount of wheat farmers could harvest on their land). The Court's recent commerce clause cases have not overturned the *Wickard* test with respect to "economic activity" such as manufacturing, agriculture, or labor relations. See, e.g., United States v. Lopez, 514 U.S. 549, 559–60 (1995).
17. See United States v. Coombs, 37 U.S. (12 Pet.) 72, 78 (1838) (Story, J.); see also Willson v. Black Bird Creek Marsh Co., 27 U.S. (2 Pet.) 245, 251–52 (1829) (Marshall, C.J.); Gibbons v. Ogden, 22 U.S. (9 Wheat.) 1, 197 (1824) (Marshall, C.J.) ("All America understands, and has uniformly understood, the word 'commerce,' to comprehend navigation. It was so understood, and must have been so understood, when the constitution was framed. The power over commerce, including navigation, was one of the primary objects for which the people of America adopted their government. . . ."). Regulation of navigable waters was the primary concern of Madison's resolutions for the Annapolis Convention and of the 1785 compact between Maryland and Virginia, both of which were understood to be important precursors of the commerce power written into the Constitution. See, e.g., 2 John Randolph Tucker, *The Constitution of the United States* 520–21 (Henry St. George Tucker, ed., Chicago, Callaghan & Co. 1899).
18. E. Paramalee Prentice and John G. Egan, *The Commerce Clause of the Federal Constitution* 109 (Chicago, Callaghan & Co. 1898) (quoting Pennsylvania v. Wheeling & Belmont Bridge Co., 59 U.S. [18 How.] 421, 442 [1856] [McLean, J., dissenting]).
19. 317 U.S. 111 (1942).
20. Id. at 127–28.

21. See, e.g., Bork, *The Tempting of America*, at 56–57; Berger, "Judicial Manipulation"; Epstein, "The Proper Scope of the Commerce Clause," at 1451.

22. Epstein, "The Proper Scope of the Commerce Clause," at 1451.

23. Carter v. Carter Coal Co., 298 U.S. 238, 317 (1936) (separate opinion of
Hughes, C.J.). Despite this formulation, Hughes still held, in 1936, that the
Court would "amend the Constitution" if it declared that Congress had "the
power to regulate industries within the State, and the relations of employers
and employees in those industries." Id. So long as it was empirically possible
for labor relations in in-state industries to threaten injury to interstate
commerce, it is hard to see how Hughes could maintain both positions at the
same time; he did not do so for long. See NLRB v. Jones & Laughlin Steel
Corp., 301 U.S. 1, 43 (1937) (upholding National Labor Relations Act)
(Hughes, C.J.) (due to industry's effects on commerce, "we have no doubt
that Congress has constitutional authority" to regulate employer/employee
relations).

24. See, e.g., Kidd v. Pearson, 128 U.S. 1 (1888) (upholding Iowa law prohibiting
manufacture of spirits as applied to Iowa distillery that sold its entire output
in other states). The Court in *Kidd,* clearly presupposing that Congress's
commerce power was exclusive, upheld Iowa's law on the ground that
manufacturing was not commerce. Indeed the exclusive-power premise was
central to the Court's reasoning: "If it be held that the term [commerce]
includes the regulation of all . . . productive industries," the "result would be
that Congress would be invested, to the exclusion of the States, with the
power to regulate, not only manufactures, but also agriculture, horticulture,
stock raising, domestic fisheries, mining—in short, every branch of human
industry. . . . The power being vested in Congress and denied to the States,
it would follow as an inevitable result that the duty would devolve on Congress
to regulate all these delicate, multiform and vital interests—interests which in
their nature are and must be, local in all details of their successful management."
Id. at 21.

25. See, e.g., Schecter Poultry Corp. v. United States, 295 U.S. 495, 529 (1935)
("Congress is not permitted to abdicate or to transfer to others the essential
legislative function with which it is thus vested.").

26. One famous example is the *Steel Seizure Case,* in which the Supreme Court
struck down President Truman's attempt, in the face of strike threats, to seize
control of most of the nation's steel mills in order to keep them in operation
during the Korean War. See Youngstown Sheet & Tube Co. v. Sawyer, 343
U.S. 579 (1952). The Court's opinion repeatedly used the rhetoric of strict
separationism. The President's action, the Court found, were an exercise of
the "lawmaking power." "In the framework of our Constitution, the President's
power to see that the laws are faithfully executed refutes the idea that he is to
be a lawmaker." "Congress has not . . . lost its exclusive constitutional authority to make laws." Id. at 587–88. Another decision employing the logic of
strict separationism is *I.N.S. v. Chadha,* 462 U.S. 919 (1983).

27. E.g., Mistretta v. United States, 488 U.S. 361 (1989).

28. E.g., Morrison v. Olson, 487 U.S. 654 (1988).

29. See, e.g., Steven G. Calabresi & Saikrishna B. Prakash, "The President's Power to Execute the Laws," 104 *Yale L.J.* 541 (1994); John C. Yoo, "Interpretation and the False Sirens of Delegation," 90 *Cal. L. Rev.* 1305, 1325-28 (2002).

30. See The Prize Cases, 67 U.S. (2 Black) 635, 668 (1863) ("By the Constitution, Congress alone has the power to declare a national or foreign war."); see, e.g., Doe v. Bush, 323 F.3d 133 (1st Cir. 2003) (refusing to hold that President could not make war on Iraq where there was no "clear evidence of congressional abandonment of the authority to declare war to the President").

31. See *Youngstown*, 343 U.S. at 634-36 (Jackson, J., concurring).

32. Geoffrey R. Stone et al., eds., *Constitutional Law* ch. IX(A), at 1629 (3rd ed. 1996).

33. 290 U.S. 398 (1934).

34. The *Blaisdell* dissenters emphatically criticized the majority for violating the foundational Application Understanding. Id. at 454–65 (Sutherland, J., dissenting). It is possible to argue that the debt-relief law at issue in *Blaisdell* was different in relevant respects from the laws at which the contracts clause was directed. For an insightful statement of this argument, see Paul Brest et al., *Processes of Constitutional Decisionmaking* 425 (4th ed. 2000). If this argument is correct, then *Blaisdell* was not a counterexample after all.

4. The Paradox of Commitment

1. Edward F. McClennen and Scott Shapiro, "Rule-Guided Behaviour," in 3 *The New Palgrave Dictionary of Economics and the Law* 363, 366 (1998).

2. Michael E. Bratman, *Faces of Intention* 41 (1999).

3. Thomas Hobbes, *Leviathan* pt. 2, ch. 26, at 204 (1965) [1651] ("Nor is it possible, for any person to be bound to himself; because he that can bind, can release; and therefore, he that is bound to himself only, is not bound.").

4. Bratman, *Faces of Intention*, 41.

5. Alexander Bickel, *The Least Dangerous Branch* 16–17 (1962).

6. Id. at 17.

7. Jean-Jacques Rousseau, "On the Social Contract or Essay About the Form of the Republic" (Geneva Manuscript) (1762), in *On the Social Contract* 157, 168 (R. D. Masters, ed., and J. R. Masters, trans., 1978).

8. Jean-Jacques Rousseau, "Sur le Gouvernement de Pologne" (1782), in 3 *Œuvres Complètes* 981 (B. Gagnebin and M. Raymond, eds., 1964).

9. Letter to James Madison (Sept. 6, 1789), in 15 Thomas Jefferson, *The Papers of Thomas Jefferson* 392, 395, 396 (Julian Boyd, ed., 1958).

10. See, e.g., Robert Dahl, *Democracy and Its Critics* 50 (1989) (the "true consent" of the governed "would have to be continuous—of the living now subject to the laws, not of the dead who enacted them"); Jürgen Habermas, *Between*

Facts and Norms: Contributions to a Discourse Theory of Democracy 264–66, 274–79 (W. Rehg, trans., 1996) ("insist[ing]" on a process of "democratic will-formation" that "does not draw its legitimating force from . . . *prior*" expressions of democratic will); Jon Elster, "Introduction," in Jon Elster and Rune Slagstad, eds., *Constitutionalism and Democracy* 1 (1993) (defining democracy as "simple majority rule, based on the principle of 'One person, one vote.'").

11. Franck offers a characteristically incisive statement. See Thomas M. Franck, "The Democratic Entitlement," 29 *U. Rich. L. Rev.* 1, 3 (1994) ("Judicial governance is not democratic, and no nation on earth has more government by judiciary than the United States: with India and Germany, their constitutions patterned after ours, the distant runners-up. Bear in mind, too, that our nation's elected federal legislature and elected presidency are confined, in their exercise of political power, by a constitution that we, contemporary Americans, neither wrote nor are able to amend except with great difficulty."). See also, e.g., Jeremy Waldron, *Law and Disagreement* 255–62 (1999) (arguing against American-style constitutionalism because of its conflict with the imperatives of [present-oriented] democracy).

12. Christopher G. Tiedeman, *The Unwritten Constitution of the United States: A Philosophical Inquiry into the Fundamentals of American Constitutional Law* 144 (1890).

13. James Bradley Thayer, "The Origin and Scope of the American Doctrine of Constitutional Law," 7 *Harv. L. Rev.* 129, 144 (1893).

14. See Bickel, *The Least Dangerous Branch,* 16–17, 24.

15. See John Hart Ely, *Democracy and Distrust: A Theory of Judicial Review* (1980).

16. Jon Elster, *Ulysses and the Sirens: Studies in Rationality and Irrationality* 93–103 (rev. ed. 1984).

17. Jon Elster, *Ulysses Unbound: Studies in Rationality, Precommitment, and Restraints* (2000).

18. Id. at ix.

19. Id. at 93.

20. Id.

21. Id. at 170.

22. Id.

23. Id. at 96 (original emphasis).

24. Id.

25. Id. (original emphasis).

26. Id. at 168.

27. Scott J. Shapiro, "The Difference That Rules Make," in Brian Bix, ed., *Analyzing Law: New Essays in Legal Theory* 33–62 (1998).

28. See Michael E. Bratman, *Intentions, Plans, and Practical Reason* 48 (1987).

29. Id. at 107.

30. See Edward F. McClennen, *Rationality and Dynamic Choice* 14, 211–13 (1990).
31. See George Ainslie, *Picoeconomics: The Strategic Interaction of Successive Motivational States within the Person* 156–62 (1992).
32. See Frank Döring, "Le 'Choix résolu' selon McClennen," in 1 J.-P. Dupuy and P. Livet, eds., *Les Limites de la Rationalité* 111, 113 (1997); see also Bratman, *Intentions, Plans, and Practical Reason*, 48.
33. Ainslie, *Picoeconomics*, 161.
34. Laurence H. Tribe, "Ways Not to Think About Plastic Trees: New Foundations for Environmental Law," 83 *Yale L.J.* 1315, 1326–27 (1974) (footnotes omitted).
35. For my elaboration of these ideas, see Jed Rubenfeld, *Freedom and Time: A Theory of Constitutional Self-Government,* chs. 1, 5–7 (2001).
36. See Patrick O. Gudridge, "Public Privacy (Self-Government)," 53 *U. Miami L. Rev.* 395, 408 (1999) ("Self-government . . . may be understood to be especially concerned with the decisions that individuals make that they regard as exclusionary or preemptive—that, once made, they know will substitute and thus block decisionmaking anew.").
37. Immanuel Kant, *Grounding for the Metaphysics of Morals* * 459–60 (J. W. Ellington, trans., 1981) [1785].
38. Id. at * 461–63.
39. See Rubenfeld, *Freedom and Time,* chs. 2, 9.
40. But I do make an argument of logical untenability in id., ch. 4, which shows that the idea of democracy as government by the present voice of the governed necessarily, if covertly, presupposes government by some kind of constitutional text laid down in the past.

5. Commitments and Original Understandings

1. I say that understandings "at most" reflect intentions because of the following well-known possibility. An agent may understand that certain consequences will follow from his actions without intending those consequences. I understand that my late-night drinking will cause me headaches in the morning, but that is not my intention in drinking. This means: producing headaches forms no part of my reasons for drinking. If we accept this standard way of thinking about intentions and unintended but foreseeable consequences, an original No-Application Understanding would *not* be an intention if it was not a reason for the agent in deciding to commit himself. But the No-Application Understanding *would* count as an intention if, for example, the agent would not have made the commitment but for the No-Application Understanding. In this sense, a No-Application Understanding can be an intention, but even so, it is still not a commitment.
2. In fact, Section 2 of the Fourteenth Amendment, which was designed to deter racial discrimination in the suffrage, targeted such discrimination only

in the case of men, not women. See U.S. Const. Amend. XIV, §2 (attaching constitutional penalties to a state's denial of the suffrage to any of its adult "male" inhabitants).

3. It may be objected that the unintended obligations I undertake by having a child are not entailed by a commitment I have made, but rather by the duties I owe to the child. But the argument just made would have worked just as well if I had chosen as an example a commitment involving no duties running to any other specific person, such as a commitment to becoming a great pianist. I might have made such a commitment utterly misunderstanding how much time this would take. Upon discovering the truth, I might repudiate or modify my commitment (perhaps I will downgrade my commitment, to becoming a not-horrible pianist). If, however, I mean to honor the commitment, then my interpretive task is to decide in good faith what the commitment requires, whatever my original understanding may have been.

4. Note that this approach differs sharply from Dworkin's distinction between "semantic" intentions and "application" or "concrete" or "expectation" intentions, which he equates with his distinction between "concepts" and "conceptions." See Ronald Dworkin, *A Matter of Principle* 48 et seq. (1985). Dworkin's argument is that interpretation always properly aims at vindicating the "concepts" used in legal language (and thus is bound to adhere to the original "semantic intentions"), not the particular "conceptions" of those concepts that the framers may themselves have entertained (and thus is not bound to adhere to their "inten[ded] applications"). But Dworkin has never adequately come to grips with the simple fact that individuals have (and have good reason for having) a number of different rule-making practices at their disposal, in some of which their original, specific, intended applications count for a great deal more than they do in others. A and B may have had no shared "conception" of deception, but in the story just told, they did have a set of original, specific intentions—presumably of both the Application and No-Application variety, to use my terms—and they engaged in a particular normative practice (called "contract") that privileges these original, specific understandings in interpreting the concept of "deception" in their agreement.

6. Two Objections

1. For an argument of this kind against paradigm-case theories of meaning in general, see Michael Moore, "A Natural Law Theory of Interpretation," 58 *S. Cal. L. Rev.* 277, 298–99 (1985). For an argument of this kind against my account of constitutional interpretation in particular, see Christopher L. Eisgruber, "Theories of Constitutional Self-government: Dimensions of Democracy," 71 *Fordham L. Rev.* 1723 (2003).

2. See, e.g., Bork, *Tempting of America,* 82 (conceding that *Brown* contradicted the original understanding of the Fourteenth Amendment, but arguing that *Brown* can nonetheless be rested on original meaning, because "equality and

segregation were mutually inconsistent," and that as a result, courts must "choose equality," the original "purpose" behind the clause).

3. See, e.g., Lawrence Lessig, "Fidelity in Translation," 71 *Tex. L. Rev.* 1165 (1993). Discussing statutory interpretation, Archibald Cox distinguished between general-purpose and specific-intention originalism over fifty years ago. See Archibald Cox, "Judge Learned Hand and the Interpretation of Statutes," 60 *Harv. L. Rev.* 370, 370–71 (1947) (distinguishing between a statute's "purpose" or the "general aim or policy which pervades it," and "the specific, particularized application[s] which the statute was 'intended' to be given").

4. For an argument of this form, see Ronald Dworkin, *Freedom's Law* 291–92 (1996).

5. See, e.g., Michael Bratman, *Faces of Intention: Selected Essays on Intention and Agency* (1999); Christopher Kutz, *Complicity: Ethics and Law for a Collective Age,* ch. 3–5 (2000); Philip Pettit, *A Theory of Freedom,* ch. 5 (2001); John Searle, "Collective Intentions and Actions," in Philip R. Cohen et al., eds., *Intentions in Communication* 405 (1990); David J. Velleman, "How to Share an Intention," 57 *Phil. & Phenomenological Res.* 29 (1997).

7. Has Constitutional Law Stopped Making Sense?

1. Adarand Constructors, Inc. v. Peña, 515 U.S. 200 (1995).

2. See, e.g., Bush v. Vera, 517 U.S. 952, 993 (1996); Miller v. Johnson, 515 U.S. 900 (1995). In light of these decisions, lower courts also struck down many majority-minority voting districts. See Moon v. Meadows, 952 F. Supp. 1141, 1150 (E.D. Va. 1997) (three-judge panel) (Virginia); Hays v. Louisiana, 936 F. Supp. 360, 371 (W.D. La. 1996) (three-judge panel) (per curiam) (Louisiana); Johnson v. Mortham, 926 F. Supp. 1460, 1495 (N.D. Fla. 1996) (three-judge panel) (per curiam) (Florida); Johnson v. Miller, 922 F. Supp. 1552, 1553 (S.D. Ga. 1995) (three-judge panel) (Georgia).

3. Rice v. Cayetano, 528 U.S. 495, 517 (2000).

4. See United States v. Lopez, 514 U.S. 549 (1995).

5. Gerald Gunther and Kathleen M. Sullivan, *Constitutional Law* 142 (13th ed. 1997). Actually, the honor seems to belong to New York v. United States, 505 U.S. 144 (1992), which struck down a federal statute that ordered state governments in certain circumstances to pass nuclear waste cleanup laws, in part on the ground that the commerce clause "authorizes Congress to regulate interstate commerce," not to "regulate state governments' regulation of interstate commerce." Id. at 166.

6. United States v. Morrison, 529 U.S. 598 (2000).

7. See, e.g., Bd. of Trs. of the Univ. of Ala. v. Garrett, 531 U.S. 356 (2001); Kimel v. Fla. Bd. of Regents, 528 U.S. 62, 72–73 (2000); Coll. Sav. Bank v. Fla. Prepaid Postsecondary Educ. Expense Bd., 527 U.S. 666, 675–87 (1999); Seminole Tribe v. Florida, 517 U.S. 44, 54–55 (1996).

8. Employment Division, Department of Human Resources of Oregon v. Smith, 494 U.S. 872 (1990).

9. Boy Scouts of America v. Dale, 530 U.S. 640 (2000).

10. For a range of viewpoints, see *Bush v. Gore: The Question of Legitimacy* (Bruce Ackerman, ed. 2002).

11. See Grutter v. Bollinger, 123 S. Ct. 2325 (2003); Gratz v. Bollinger, 123 S. Ct. 2411 (2003).

12. Lawrence v. Texas, 123 S. Ct. 2472 (2003).

13. See Rasul v. Bush, 124 S. Ct. 2686 (2004); Hamdi v. Rumsfeld, 124 S. Ct. 2633 (2004).

14. E.g., Carter v. Carter Coal Co., 298 U.S. 238 (1936); A.L.A. Schechter Poultry Corp. v. United States, 295 U.S. 495 (1935); R.R. Ret. Bd. v. Alton R.R. Co., 295 U.S. 330 (1935).

15. *Schechter Poultry,* 295 U.S. at 549.

16. *Carter Coal,* 298 U.S. at 295–96.

17. E.g., Adkins v. Children's Hosp., 261 U.S. 525 (1923) (minimum wage); Coppage v. Kansas, 236 U.S. 1 (1915) (right to join union); Lochner v. New York, 198 U.S. 45 (1905) (maximum hours).

18. Berea College v. Kentucky, 211 U.S. 45 (1908). To be sure, *Berea College* involved a corporation, and there are indications in the Court's opinion that if the state law had directly prohibited individuals from mixing racially in schools, the case might have come out differently.

19. Lochner v. New York, 198 U.S. 45, 63–64 (1905).

20. Id. at 64.

21. Coppage v. Kansas, 236 U.S. 1, 17–18 (1915).

22. 268 U.S. 295 (1925).

8. The Anti-Anti-Discrimination Agenda

1. See, e.g., Scott Fruehwald, "If Men Were Angels: The New Judicial Activism in Theory and Practice," 83 *Marq. L. Rev.* 435 (1999); Donald H. Zeigler, "The New Activist Court," 45 *Am. U. L. Rev.* 1367 (1996); Larry D. Kramer, "No Surprise. It's an Activist Court," *N.Y. Times,* Dec. 12, 2000, A33.

2. See, e.g., Steven G. Calabresi, "Textualism and the Countermajoritarian Difficulty," 66 *Geo. Wash. L. Rev.* 1373, 1389–90 (1998).

3. Larry D. Kramer, "The Supreme Court, 2000 Term—Foreword: We the Court," 115 *Harv. L. Rev.* 4, 14 (2001).

4. Id.

5. Editorial, "A Court Running in the Wrong Direction," *N.Y. Times,* July 6, 1995, A20.

6. Jeremy Waldron, "A Question of Judgment," *Times Literary Supplement,* Sept. 28, 2001, 17.

7. John O. McGinnis, "Reviving Tocqueville's America: The Rehnquist Court's Jurisprudence of Social Discovery," 90 *Cal. L. Rev.* 485, 491 (2002).

8. See Richard H. Fallon, Jr., "The 'Conservative' Paths of the Rehnquist Court's Federalism Decisions," 69 *U. Chi. L. Rev.* 429, 432, 462–63 (2002) (observing that since 1991, "the Court has decided thirty-five preemption cases and found state statutes or causes of action to be preempted, either in whole or in part, in twenty-two. Indeed, during the Court's 1999 and 2000 Terms, the Court decided seven preemption cases and held that federal law preempted state law in all of them," and that these results conflict with the putative federalism associated with the current Court). The Court has, however, at least ostensibly limited the scope of ERISA preemption.

9. Bd. of Trs. of the Univ. of Ala. v. Garrett, 531 U.S. 356 (2001).

10. Id. at 362.

11. See, e.g., Kimel v. Fla. Bd. of Regents, 528 U.S. 62, 72–73 (2000); Coll. Sav. Bank v. Fla. Prepaid Postsecondary Educ. Expense Bd., 527 U.S. 666, 675–87 (1999); Seminole Tribe v. Florida, 517 U.S. 44, 54–55 (1996).

12. U.S. Const. amend. XI ("The Judicial power of the United States shall not be construed to extend to any suit . . . commenced . . . against one of the United States by Citizens of another State, or by . . . Subjects of any Foreign State.").

13. U.S. Const. amend. XIV, §5; see Fitzpatrick v. Bitzer, 427 U.S. 445, 456 (1976) (holding that the Eleventh Amendment is "necessarily limited by the enforcement provisions of §5 of the Fourteenth Amendment").

14. *Garrett,* 531 U.S. at 360.

15. See id. at 374 n.9 ("Title I of the ADA still prescribes standards applicable to the States.").

16. *Garrett* came to the Supreme Court on appeal from an order granting summary judgment to the University of Alabama, id. at 362–63, so Garrett's allegations were assumed true for purposes of the decision.

17. See, e.g., Larkins v. Dep't of Mental Health & Mental Retardation, 806 So. 2d 358 (Ala. 2001) (dismissing on sovereign immunity grounds an employee's suit against a state employer alleging violations of a federal statute).

18. 5 U.S. (1 Cranch) 137 (1803).

19. Id. at 166.

20. Id.

21. Id. at 163.

22. See *Garrett,* 531 U.S. at 374 n.9.

23. U.S. Const. amend. XI.

24. See, e.g., Vicki C. Jackson, "*Coeur d'Alene,* Federal Courts and the Supremacy of Federal Law: The Competing Paradigms of Chief Justices Marshall and Rehnquist," 15 *Const. Comment.* 301 (1998).

25. See Garrett v. Bd. of Trs. of the Univ. of Ala., 989 F. Supp. 1409 (N.D. Ala. 1998), rev'd, 193 F.3d 1214 (11th Cir. 1999), rev'd, 531 U.S. 356 (2001).

26. The Fifth Amendment provides that no person "shall . . . be subject for the same offence to be twice put in jeopardy of life or limb." U.S. Const. amend. V.

27. Alden v. Maine, 527 U.S. 706 (1999).

28. *Garrett,* 531 U.S. at 363.

29. Whitney v. California, 274 U.S. 357, 373 (1927) (Brandeis, J., concurring) ("Despite arguments to the contrary which had seemed to me persuasive, it is settled that the due process clause of the Fourteenth Amendment applies to matters of substantive law as well as to matters of procedure.").

30. See Kimel v. Fla. Bd. of Regents, 528 U.S. 62, 72–73 (2000); Coll. Sav. Bank v. Fla. Prepaid Postsecondary Educ. Expense Bd., 527 U.S. 666, 669–70 (1999); Seminole Tribe v. Florida, 517 U.S. 44, 54 (1996); Hans v. Louisiana, 134 U.S. 1, 15 (1890). In favor of these cases, it is sometimes said that it would be absurd to take the Eleventh Amendment at its word. If the Eleventh Amendment is taken literally, it is said, federal judicial review would be barred for suits against a state brought by *out-of-state* citizens ("citizens of another state") but allowed for suits against a state brought by *in-state* citizens. This result would be topsy-turvy; federal jurisdiction has always been favored in cases involving out-of-state parties, to protect against potential bias in the home state's courts. According to this argument, it is better to read "same" as "other" than to permit the absurd result that a citizen of Georgia can sue Georgia in a federal court, while out-of-state citizens, the parties with a much better claim to the protections of federal jurisdiction, cannot.

But as many have pointed out, this argument dissolves if one recognizes that the Eleventh Amendment is directed only at the federal courts' *diversity* jurisdiction—that is, cases in which federal jurisdiction is based solely on the fact that the plaintiff comes from a state different from the defendant—as opposed to the federal courts' jurisdiction over cases *arising under federal law.* On this view, in-state and out-of-state plaintiffs trying to sue a state receive identical treatment. Neither would have recourse to the federal courts if the suit arose under state law, while both could sue in federal court if the suit arose under federal law. True, the diversity-jurisdiction-only reading of the Eleventh also produces strains on its text, but the strain is far less than reading "other" to include "same," and, more significantly, the diversity-only reading is fully supported by the Eleventh Amendment's foundational paradigm case. Chisholm v. Georgia, 2 U.S. (2 Dall.) 171 (1793), involved an out-of-state citizen suing Georgia for simple payment of a debt (not a federal law cause of action). The Supreme Court upheld jurisdiction based on the diversity of the parties. The case led to a national outcry (Georgia threatened to hang anyone who sought to enforce the Court's judgment) and the passage of the Eleventh Amendment, the core Application Understanding of which was that it would overturn *Chisholm.*

31. See Alden v. Maine, 527 U.S. 706, 713 (1999) ("We have, as a result, sometimes referred to the States' immunity from suit as 'Eleventh Amendment immunity.' The phrase is convenient shorthand but something of a misnomer,

for the sovereign immunity of the States neither derives from nor is limited by the terms of the Eleventh Amendment.").

32. Boy Scouts of Am. v. Dale, 530 U.S. 640 (2000).

33. Id. at 646.

34. Jed Rubenfeld, "The First Amendment's Purpose," 53 *Stan. L. Rev.* 767 (2001).

35. A. L. A. Schechter Poultry Corp. v. United States, 295 U.S. 495, 549 (1935).

36. United States v. Morrison, 529 U.S. 598 (2000).

37. Id. at 613.

38. Id. at 619, 627.

39. See, e.g., City of Boerne v. Flores, 521 U.S. 507, 519 (1997) ("Congress' power under § 5 . . . extends only to 'enforc[ing]' the provisions of the Fourteenth Amendment. . . . Legislation which alters the meaning of the Free Exercise Clause cannot be said to be enforcing the Clause. Congress does not enforce a constitutional right by changing what the right is. It has been given the power 'to enforce,' not the power to determine what constitutes a constitutional violation.").

40. See id.

41. *Morrison,* 529 U.S. at 626–27.

42. See id. at 613–14.

43. See id. at 617–18 ("We . . . reject the argument that Congress may regulate noneconomic, violent criminal conduct based solely on that conduct's aggregate effect on interstate commerce. The Constitution requires a distinction between what is truly national and what is truly local.").

44. Compare U.S. Const. amend. XIV, §5 ("The Congress shall have power to enforce, by appropriate legislation, the provisions of this article."), with id. amend. XIII, §2 ("Congress shall have power to enforce this article by appropriate legislation.").

45. See, e.g., Jones v. Alfred H. Mayer Co., 392 U.S. 409 (1968) (upholding a federal statute prohibiting racial discrimination in housing).

46. See *Morrison,* 529 U.S. at 621 (relying on and reaffirming the *Civil Rights Cases,* 109 U.S. 3 [1883]).

47. 163 U.S. 537 (1896) (finding that the Fourteenth Amendment protects only "civil" equality, not "social" equality, and therefore upholding a state statute segregating railway cars by race).

48. 83 U.S. (16 Wall.) 130 (1872) (upholding a state statute barring women from the practice of law).

49. 83 U.S. (16 Wall.) 36 (1872) (rendering the Privileges or Immunities Clause of the Fourteenth Amendment essentially a nullity).

50. See, e.g., NAACP v. Alabama, 357 U.S. 449 (1958). A supporter of both the Court's federalism decisions and the *Boy Scouts* case might try to explain this discrepancy by claiming that the Constitution's *federalism provisions* should be read narrowly, while the Constitution's *individual rights provisions* should

be read expansively. Whatever may be said in theory for this idea, it cannot make sense of the Court's new case law. As already discussed, the Court's "Eleventh Amendment" cases show that the five Justices who make up the present majority are prepared to shift into expansive, textually cavalier mode—to the point of creating wholly unwritten constitutional law—in interpreting the Constitution's federalism provisions too. See also, e.g., Printz v. United States, 521 U.S. 898, 905 (1997) (striking down a federal statute on federalism grounds even though "there is no constitutional text speaking to this precise question").

51. See *Boy Scouts*, 530 U.S. at 658–59.

52. See Lochner v. New York, 198 U.S. 45 (1905).

53. See, e.g., id. at 72 (Harlan, J., dissenting) ("What the precise facts are it may be difficult to say. It is enough for the determination of this case, and it is enough for this court to know, that the question is one about which there is room for debate and for an honest difference of opinion."); id. at 75 (Holmes, J., dissenting) ("This case is decided upon an economic theory which a large part of the country does not entertain. If it were a question whether I agreed with that theory, I should desire to study it further and long before making up my mind. But I do not conceive that to be my duty, because I strongly believe that my agreement or disagreement has nothing to do with the right of a majority to embody their opinions in law.").

54. Bd. of Trs. of the Univ. of Ala. v. Garrett, 531 U.S. 356, 368 (2001); see also, e.g., Kimel v. Fla. Bd. of Regents, 528 U.S. 62, 91 (2000) (holding that a federal age-discrimination statute exceeded the reach of the Fourteenth Amendment prohibition of discrimination). The more recent *Hibbs* decision may portend a slight retreat from these cases, but in principle *Hibbs* is consistent, because in *Hibbs* the Court concluded that Congress acted to protect against a form of discrimination that the Constitution itself prohibited. See Nevada Department of Human Resources v. Hibbs, 123 S. Ct. 1972 (2003).

55. City of Boerne v. Flores, 521 U.S. 507, 519 (1997). Needless to say, not all of the Court's new "federalism" cases have involved antidiscrimination statutes. See, e.g., Fla. Prepaid Postsecondary Educ. Expense Bd. v. Coll. Sav. Bank, 527 U.S. 627 (1999) (addressing an intellectual property statute as applied to infringement by a state actor); Printz v. United States, 521 U.S. 898 (1997) (involving a gun sale background-check statute); United States v. Lopez, 514 U.S. 549 (1995) (involving a "gun-free school zones" statute).

56. *Boy Scouts*, 530 U.S. at 640.

57. Id. at 648.

58. Id. at 655.

59. Id. at 640–41.

60. Id. at 653.

61. Cf. Hyman v. City of Louisville, 132 F. Supp. 2d 528, 543–44 (W.D. Ky. 2001) (rejecting a *Boy Scouts*–like claim under "the Freedom of Association Clause of the First Amendment" where the plaintiff's "medical practice [was]

simply a commercial enterprise" and where the doctor asserting a right not to hire homosexuals "made no allegation that . . . his practice ha[d] as a purpose the exercise of his religion"), vacated on other grounds, 53 Fed. Appx. 740 (6th Cir. 2002).

62. See, e.g., German Alliance Ins. Co. v. Lewis, 233 U.S. 389, 406 (1914).

63. See, e.g., Bd. of Trs. of the Univ. of Ala. v. Garrett, 531 U.S. 356 (2001).

64. Kimel v. Fla. Bd. of Regents, 528 U.S. 62 (2000).

65. See, e.g., United States v. Morrison, 529 U.S. 598 (2000).

66. See cases cited at notes 2–3 of Chapter 7.

67. Employment Division, Department of Human Resources of Oregon v. Smith, 494 U.S. 872 (1990).

68. See pp. 168–70.

69. See Wards Cove Packing Co. v. Atonio, 490 U.S. 642 (1989). The five Justices were Rehnquist, Scalia, Kennedy, O'Connor, and White.

70. Pub. L. No. 102–166, 105(a), 105 Stat. 1071, 1074–75 (1991) (codified at 42 U.S.C. 2000e-2(k) (2002).

71. See Alexander v. Sandoval, 532 U.S. 275 (2001). The five Justices were, as in so many of the cases discussed here, Rehnquist, Scalia, Kennedy, O'Connor, and Thomas.

72. See Nguyen v. INS, 533 U.S. 53 (2001). The *Nguyen* Court upheld the statute on the ground that it "serves 'important governmental objectives and that the discriminatory means employed' are 'substantially related to the achievement of those objectives.'" Id. at 60. Previous cases had emphasized that state actors had to prove "at least" this much and had, moreover, held that the state's showing had to be "exceedingly persuasive," a test that the *Nguyen* majority seemed, if not in form, at least in content, to abandon. Cf. *Nguyen*, 533 U.S. at 74 (O'Connor, J., dissenting); United States v. Virginia, 518 U.S. 515, 533 (1996); J.E.B. v. Alabama ex rel. T.B., 511 U.S. 127, 137 n.6 (1994) (emphasizing that sex-based classification had *at least* to satisfy the important-governmental-interest test, and leaving open the question of whether a more stringent test might be appropriate).

73. Alfred Avins, "Freedom of Choice in Personal Service Occupations: Thirteenth Amendment Limitations on Antidiscrimination Legislation," 49 *Cornell L.Q.* 228 (1964) (arguing that state legislation requiring nondiscrimination in public accommodations and various personal service occupations violates the Thirteenth Amendment by forcing one person to serve another); Roger Pilon, "Discrimination, Affirmative Action, and Freedom: Sorting out the Issues," 45 *Am. U.L. Rev.* 775, 778–79 (1996) (arguing that the Thirteenth and Fourteenth Amendments guarantee a right to discriminate).

74. See, e.g., Roberts v. U.S. Jaycees, 468 U.S. 609 (1984) (distinguishing "freedom of intimate association" from "first amendment right of association").

75. See, e.g., NAACP v. Button, 371 U.S. 415 (1963); NAACP v. Alabama, 357 U.S. 449 (1958).

76. Price v. Evergreen Cemetery Co., 357 P.2d 702, 704–05 (Wash. 1959) (Mallery, J., concurring). The case struck down a local antidiscrimination law that banned the practice of excluding blacks from "whites-only" cemeteries. For other judicial examples, see Boman v. Birmingham Transit Co., 292 F.2d 4, 14 (5th Cir. 1961) (Cameron, J., dissenting) ("The question is not whether appellants are entitled to seats which are equally as safe, comfortable, desirable and adequate as those [of] white people . . .; it is whether appellants are entitled to sit in the same seat or mingle in close contact with passengers who may not choose to have such association. Freedom of association and choice of social companions have always been considered among the things which cannot be enforced by judicial decree."); Wood v. Vaughan, 209 F. Supp. 106, 114 (W.D. Va. 1962) ("'It has not yet been held to be unconstitutional for individuals to prefer to associate with others of their own race, class, background or, if you like, prejudices.' And there is no reason for the City to interfere with such free-dom of choice—or freedom of association as it is sometimes called."); Bell v. Hill, 74 S.W.2d 113 (Tex. 1934) (upholding right of Democratic Party to ex-clude blacks on "freedom of association" grounds).
77. 163 U.S. 537, 544 (1896).
78. Herbert Wechsler, "Toward Neutral Principles of Constitutional Law," 73 *Harv. L. Rev.* 1, 34 (1959).
79. 517 U.S. 620, 624 (1996).
80. 518 U.S. 515 (1996).
81. Grutter v. Bollinger, 123 S. Ct. 2325 (2003). At the same time, the Court simultaneously struck down a different affirmative action program. Gratz v. Bollinger, 123 S. Ct. 2411 (2003).
82. Nevada Department of Human Resources v. Hibbs, 123 S. Ct. 1972 (2003).
83. Lawrence v. Texas, 123 S. Ct. 2472 (2003).

9. Sex, Commerce, Preferences

1. Lawrence v. Texas, 123 S. Ct. 2472 (2003) (overruling Bowers v. Hardwick, 478 U.S. 186 [1986]).
2. *Lawrence*, 123 S. Ct. at 2481–82 (quoting Planned Parenthood of Southeastern Pa. v. Casey, 505 U.S. 833, 851 [1992]).
3. Id. at 2842, 2844.
4. See Jed Rubenfeld, "The Right of Privacy," 102 *Harv. L. Rev.* 737 (1989). The argument here is not that anti-abortion laws constitute "involuntary servitude" and therefore violate the Thirteenth Amendment. It is that the Fourteenth Amendment's foundational paradigm case—the black codes—can be compellingly interpreted as an effort to recreate through legal means the conditions of slavery without actually, formally enslaving anyone. Because one of the defining elements of female slavery involved forcing women to bear chil-dren against their will, a constitutional rule prohibiting anti-abortion laws, which have the same effect, can claim a powerful paradigm-case justification.

5. See Richard A. Epstein, *Forbidden Grounds: The Case Against Employment Discrimination Laws* (1992).

6. The "economic in nature" test was first suggested in United States v. Lopez, 514 U.S. 549, 559–60 (1995), and then cemented in United States v. Morrison, 529 U.S. 598, 610, 613 (2000).

7. Notwithstanding the *Lopez* rule, the current Court would still presumably uphold a law prohibiting the construction of a bridge obstructing navigable waters, on the ground that Congress was exercising its power to regulate the "channels" of interstate commerce. See *Lopez*, 514 U.S. at 558. The point remains, however, that the *Lopez* rule misunderstands the circumstances in which an effect on commerce justifies an exercise of Congress's commerce clause power. For more on the *Lopez* Court's exemption of laws regulating the "channels" of interstate commerce, see note 10 below.

8. Carter v. Carter Coal Co., 298 U.S. 238, 317 (1936) (separate opinion of Hughes, C.J.).

9. United States v. Darby, 312 U.S. 100, 115 (1941).

10. The absence of a purpose-based limitation explains what is wrong with both the *Lopez* Court's economic-activity rule and its exemption for laws regulating the "use of the channels" of interstate commerce (see note 7 above). A federal statute forbidding persons who enter into homosexual marriages from using the nation's waterways or airways would be a regulation of the use of the channels of interstate commerce, but it would not be a valid exercise of the commerce power—precisely because its purpose was not genuinely commercial or economic in nature. Conversely, a law prohibiting the noncommercial transport of dangerous explosives on airplanes *is* a valid exercise of the commerce power—not because the activity regulated is "economic in nature," and not because a "channel" of commerce is involved, but because the law is clearly aimed at preventing harm to interstate commerce (not to mention people and things in interstate commerce). Neither the "economic nature" of the activity regulated, nor the use of a "channel" of commerce, is properly dispositive.

11. See Grutter v. Bollinger, 123 S. Ct. 2325 (2003); Gratz v. Bollinger, 123 S. Ct. 2411 (2003). The *Grutter* program was of the all-things-considered variety, in which race counted as just one factor among all others, with no formal weighting of factors, and no official quotas were in place.

12. For a brief summary, see Jed Rubenfeld, "Affirmative Action," 107 *Yale L.J.* 427, 430–32 (1997).

13. See, e.g., City of Cleburne v. Cleburne Living Center, 473 U.S. 432 (1985).

14. 426 U.S. 229 (1976).

15. For more on this argument, see Jed Rubenfeld, *Freedom and Time* ch. 11 (2001); Rubenfeld, "Affirmative Action."

Index

Abortion, 187–188, 230n4

Abrams v. U.S., Justice Holmes's dissent in, 24, 209n19

Abusive language, and freedom of speech, 28

Academic schools of interpretation, 10

Ackerman, Bruce, 10–11

Adams, John, 23

Adams, John Quincy, on public works appropriations, 51

Adarand Constructors, Inc. v. Peña, 145, 177, 195–201, 202

Affirmative action, 195–201; equal protection clause and, 126–127; strict scrutiny standard of review, 8, 145, 195, 198, 206n19; University of Michigan admissions procedures, 147, 177, 195; and welfare compared, 198

Age Discrimination Act, 177, 178

Ainslie, George, 87

Amar, Akhil, 32

American Socialist Party, 152

Americans with Disabilities Act (ADA), 162–163, 172, 177

Anti-abortion laws, 187–188, 230n4

Anti-anti-capitalist agenda, 149, 153–154, 156, 176

Anti-anti-discrimination agenda, 149, 158, 175–183; corrosive ideas espoused by, 175, 176; disparate impact discrimination, 178–179; expressive association, 177; Fourteenth Amendment, section 5, 178; sex discrimination, 179

Anticapitalist legislation, 176

Antidiscrimination laws: constitutionality of, 146; court hostility toward, 161;

freedom of association and, 6; as laws regulating association, 174; suspect classes in, 16

Anti-inferiorization principle, 43, 44

Anti-instrumentalization account of privacy, 188

Antitrust statutes, 156

Application Understandings: as commitments, 114–119, 124, 130; deception vs. omission, 116–118; defined, 14, 115; in freedom of speech, 23; mistaken, 125–127; mistakes of fact, 127–130; mistakes of interpretation, 130–134; and No-Application understandings compared, 115; precedent-based, 16; subsequent paradigm cases, 120–124

Atheistic speech, 28

Authority, self-given, 83

Authorizing text, 49

Autonomy, 91

Bargained-for exchange, 111, 113

Barnette case. See *West Virginia State Board of Education v. Barnette*

Bickel, Alexander, 12, 77–78, 96

Bigamy laws, 188

Black codes: abolishment of, 15, 16, 41, 42, 44, 119, 153; constitutionality of, 131; *Plessy v. Ferguson*, 45–46; rationale for, 41, 196

Blasphemy: *Cantwell v. Connecticut*, 209n31; *People v. Ruggles*, 28, 209n28; prohibition of, 14, 208n11; protection of, 21, 28–29

Bootstrapping, 85

Bork, Robert, 126, 222n2

233

works appropriations, 51; separation of powers, 56–67; spending, 50–53; treaties, 62–63; vesting clauses, 60–61

Consensual conduct, protection of, 186, 188, 190

Consequentialist-pragmatic style of constitutional interpretation, 12

Constitution: as a bargain among individuated actors, 112–113; as a contract among the states, 113; framers' death, 135–141; moral reading of, 7, 19, 44, 126–127, 134; constitutional commitments, 76–79, 97, 137

Constitutional democracy, paradox of commitments in, 76–79, 96–98

Constitutional law: ahistorical views of, 17, 19; Application and No-Application Understandings of, 14–15, 64; changed-circumstances approach to, 9, 10, 205n11; conformance of to interpretive structure, 12–15; constitutional moments theory, 10–11; as contract making, 111–112; descriptive perspective on, 18; doctrinal changes, recent, 145–146; evaluative perspective on, 19; framers' death and, 135–141; general-purpose interpretation of, 126; historical meaning in, 13; holistic approach to interpretation of, 65; interpretive styles, 12; level-of-generality objections, 126; paradigm cases, shifts in, 15–18, 206n20; paradox of commitments in, 76–79; politics and, 4; radical reinterpretation of, 3–4; as recovery of lost meaning, 8; rhetoric of restoration, 8–9; rulings based on nonexistent clauses, 6; self-governance and, 97–98, 112; standard interpretation of, 4; statutory interpretation, protocols for, 4–5; theoretical perspective on, 19

Constitutional moments, 10–11

Constitutional powers, 48

Constitutional rights, 48

Constitutional theory, purpose of, 201–202

Contempt, 34

Contraband laws, 36

Contract, 110

Contracts clause, 67–68

Coordination benefits, 92

Core applications, 14, 15, 119

Coronado Coal Co. v. United Mine Workers, 156

Counter-majoritarian difficulty, 77, 96

Creeping redistributive bias, 155

Criminal procedure: *Miranda* rights, reading of, 32, 34; searches and seizures, 20, 32–33

"Cruel trilemma," Fifth Amendment, 15, 34

Debs, Eugene, 152

Decentralization, 158, 160–161

Deception, 105

Declaration of Independence, 48, 57–58, 68, 97–98

Declaration-of-war power, 57, 59, 68

Deliberation costs, 92

Democracy, as paradox of commitment, 77

Democratic constitution, original understanding of, 97

Destruction of property, 40

Differential treatment, exceedingly persuasive proof of, 179, 229n72

Disparate impact discrimination, 178–179

Diversity jurisdiction, 226n30

Doctrinal changes: list of major, 145–146, 177–179; over time, 11

Dred Scott v. Sandford, 3–4

Due process clause, 166

Electoral outcomes, effect of on constitutional interpretation, 10

Eleventh Amendment, 145–146, 158, 161, 177; diversity jurisdiction and, 226n30; same/another in, 165–167; *University of Alabama v. Garrett*, 162–167, 172

Elster, Jon, 79–84, 98

Ely, John Hart, 12, 78, 96, 187

Emancipation, and freedom compared, 89

Eminent domain, 14–15, 38, 213n78. *See also* Takings clause

Employment Division, Department of Human Resources of Oregon v. Smith, 146, 160, 177

Endangered Species Act, constitutionality of, 146, 187

Enemy combatants, detaining of, 147

English-only policy, 178

Enumerated powers, congressional, 49, 192

Enumerated rights, Supreme Court decisions on, 4

compared, 48; separation of, 56–67; spending, 50–53; strict separationist view, 56, 57, 60–61; treaty, 62–63, 65

Pragmatism, 10

Prayer in public schools, 31

Precommitments, 75–76, 86, 91–92

Preemption doctrine, 160, 225n8

Preferential treatment, 197–198, 200, 201

Price regulation, 155

Prior restraint, freedom of speech, 14–15, 21–23, 25–26, 119, 207n5

Privacy. *See* Right of privacy

Private property system, and inequalities of wealth, 154

Probable cause, warrants and, 33

Proceduralism, 10

Production of goods, commerce clause and, 53

Profanity, 21

Prohibition laws, 152, 155

Prohibitory rights, 13, 14

Prohibitory text, 49

Pro-labor bias, 155

Pro-labor legislation, 154

Property, regulation of, 35

Prostitution laws, 152, 155, 188

Public-choice theory, 112

Public use, 39–41, 213n81

Public works, appropriations for, 51

Racial classification, 8

Racial discrimination, 173, 196. *See also* Black codes

Racial inferiority, 42, 198

Racial justice, 131

Racial quotas, 231n9

Racial separation laws, 45

Racial stereotypes, 198

Radical reinterpretation: in the absence of amendment, 3–4; changed-circumstances idea and, 9, 205n11; constitutional moments and, 10–11; explanations for, 8–12; foundational paradigm cases and, 148; judicial motivations for, 20–21; living Constitution, 9–10, 206n12

Rational slave, 90

Realist-cynical style of constitutional reinterpretation, 12

Recentralization, 160

Reconstruction Amendments, 114, 119, 180. *See also* Fifteenth Amendment;

Fourteenth Amendment; Thirteenth Amendment

"Recovery of lost meaning," 8

Rehnquist Court: *Boy Scouts v. Dale*, 4, 6, 146, 167, 170–175, 177, 180, 184, 202; *Bush v. Gore*, 4, 6, 146, 147, 161–162; decentralization in, 158, 160–161; effects of pivotal events on, 202; federalism cases, 167–170, 176, 227n50; future directions, predicting, 183, 202; judicial sovereignty in, 158, 159–161; preemption doctrine in, 160, 225n8; textualism and activism in, 158; Toquevillian view of, 160–161; *University of Alabama v. Garrett*, 162–167, 172. *See also* Anti-anti-discrimination agenda

Religion, 102; state laws supporting, 29, 210n34; taxes for the support of Protestant ministries, 30

Religious exemptions, 146, 160, 177

Religious freedom. *See* Freedom of religion

Religious Freedom Restoration Act of 1990, 172, 177

Religious fundamentalism, 187

Reverse discrimination, 177

Rhetoric of restoration, 8–9

Right of privacy, 3, 166, 184–190, 230n4

Rights, 20–47; of conscience, violation of, 29–30; equal protection, 20, 41–47; freedom of speech, 20, 21–29; human, 97; and powers compared, 48; religious freedom, 20, 29–32; searches and seizures, 20, 32–33; self-incrimination, 20, 33–35; takings clause, 20, 35–41; unenumerated, 6; universal, 97

Roe v. Wade, 4, 6, 159, 187–188

Romer v. Evans, 182

Rousseau, Jean-Jacques, 78

Rule-making practices, 109–114, 222n4

Searches and seizures, 20, 32–33; *Miranda* rights, 32; original understanding of, 32; warrantless, 32–33

Sedition Act of 1798, 16–17, 23–24, 25, 27, 123, 208n15

Seditious libel laws, 23–24, 27, 119

Segregation; *Brown v. Board of Education*, 43, 44, 47; equal protection clause and, 43–44; Fourteenth Amendment and, 100, 102–103, 197; majority consensus against, 7